From the Institute of Policy Studies'
Singapore Perspectives

Insights on Singapore's Economy and Society from Leading Thinkers

From the Institute of Policy Studies'
Singapore Perspectives

Insights on Singapore's Economy and Society from Leading Thinkers

Institute of Policy Studies, Singapore

Lee Kuan Yew
School of Public Policy
National University of Singapore

Institute of
Policy Studies

World Scientific

Published by

World Scientific Publishing Co. Pte. Ltd.

5 Toh Tuck Link, Singapore 596224

USA office: 27 Warren Street, Suite 401-402, Hackensack, NJ 07601

UK office: 57 Shelton Street, Covent Garden, London WC2H 9HE

British Library Cataloguing-in-Publication Data
A catalogue record for this book is available from the British Library.

INSIGHTS ON SINGAPORE'S ECONOMY AND SOCIETY FROM
LEADING THINKERS
From the Institute of Policy Studies' Singapore Perspectives

ISBN 978-981-120-487-6
ISBN 978-981-120-503-3 (pbk)

For any available supplementary material, please visit
https://www.worldscientific.com/worldscibooks/10.1142/11402#t=suppl

Desk Editor: Jiang Yulin

Contents

Contents

CHAPTER 1

Migration and Social Diversity in Singapore[1]

BRENDA S A YEOH

INTRODUCTION

Singapore as a small, natural resource-scarce city-state has been part of global enterprise and global service capitalism since its very birth. As a child of imperial and labour diasporas in the colonial era, our story is very much intertwined with migration and migrants. An openness to migrants is how we have gained importance and stature in the world. With the colonial era behind us, we are a "wannabe" global city, competing very hard for a place in the top league of globalising nations. Once again we are a convergence node for transnational flows of different sorts of migrants from many parts of the world.

A migrant history is thus where we come from and that gives us, hopefully, a sense of empathy for migrants. We know the inside story of migration because it is part and parcel of our being, our histories, our families perhaps, and our place in Singapore today. And as part of the story of migration, a dependence on foreign labour is also very much part and parcel of our economic survival through the times, from the colonial era right up to today.

Our economy today is restructuring and transiting to services, financial and high-technology areas. Migrant labour continues to be crucial. The Ministry of Manpower puts it in a nutshell when it says in the Manpower 21 statement that the employment of foreign manpower is a "deliberate strategy to enable us to grow beyond what our indigenous resources can produce". In Singapore, a city-state that is very well managed in many regards, leveraging on migrant labour is part of this carefully managed, "deliberate strategy" of growth.

CHANGING POPULATION COMPOSITION

So what implications do the increased flows of migrants have on the social landscape of Singapore? Let us first take a look at Table 1 which shows population figures compiled from census reports.

Table 1 Changing proportion of citizens to non-citizens in Singapore

Census Year	Citizens		Permanent Residents		Non-resident Population		Total	
	No.	%	No.	%	No.	%	No.	%
1970	1,874,778	90.4	138,785	6.7	60,944	2.9	2,074,507	100
1980	2,194,280	90.9	87,845	3.6	131,820	5.5	2,413,945	100
1990	2,595,243	86.0	109,872	3.6	311,264	10.3	3,016,379	100
2000	2,973,091	74.0	290,118	7.2	754,524	18.8	4,017,733	100

SOURCE   Adapted from Yeoh, 2006, page 28, Table 1.

As of the year 2000, the non-resident population makes up 18.8 per cent of a population of just over four million, in other words, one in five people on this island. If we focus on the division between citizens and non-citizens instead, then basically every one in four people on the streets that we meet today is a non-Singaporean.

Turning now to changes over the decades, it is obvious that the non-resident population is the part of the population that is growing in the most rapid fashion, almost doubling every decade in terms of its percentage of the total population. In short, from the 1970 census to the 2000 census, the population of Singapore has doubled from about two million to four million. The non-resident population has grown from 2.9 per cent in 1970 to a hefty 18.8 per cent of the population of four million today. The non-citizen population has likewise grown from 9.6 per cent in 1970 to 26 per cent in 2000. The 2005 figures also show a further increase of the non-citizen population to 28.4 per cent out of a total population of 4.3 million.

Table 2 Resident population by ethnic group and residential status

	Total	Chinese		Malays		Indians		Others	
Total	**3,263,209**	**2,505,379**	**76.8%**	**453,633**	**13.9%**	**257,791**	**7.9%**	**46,406**	**1.4%**
Singapore Citizens (91.1%)	2,973,091	2,284,617	76.8%	441,737	14.9%	214,642	7.2%	32,095	1.1%
Permanent Residents (8.9%)	290,118	220,762	76.1%	11,896	4.1%	43,149	14.9%	14,311	4.9%

SOURCE   Department of Statistics, 2000.

In terms of ethnic composition, the CMIO (Chinese, Malays, Indians and Others) model that is foundational to Singapore's multi-ethnic philosophy remains more or less in place despite the decades of in-migration. However, there are dips in the Chinese and Malay percentages and increases in the Indian and Others percentages. This may be accounted for if we look at the differences in the ethnic profile between Singapore citizens and Permanent Residents (see Table 2). Among the Permanent Residents, the Indian population is 14.9 per cent, which is twice the percentage of Indians within the Singapore citizen pool. The Others category, of course, features as a larger percentage of the Permanent Resident population than of the Singapore citizenry.

"NEW" SOURCES OF SOCIAL DIVERSITY

Clearly, then, we have been an immigrant society of considerable diversity since our beginnings as a port-city. Today, under conditions of globalisation, what sorts of new social diversity do we confront? As Singapore fashions itself as a magnet for foreign manpower, we have in our midst different categories of migrant labour. "Foreign workers" is the term we tend to use to refer to the large numbers of low-skilled labourers in construction, manual work, cleaning and domestic work. A category that is much smaller in number but of importance is skilled labour — employees at the professional and managerial level, whom we commonly refer to as "foreign talent". A third group that is increasingly important — because they are the future manpower — and growing in numbers is the foreign students. At all levels there has been an increase in foreign students in our schools and institutions of higher learning. In sum, the non-resident workforce of over 600,000 in 2000 makes up about 30 per cent of total employment in Singapore, the highest figure in Asia.

Managing "Foreign Workers"

We first turn to the category of foreign labour that has the largest number. Foreign workers, who number more than half a million in the industries mentioned before, come from a wide range of countries and include Chinese, Indians, Filipinos, Thais, Malaysians, Indonesians, and Sri Lankans. These workers perform the kinds of work that Singaporeans themselves have been reluctant to do.

Our changing social landscape shows signs of their presence. We see them in Little India, the Golden Mile Complex, Orchard Road, and other public places when they leave the confines of construction sites, workers' dormitories and employers' homes on their days off.

On 3 March 2002, a photograph which appeared in *The Straits Times* showed a scene rarely seen in Singapore. A group of Chinese nationals working in the construction industry had staged a protest outside Parliament House to remonstrate against what they felt was the slow pace of investigations into the case of a remittance agent who fleeced them of large sums of money. Riot police had to be deployed to break up the protest — certainly something of a head-turner in Singapore, for how many Singaporeans would stage a protest outside Parliament House to demand justice? This is perhaps a sign that things are changing, not just in the economic sphere, but also in the socio-political sphere.

Socio-political change is, however, also kept carefully in check. Foreign workers are "managed" through a whole series of control measures — including the Work Permit system, the dependency ceiling, government levies and the security bond — to ensure that they remain a transient population, carefully regulated in order to avoid what may seem to be disruptive social effects. State policy is opposed to the long-term immigration of low-skilled workers and is directed at ensuring that they remain temporary and easily repatriated in times of recession. As part of this overall policy of transience, family formation is circumscribed, dependents are barred, and marriage to Singaporeans or Singapore Permanent Residents is not allowed. And for the women — that is, foreign domestic workers — getting pregnant amounts to repatriation. In short, state policy treats foreign workers as disposable labour which must not remain threaded into the basic fabric of Singapore society.

Attracting "Foreign Talent"

Cities which are seriously competing in the globalising game are very much concerned with what has been called a "global war for talent". Singapore is no exception and there is an all-out effort to build Singapore into a "brains service node", an "oasis of talent", or the "Talent Capital of the New Economy", to use some of the catchphrases contained in government documents and speeches. While foreign talent comes from a wide spectrum of countries, numbers from China and India in particular have been growing rapidly in the last decade or so.

Major initiatives have been launched to attract, retain and absorb foreign talent, such as the liberalisation of immigration policies, recruitment missions, Permanent Residency schemes and company grant schemes which ease the cost of employing skilled labour. The whole re-imaging of the architectural and cultural frameworks of urban development is yet another major initiative that serves the purpose of attracting and retaining talent. Efforts to remake Singapore into a "Global City for the Arts" are at least partly aimed at retaining foreign talent who might not want to stay on if Singapore remains a cultural desert.

Skilled individuals in arenas ranging from science and technology to sports — including their family members and dependents — are hence part and parcel of our everyday social landscape. Living in a globalising city means that we encounter these individuals regularly beyond the workplace, on the streets, in shopping centres, schools and so on.

Investing in "Foreign Students"

Another source of social diversity takes the form of international students as Singapore seeks to fashion itself as an education hub for the region. The "Global Schoolhouse" project, as it is called, involves creating Singapore as a world class educational hub, known for its intellectual capital and creative energies. Investing in foreign students is another way of augmenting our pool of skilled manpower for the near future. This is a strategy that affects the whole education landscape from schools to universities. Here, Singapore is capitalising on its various strengths, including its English-speaking environment, high standards of education, low crime rates, high order of social discipline, as well as what has been called our "squeaky clean", "nanny state" reputation, to make parents feel assured about sending their children here.

The aim is to more than double the number of foreign students coming to our schools and universities from about 66,000 in 2005 to 150,000 by 2012. The main targets are China and India as well as neighbouring Southeast Asian countries.

Turning to "Foreign Spouses"

Social diversity in Singapore is not just a product of the nation's labour policy. While manpower needs are the main drivers for the increasing social diversity we are experiencing in the population, there are other pressures at work. One of these has to do with the falling marriage rates in Singapore.

As seen in Table 3, the proportion of singles has gone up over the decade (1990–2000) in nearly all age groups among both Singapore citizens and residents. The increase in the rate of non-marriage as well as delayed marriage has been the subject of much public discussion as well as the source of state anxiety in recent years. Various reasons have been propounded, including the hectic pace of life in a globalising city that squeezes out time for love, sex and marriage, as well as the higher levels of education, financial independence and career-mindedness among Singaporean women. Social perceptions of singlehood are apparently also changing, becoming more acceptable than before.

Table 3 Proportion single by residential status, sex and age group

Per Cent

Age Group	Singapore Residents		Singapore Citizens	
	1990	2000	1990	2000
Males				
20–24	94.2	95.2	94.1	95.4
25–29	64.1	64.2	64.0	66.4
30–34	34.0	30.7	33.9	33.3
35–39	18.1	19.7	17.8	21.5
40–44	10.9	14.8	10.4	15.5
Females				
20–24	78.5	83.8	79.0	86.6
25–29	39.3	40.2	39.6	45.5
30–34	20.9	19.5	20.9	21.9
35–39	14.8	15.1	14.7	16.2
40–44	11.5	13.6	11.4	14.1

SOURCE   Singapore Department of Statistics, 2000.

Linked to these trends, Singaporeans searching for suitable marriage partners are increasingly turning to sources from abroad. As with globalising cities elsewhere, for example, Taiwan, Japan and South Korea, turning to "foreign brides" from the region appears to be a growing trend in Singapore. Foreign spouses are hence an important source of social diversity that affects the basic social fabric of Singapore.

According to the Department of Statistics, there were 8,116 marriages (35.3 per cent) between residents and non-residents in 2005. This can be broken down into 6,520 male Singaporeans and Permanent Residents wedded to foreign brides and 1,596 of their female counterparts marrying foreign grooms. As the actual nationalities involved in these cross-nationality marriages are not released to the public, one can only speculate that the foreign brides are largely Chinese, Indian or Southeast Asian, perhaps, Vietnamese, Filipinos and so forth. Looking at the websites of matchmaking agencies, it appears that marriages to foreigners can be facilitated by packaged tours to Vietnam, for instance, to handpick one's partner from a wide range of applicants.

CURRENT DEBATES — MIGRATION AND INCREASING SOCIAL DIVERSITY IN GLOBALISING SINGAPORE

Migration, and the increasing social diversity it brings, have been very much in the news in recent years. Prime Minister Lee Hsien Loong gave these issues a central place in his 2006 National Day Rally, emphasising a three-pronged approach: encouraging procreation among citizens, engaging overseas Singaporeans in order to help them fit in when they return, and attracting foreigners who can contribute to Singapore to work, live and settle in the city-state. Apparently, efforts to recruit and retain foreigners and convert them to Singaporeans are bearing fruit because in 2005, there were 12,900 new citizens, compared to the usual 6,000 to 7,000 new citizens in the last four years before 2005. This gain seems substantial compared to the average figure of 800 Singaporeans giving up their citizenship each year.

SINGAPORE AS PERMANENT MAGNET FOR TALENT OR TRANSNATIONAL REVOLVING DOOR?

A key issue I would like to raise for discussion relates to the question of the permanence of the foreign population within our workforce. There is, of course, a major differentiation between the unskilled workers and elite transnational workers. For the unskilled workers, the revolving door is one that turns systematically and continually. "Use and discard" is the underlying philosophy behind a range of policies such as the Work Permit system which have been put in place to prevent unskilled workers from gaining a foothold in Singapore as socio-political subjects. Basically, we extract their labour for a certain number of years and then we send them back to their home countries.

In contrast, among the elites with talent and skills, the state tries to slow down this revolving door as much as possible and in fact encourages them to put down roots in Singapore, if not by becoming citizens, then as Permanent Residents, or at least as individuals willing to work in and contribute to Singapore for a good number of years.

Studies, however, seem to indicate that international talent is highly mobile. Even when Permanent Residency status and Singapore citizenship are used as carrots, they will not necessarily guarantee the integration of talented individuals into the fabric of Singapore society. In fact, attaining Singapore citizenship or Permanent Residency may confer a higher degree of potential mobility on them, enabling them to gain entry more easily as tourists and immigrants in other gateways around the world. In fact, people in a globalised world live transnational lives, negotiating a whole range of gateways and taking on multiple identities as part of the strategy to cope with the conditions of globalisation. Globalising cities such as Singapore are thus sites with a very high density of interactions between all kinds of locals and transnationals, not just in the economic sphere, but in all spheres at all scales, from the family to the nation-state.

In this globalising city, some key questions pertain to how best we cope with living in the kind of society where constant mobility is taken for granted. In this context, are we are fashioning Singapore as a transnational revolving door or an immigrant gateway? And if we want Singapore to be a gateway where people come and stay and contribute, is this to be done on a highly selective basis, and if so, what will the selection criteria be based upon? Is the globalising city only a place of welcome for those with talent and skills? How can we manage this divide mentality between welcoming the skilled and guarding against the unskilled and, at the same time, pay heed to upholding high standards of human rights and dignity congruent with a developed nation like ours? How do we ensure that the way we treat foreigners in our midst is not just calibrated according to, and polarised by, the market value of their skills? We need to remember that when we import a human being to work in our country, we are not just importing a skill or labour power, but socio-political subjects who carry with them their own cultures, values, hopes and dreams.

There is thus a need to take a harder look at the social integration and support mechanisms that we have, not just for the talented but also for all levels of skills, and perhaps evolve an integration policy which matches the complexity of our immigration and labour policies. While we have carefully calibrated immigration-labour categories, we also need an equally complex way to integrate human beings of all skill levels after they have entered Singapore. Integration and support mechanisms should go beyond foreign talent to include foreign students, foreign workers and foreign spouses, and each category deserves careful consideration for better-tailored support mechanisms. For example, there are hardly any support groups for foreign spouses who arrive in Singapore and who do not speak any of the mainstream languages here.

Finally, it leaves me to stress that debates about migration and migrants are significant, not just because of their importance in the labour force, but certainly also because of the way migrants of all categories shape the contemporary social landscape, as well as our demographic future.

ENDNOTES

1. Parts of the discussion in this paper can be found in expanded form in Lam, T., Yeoh, B. S. A. and Huang, S. " 'Global Householding' in a City-State: Emerging Trends from Singapore," *International Development Planning Review*, Vol. 28, No. 4 (2006) and Yeoh, B. S. A. "Singapore: Hungry for Foreign Workers at all Skill Levels," *Migration Information Source*, January 2007. Available online at http://www.migrationinformation.org/Profiles/display.cfm?ID=570.

REFERENCES

Singapore Department of Statistics. "Singapore Census of Population, 2000. Advance Data Release No. 8: Marriage and Fertility," accessed 28 February 2007 from http://www.singstat.gov.sg/papers/c2000/adr-marriage.pdf.

Yeoh, B. S. A. "Bifurcated Labour: The Unequal Incorporation of Transmigrants in Singapore," *Tijdschrift voor Economische en Sociale Geografie* (*Journal of Economic and Social Geography*), Vol. 97, No. 1 (2006): 26–37.

CHAPTER 2

The Future Singapore Economy: An Alternative Approach Needed

INDERJIT SINGH

INTRODUCTION

The topic about a high-cost Singapore is indeed timely as we grapple with the issues caused by the worst downturn the world has ever seen. Singapore's issue is not only one caused by a recession, but also one complicated by a preceding era of rapid cost increases and very high inflation. Unless we can rapidly bring down our costs in Singapore for individuals and for companies, we will have a difficult time coming out of the downturn and we will see unprecedented corporate failures and personal hardships faced by Singaporeans. I say this because I do not see demand coming back fast or incomes of Singaporeans rising again for quite some time to come. The government has a challenge in handling both sides of an equation: income and demand on one side and cost on the other.

As Singapore continues to expand economically, the lack of space will drive business costs up. Another factor that is likely to add pressure on rising costs in Singapore is the government's plans to increase the country's population over the coming years. This will increase the demand for key factors of production, and the competition for factors of production will accelerate increasing business costs further. One argument to this is that high costs are inevitable in resource-scarce Singapore. We need to move up the value chain of businesses and not depend on lower value-added activities to drive our economy and earn our incomes. Everyone needs to upgrade their skills and businesses need to upgrade their capabilities and to engage in activities further up the value chain. This has been the direction the government has taken to transform our economy and our workforce. This is done by either focusing on skills upgrading or by bringing in foreign talent.

GROWTH-AT-ALL-COSTS POLICY

Could rising costs in Singapore be avoided? Is the government's growth-at-all-costs policy the most effective for Singapore? One implication of rising costs is the low viability of low-cost industries operating in Singapore. This is accentuated by more cost-competitive countries, such as China and Vietnam in the region. Consequently, the government has opted to move the level of economic activity in Singapore up the value chain and force lower value-added activities to relocate in lower-cost countries. At many levels, this is very much like the business outsourcing strategy that multinationals have adopted in decentralising production processes.

This was how most developed nations progressed when they experienced high costs. They looked elsewhere for their low-cost production needs to support their higher value-added activities in their respective home economies. With regard to textile, steel, automobiles and light electronics industries, there was a distinctive point in each industry's life cycle where it was more profitable to let another country provide the labour or to take over the production process. In East Asia, Taiwan and Korea have in the past been beneficiaries of declining Japanese industries. Leading economies move into higher value-added activities as their own cost structures rise, thus allowing their lower-cost partners to take over the lower value-added activities.

It is not surprising that Singapore, like other more-developed countries in the region, has adopted a similar strategy. However, the point of contention here is the rate at which this movement up the value chain has occurred in Singapore. From the United Nations Conference on Trade and Development (UNCTAD)'s Trade Development Report, the Manufacturing Value-Added (MVA) indicator gives the composition of a country's higher value-added activities in its aggregate production. Even though Singapore's MVA has risen rapidly, its productivity has grown at a lower rate thus showing that it has moved too quickly up the value chain without achieving equivalent improvements in efficiency (see Table 1).

Table 1 Singapore's rise in MVA does not commensurate with its productivity growth rates

Manufacturing Value-Added (MVA) in Selected Countries				
Country	MVA (% of world total)		MVA Ratio 2003/1980	Productivity Growth Rates (1980–2002) (%)
	1980	2003		
China	3.3	8.5	2.6	5.2
Taiwan	0.6	1.1	1.8	4.3
Korea	0.7	2.3	3.3	4.9
ASEAN 4	1.2	2.8	2.3	2
Developed Countries	64.5	73.3	1.1	1.6
Singapore	0.1	0.45	4.5	3.7

Source: UNCTAD

Using these statistics, Singapore's MVA, which was 0.1 percent of the world's share in 1980, had grown to 0.45 percent of the world's share by 2003. This means that Singapore's share of medium and high value-added activities in the world has increased to 4.5 times its 1980 share in these 23 years. Singapore's rate of transition is more than other developing Asian countries over the same time period with Korea increasing to 3.3 times, Taiwan to 1.8 times and the ASEAN Four (ASEAN Five excluding Singapore) to 2.3 times 1980 levels. Even China, which experienced an unprecedented level of industrialisation and technological adoption over this time period, increased its MVA to 2.6 times of 1980 levels. The group of developed countries' share of global MVA rose from 64.5 percent in 1980 to 73.3 percent in 2003, with latter numbers only 1.1 times of 1980 figures.

From the statistics, Singapore's transition from low value-added industries to high value-added sectors has exceeded the rate of other developed countries and has happened too rapidly. You may ask: why is this a problem? After all, having a higher MVA faster means we are progressing better and moreover; why should we turn away opportunities to upgrade ourselves? The point is that moving up the value chain has forced business costs in Singapore to rise (see Chart 1). Singapore has the highest unit business costs which had exceeded productivity rates and the rate of increase in Singapore's business costs from 2006 to 2008 is sharpest.

Chart 1 Business costs in Singapore rose at an extremely high rate between 2006 and 2008

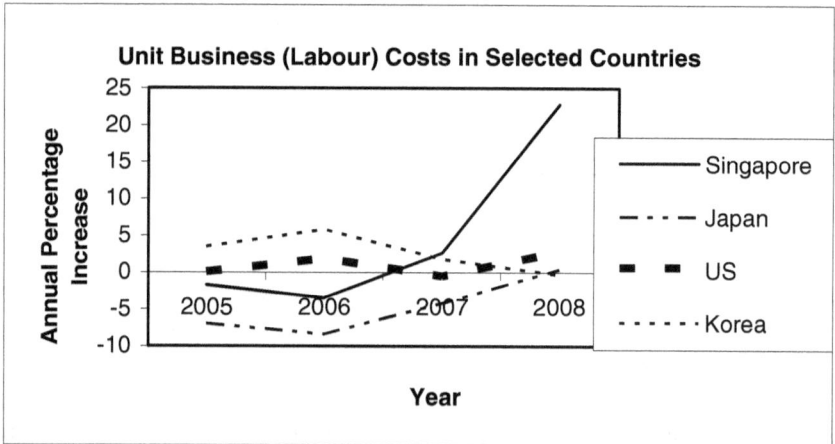

Source: International Labour Organization

From 2007 to 2008, unit labour costs in Singapore increased by 22.8 percent compared to 0.4 percent and 2.8 percent in Japan and US respectively. At the other end, Korea's unit labour costs fell by 0.3 percent during the same period. To emphasise the severity of the problem, the rising labour costs in Singapore were not directly a result of higher productivity. From the productivity growth rates released by the International Labour

Organization, Singapore's productivity increased by 3.7 percent from 1980 to 2002, suggesting that its productive efficiency was increasing at a slower rate than its MVA growth as well as its rising business costs. It is therefore moving too quickly up the value chain of activities. Singapore has the sharpest rise in rankings from the 46th position in 2004 to the 13th position in 2008 (see Table 2).

Table 2 Singapore rose from 46th position to 13th position in a ranking of the world's most expensive cities between 2004 and 2008

Ranking of Expensive Cities		
2008	Country	2004
1	Moscow	3
2	Tokyo	1
3	London	2
4	Oslo	15
5	Seoul	7
6	Hong Kong	5
7	Copenhagen	8
8	Geneva	6
9	Zurich	9
10	Milan	13
11	Osaka	4
12	Paris	17
13	Singapore	46
14	Tel Aviv	33
15	Sydney	20

Source: Mercer's 2008 Cost of Living Survey

DISLOCATION OF INDUSTRIES AND CAPABILITIES

Why does the rate of transition matter? After all, is it not a positive reflection of Singapore's technological capabilities if our rate of moving up the value chain is faster than other Asian economies? The implication of a high rate of development is that it dislodges Singapore's economy, workforce and other infrastructure. A slower rate of development would encourage domestic industries to improve on their capabilities and technologies. This would keep industries in Singapore for a longer period of time. The textile industry in Belgium is a good example. Till today, it has a turnover of 6.6 billion Euros and has been able to maintain its volume of output despite lower-cost competition from other countries and the strengthening of the Euro. The relative good performance and continued viability of the textile industry in Belgium is a result of a high degree of specialisation and more importantly, due to the increasing efficiency of high capital-intensive enterprises. By being capital-intensive, production processes are automated and highly advanced. This has resulted in increasing returns to scale for the Belgian textile industry. The same output is achieved by only a third of the workforce compared to 30 years ago.

Singapore, on the other hand, had moved on to newer industries quickly such as electronics production instead of developing the competencies of its domestic textile industries. Textile companies were forced to relocate in lower-cost countries and Singapore lost out on potential dividends from a viable industry. The approach had led Singapore to lose many of its core competencies each time it started afresh with a new industry. The result was the dislocation of relevant infrastructure, skills workers had gained and the knowledge required of each industry. If Singapore had focused on productivity and innovation, it could have stretched capabilities and allowed lower value-added industries, like textiles, to be viable by being highly automated. This would have allowed Singapore to keep, and benefit from, its core competencies for a longer period. The government's approach was to de-incentivise companies from trying to keep many of what the government considered as 'no-longer-attractive' capabilities in Singapore so that land and manpower can be freed up for a newer group of industries.

IMPACT OF POPULATION GROWTH

As I mentioned earlier, while cost increases are inevitable, the government could have slowed down the rate of increase. Here, the issue of population growth is another point of contention. Based on the United Nations' World Urbanization Prospects Report, Singapore's rate of population growth exceeded that of most other small countries. From 1995 to 2005, Singapore grew at an average of 2.285 percent, while Luxembourg and Belgium grew at 1.73 and 0.265 percent respectively. Even densely-populated entities like Hong Kong and Monaco grew at 1.495 and 0.98 percent respectively. Singapore's average population growth clearly increased at an over-rapid pace between 1995 and 2005, a phenomenon that had added pressure to the rising costs in Singapore. However, a healthy rate of population growth is needed to develop a reliable workforce since population growth is essential. Given Singapore's Total Fertility Rate and immigration rate, the government should aim to achieve an average annual population increase of about 1.5 percent over the next 10 years to attain a total population of about 5.2 million. An accelerated rate of population growth may have drastic implications for the cost structure in Singapore.

THE DOUBLE WHAMMY OF THE POPULATION POLICY

While I can understand the rationale of the population policy and that of bringing in foreign labour and talent to work in our companies, I feel we may have been too impatient in wanting to see results. As I mentioned in Parliament during my Budget speech last year, we have been ramping up the population relentlessly in the last couple of years. It is like we want a tree, but are not willing to wait for it to grow. Singapore's "instant tree" mentality is pushing the pace of population growth at unrealistic rates. As we bring in more and more people, many from India and China, not just at the top level of talent, but also at various levels including unskilled workers, we depress the wages of Singaporeans. However, our costs continue to go up, because of imported inflation, and because of our policies. Hence, we cause a double whammy for Singaporeans who have no choice but to live with the high cost of living while having to accept lower wages. This is especially so for lower-income Singaporeans (see Chart 2).

Chart 2 Real wage increases of various income groups in Singapore

Real Wage Increases of Various Income Groups in Singapore

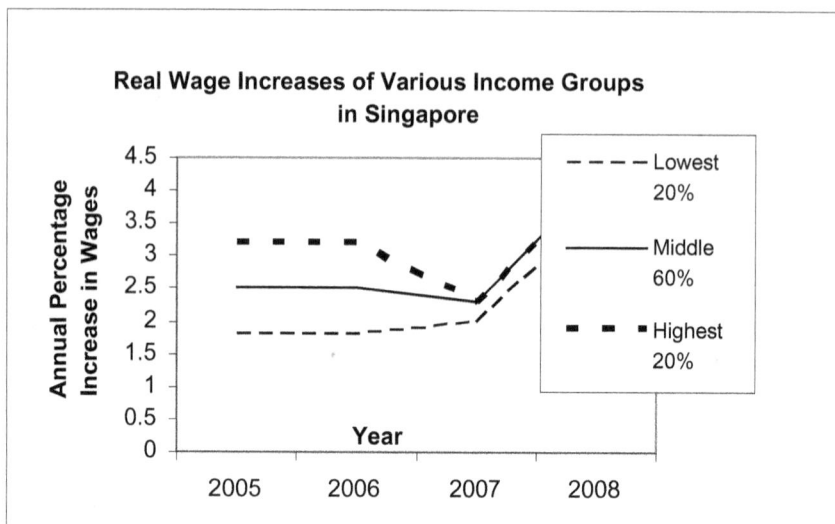

Year	2005	2006	2007	2008
Inflation Rate	0.5	1.0	2.1	5.5

Source: Singapore Department of Statistics

We had also created a problem for companies in the long term by allowing companies to access low-cost labour with a very liberal population policy and a liberal foreign worker policy. In the short term, companies benefited because they got access to workers easily and in the long term, there was no impetus for companies to inject greater productivity, innovation and automation to create real added value to the economy. We continue to rely on input factors, especially labour, to keep the economy going. Paul Krugman explained this fallacy as he sought to dispel the apparent myth of the Asian miracle. He asserted that East Asian growth models, including Singapore's, were based on mobilising resources rather than on increasing efficiency. As a result, the Singapore growth model has been predominantly built upon increased inputs, primarily of labour and capital, and not innovation and productivity. According to Krugman, unless production processes are made more efficient, diminishing marginal returns will make the use of more inputs unproductive. I believe this will be a big problem for us as cost continues to increase in Singapore because of our limited resources.

THE ALTERNATIVE APPROACH

An underlying problem is the government's growth-at-all cost policy. As a result, the rapid changes in the structure of the economy made it difficult for Singaporeans and firms to cope. How could we have otherwise managed our economic development without applying artificial restrictions which may not work? How could we have avoided the overheating of our economy and inflation drivers which are under our control?

Firstly, we could have avoided a policy that fuelled an already overheated situation. The approach taken in the last few years before the financial meltdown was to allow rapid growth where possible. We attracted many new companies by giving very attractive incentives, which in most cases favoured foreign companies and disadvantaged local ones. Secondly, we fuelled the economy in good times by trying to build two integrated resorts (IRs) at the same time, by trying to build a sports hub and by building roads and other infrastructure. We tried to do everything at the same time and as a result of market forces, costs went up and rapidly too.

A moderation of growth rates would have eased the pressure on resources and on costs in Singapore and hence, prevented a heating of the economy. For instance, the government may have chosen to pursue the development of one integrated resort at a time instead of two. It could also have opted to do some of its infrastructural development and government expenditure in lean years instead of concentrating these resources in boom years. All of these factors added to a bubble, which was already growing due to a healthy economy. The government could attempt to cool and prevent overheating of the economy in boom years instead. In the last economic cycle, the government pursued a reverse trend and made cost increases unrealistic. For example, all efforts to cool the 1996 property bubble were undone within two years, 2006 and 2007. Singapore has not recovered from this and its economy will be dealt with a bigger blow in this economic downturn.

With regard to labour, I supported the policy of greater liberalisation of our population policy and foreign worker policies. However, we should have moderated our policies. Companies will no doubt have problems getting workers. We should have compelled them to have a good mix of foreign and local workers and incentivise companies to move up the value chain and focus on productivity to attain real improvement in the quality of our economic growth factors. We could have incentivised companies to be more innovative and improve productivity instead of giving them the easy way out with easy access to foreign workers as an alternative to local workers. How could we have done this? Perhaps by giving enough tax incentives and grants to companies as a leveller so that it will make hiring foreign workers not much cheaper than hiring locals.

We may have to start thinking of a minimum wage system that applies to both local and foreign workers. While painful in the beginning, all of us will learn about the importance of productivity and innovation to do more with less. Such a system will make our companies stronger, made better use of Singaporean workers and contribute better to the economy as Singaporeans remain employed and are being paid sufficiently to cope with the higher cost of living. This might also address the complaints of employers on local workers, which is, that they are not willing to do jobs that are made available. From what I understand, they are not willing because the wages would not be sufficient to make ends meet and they continue to leave low-paying jobs to look for better-paying ones. This may not be the best approach but how does one get by when one's income is lower than one's expenditure?

SUSTAINABLE MODEL OF GROWTH FOR THE FUTURE

What is a sustainable model that Singapore can adopt? The government's strategy should be to promote innovation and strengthen local enterprises by building their capabilities. The MNC (multinational corporation) approach that has been the focus of Singapore's development should no longer be the driver of the economy as it will probably not be feasible for much longer. Developing countries with lower operating costs such as China and India will soon catch up by enhancing their core competencies, making Singapore less viable for many economic activities except for the service industries. Had we focused on the capacity-building of local enterprises, the government would have ensured that they keep moving up the value chain while they internationalise. Local companies will try to make things work and remain in Singapore for the long haul. I fear the time when multinational corporations (MNCs) will move out at a faster rate than we can bring newer ones in. Another concern is that levels of job creation for Singaporeans will be low while increasing numbers of foreign talent will be brought in to jump-start new industries and companies. As the net flow of MNCs is in an outwards direction, our local companies may not grow fast enough to keep the economy afloat or to create jobs to employ those retrenched by the exiting MNCs. We must step up our efforts to help local enterprises to become more competitive in a high-cost environment.

It is not too late to make changes. New opportunities will arise where older ones are lost in this downturn. However, these new opportunities must be effectively utilised using the correct model of growth. The suggested model should involve a moderation of cost while Singapore's core competencies are strengthened. This will allow Singapore to keep its industries for a longer period of time and to benefit from their potential specialisation and technology. Such a model would allow Singapore to grow at lower costs. By developing its human capital and the capabilities of its domestic industries, there may be fewer limits to the country's growth. We must avoid "boom-and-bust" policies. Instead, the government should tap on its ample resources to keep the economy afloat in a downturn while resisting pumping more into the economy when the economy is doing well. While we cannot control external factors, we can definitely control some of the factors that lead to inflation.

CONCLUSION

While we are all proud that Singapore progressed from a Third World to a First World nation within one generation, the question is: at what cost? While costs went up rapidly, nearing those of most developed countries, our wages did not catch up as fast for a significant group of Singaporeans. Their wages remained close to those of developing nations. This mismatch is something the government needs to address. We need to find the right balance of the cost of living we can afford and the type of capabilities our population can develop.

CHAPTER 3

Reaching Out to Low-Income Groups in Singapore

LAURENCE LIEN

INTRODUCTION

I am here to give my personal views, which are influenced by my being at the National Volunteer and Philanthropy Centre (NVPC), on the social perspectives of the issue, "Can Singaporeans afford a high-cost Singapore?" In short, the answer is "yes for some, and no for others". The issue is definitely a lot more complicated. I will first look at some factual information on how Singaporeans are coping with a high cost of living, and go on to what we can do about this.

FACTS AND REALITY

First, high-income households are getting richer and low-income households are getting poorer (see Table 1). The average income for employed households excluding retiree households decreased by 1.3 percent from 2000 to 2005. The reason for this is globalisation and having an open economy. This means we are price-takers and increasingly there are two separate labour markets, one for well-paid high-skilled individuals and another for low-skilled individuals, who have to compete with the huge supply of lower-wage workers from developing countries.

Table 1 High-income households are getting richer and low-income households
are getting poorer

Average Monthly Per Capita Household Income from Work by Deciles

Percentile	All Households				Employed Households			
	2000	2004	2005	Avg. Annual Change (%), 2000–2005	2000	2004	2005	Avg. Annual Change (%), 2000–2005
Total	1,430	1,570	1,640	2.7	1,570	1,750	1,820	3.0
1st–10th	20	0	0	-	290	280	270	-1.3
11th–20th	340	290	280	-3.7	490	490	510	0.6
21th–30th	540	530	540	-	660	690	700	1.3
31st–40th	720	740	750	0.9	820	880	900	1.8
41st–50th	910	950	980	1.5	1,010	1,080	1,120	2.1
51st–60th	1,130	1,200	1,250	1.9	1,230	1,330	1,390	2.4
61st–70th	1,410	1,510	1,580	2.4	1,500	1,640	1,720	2.7
71st–80th	1,780	1,940	2,030	2.7	1,880	2,080	2,180	3.0
81st–90th	2,420	2,700	2,830	3.2	2,530	2,870	3,000	3.4
91st–100th	5,080	5,840	6,150	3.9	5,280	6,110	6,440	4.1

Source: General Household Survey 2005: Transport, Overseas Travel, Household
and Housing Characteristics

The Gini coefficient (see Table 2), which is the standard measure of income
inequality, has worsened over time and is likely to stay as a consequence of
the increasing cost of living.

Table 2 Singapore's Gini coefficient has also become higher

Measures of Inequality in Per Capita Household Income from Work

	All Households[2]		Employed Households[3]	
	Gini Coefficient[1]	Ratio of Average Per Capita Income of Top 20% to Lowest 20%	Gini Coefficient[1]	Ratio of Average Per Capita Income of Top 20% to Lowest 20%
2000	0.490	20.9	0.442	10.0
2001	0.493	19.5	0.455	11.0
2002	0.505	25.4	0.455	11.2
2003	0.512	28.1	0.458	11.4
2004	0.517	29.6	0.463	11.6
2005	0.522	31.9	0.468	12.1

1 The Gini coefficient takes values from zero to one. The more unequal the income distribution, the larger the Gini coefficient.

2 Based on ranking of all resident households by per capita monthly household income from work.

3 Based on ranking of resident households with income earners by per capita monthly household income from work.

Source: General Household Survey 2005: Transport, Overseas Travel, Household and Housing Characteristics

Furthermore, low-income households face a double whammy as inflation has also generally been higher for them. In recent years, inflation was generally higher for the lower-income households (see Table 3). The lowest 20 percent has suffered higher rates of inflation than the other income groups. Although 2007 was better, in 2008 we saw higher food prices, higher housing rental rates and higher transport prices that might have hit the lower-income households quite badly.

Table 3 Inflation hits certain groups more badly than others

Inflation For Households by Income Groups
(Percentage change over previous year)

	2004	2005	2006	2007
Lowest 20%	2.3	1.3	1.8	2.0
Middle 60%	1.5	0.6	1.1	2.0
Highest 20%	0.3	-0.1	0.4	2.3

Source: General Expenditure Survey, 2003

What is the impact of high prices? For the high-income Singaporeans, real wages have been rising more rapidly so they can cope better with the high cost of living. For the lower-income individuals, many would struggle to meet ends meet. The adverse social impact on the lower strata in society, for example decreased self-esteem, stress on the individual and his family, and the threat of a permanent underclass emerging, cannot be underestimated. These families need help to get out of their poverty trap.

Excluding the high-income households, expenditure has been increasing faster than income from 1998 to 2003 (see Table 4). This is not sustainable.

Table 4 Expenditure has been rising faster than income

Income and Expenditure Changes for Working Households
(Per capita percentage change per annum)

	1993–1998	1998–2003	
	Income	Income	Expenditure
Lowest 20%	5.5	0.8	1.6
2nd Quintile	7.5	2.0	2.6
3rd Quintile	8.4	2.1	2.5
4th Quintile	8.5	2.6	3.3
Highest 20%	7.8	3.7	1.8

Source: General Expenditure Survey, 2003

To an extent, an ageing population may explain this. An increasingly greater number of the households in the bottom 20 percent would include retiree households. However, the rate of expenditure has also been increasing faster than that of income for the middle 60 percent of the population.

IMPACT OF HIGH COST AND INFLATION

A consequence of expenditure rising faster than income is that people will be saving less and possibly insufficiently for the future (see Table 5). Already, the low-income household has a diminished ability to save. A retirement studies conducted by AXA, a financial institution, showed that Singaporeans rely heavily on their Central Provident Fund (CPF) savings for retirement income and for many, their CPF savings would not give them a sufficiently high income-replacement ratio if they do not have other sources of savings.

Even government rebates as an income supplement may not be sufficient (see Table 5). Expenditure was still greater than income for the bottom 40 percent. One concern is the current low expenditure on merit goods, which are items that are deemed necessary by a society's norms and standards. Looking at the types of consumer durables owned by the lowest-income households for example, figures show that half the households in the lowest bracket have air-conditioners at home. This gives the

Table 5 Government rebates as an income supplement may not suffice

Income and Expenditure for Households by Income Groups ($ Per Capita)

2003	Income	Income + Rebates	Expenditure	Savings
Lowest 20%	315	339	568	-229
2nd Quintile	669	693	712	-19
3rd Quintile	1043	1068	864	204
4th Quintile	1615	1640	1129	511
Highest 20%	3857	3883	1537	2346

Source: General Expenditure Survey, 2003

impression that the low-income group may not be that badly off. However, one cannot assume that people are rational and wise in their spending choices as we often spend too much on things we do not need, and not enough on things that we do need. In my opinion, expenditure on merit goods, be it on education or health, might be affected for low-income families.

For retirees, real wealth will get eroded if inflation is high, particularly during economic downturns when returns from risky asset classes are poor. Increased longevity suggests more is needed to meet longer-term needs. A higher cost of living could also have an impact on fertility decisions.

What could we do about this? I am making assumptions that we are price-takers for our labour markets, and that there is nothing significant we can do about income levels and that we need to keep jobs. There are three things we could do: having government income-redistribution programmes, lowering costs and encouraging private giving in the form of volunteerism and philanthropy.

INCOME REDISTRIBUTION

Government subsidies do help the lower-income group. Singaporeans are no longer experiencing high rates of income growth like we did from 1993 to 1998, when almost everybody was a winner. In a competitive world with free trade, Singapore specialised in products with comparative advantage. Although we can create a larger economic pie for the nation, there are inevitably gainers and losers. There is a need to redistribute the gains from the winners to the losers through mechanisms such as the Workfare Income Supplement (WIS) (see Chart 1).

However, one problem with understanding the impact of redistribution is, the monies are given for different purposes and are not entirely fungible. This is true even if you give cash, with the use not restricted for a particular type of expenditure. We know from behavioural economics that people practise mental accounting. They would treat permanent income differently from temporary income, with each individual having a different marginal propensity to consume. In addition, consumption baskets may also differ from individual to individual. Hence, monies from a Goods and Services Tax (GST) offset package may go to the purchase of a lottery ticket, for example.

Chart 1 The Workfare Income Supplement will aid Singaporeans who need the most help

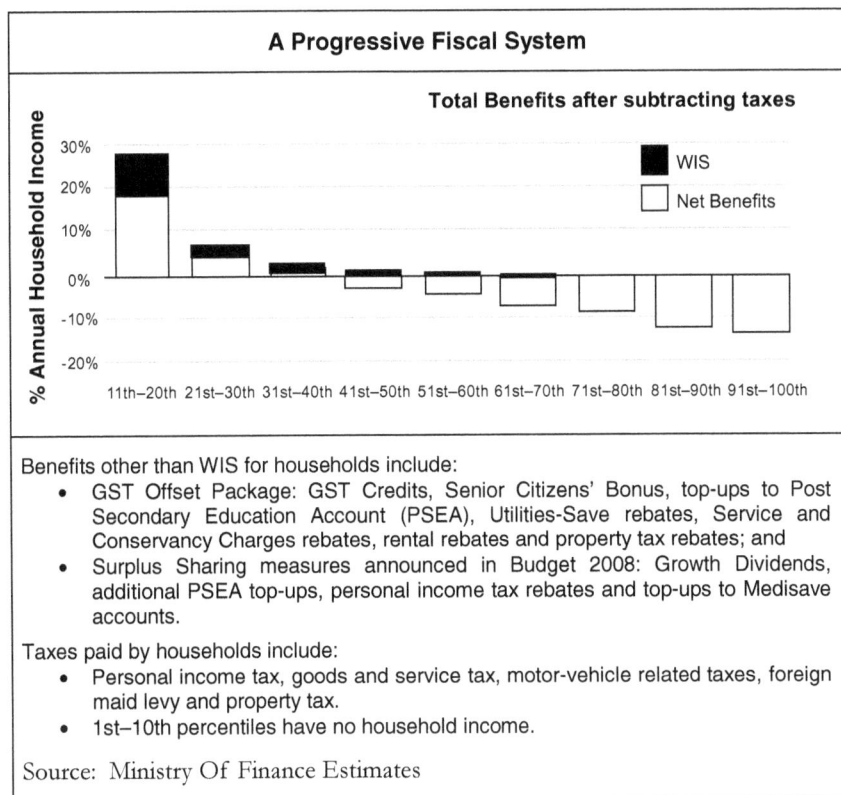

Benefits other than WIS for households include:
- GST Offset Package: GST Credits, Senior Citizens' Bonus, top-ups to Post Secondary Education Account (PSEA), Utilities-Save rebates, Service and Conservancy Charges rebates, rental rebates and property tax rebates; and
- Surplus Sharing measures announced in Budget 2008: Growth Dividends, additional PSEA top-ups, personal income tax rebates and top-ups to Medisave accounts.

Taxes paid by households include:
- Personal income tax, goods and service tax, motor-vehicle related taxes, foreign maid levy and property tax.
- 1st–10th percentiles have no household income.

Source: Ministry Of Finance Estimates

Government income redistribution works only to a limited extent. Government subsidy and redistribution schemes cannot be too customised to cater to the unique situation of each individual because that will create administrative inefficiencies. Neither can the government be too generous in its payouts to cater for the worst case because that will make aid far too costly. The latter will also create an entitlement mentality and rent-seeking behaviour. Payouts also have the effect of damaging self-esteem and self-confidence.

I see aid from the government like a big stone one uses to fill a container, but one still need small stones to fill in the gaps. That is where non-profit organisations come in.

LOWERING COSTS

With regards to keeping costs low, I think we need to have two Singapores in terms of costs. What do I mean by this? Let me give examples. In Singapore we can spend $250 per square foot for a HDB flat or $2,500 per square foot for a condominium. We can spend $3 on chicken rice at the hawker centre or $30 at a restaurant. We can spend $4.60 for a medical consultation for a child at SingHealth polyclinic or $60 for a paediatrician. There are choices. If we want to pay more, there are very high-cost options but if you want to pay less, there are good low-cost options. The focus of public policy should be to focus on items that form the largest proportions of expenditure for the low-income households such as food, transport, and housing, and healthcare, which has been the fastest growing item. (See Table 6).

Table 6 Food and Housing expenditures take up a greater proportion of household income among the lowest quintile of Singapore households

Average Monthly Household Expenditure

	1998 All (%)	2003 All (%)	2003 Lowest 20% (%)
Food	23.7	21.3	28.3
Clothing & Footwear	4.1	3.6	2.6
Housing	21.9	22.4	28.1
Transport & Communication	22.7	21.4	14.2
Education & Stationery	6.8	7.8	5.7
Health Care	3.3	5.1	7.0
Recreation & Others	16.9	17.8	13.0
Non-Assignable	0.7	0.7	1.1

Source: General Expenditure Survey, 2003

ENCOURAGE PRIVATE GIVING

Lastly, we must encourage private giving. There is a huge capacity for growth in this area, even in bad times. When compared to the United States of America, levels of private giving in Singapore appear to be low and show scope to grow more (see Table 7). Although figures of private giving in Singapore do not include donations to organisations not classified as Institutes of Public Character (IPCs) — such as religious institutions — their inclusion would still be much lower than the 2.2 percent of Gross Domestic Product (GDP) for total giving in the US.

Table 7   Singapore can do more in terms of volunteerism

Giving and Volunteerism in Singapore and the US

Singapore	US
• Total giving to Institutions of Public Character (IPC) was 0.34% of GDP in 2007 • Formal + Informal volunteerism rate was 16.9% (2008)	• Total charitable giving was 2.2% of GDP in 2007 • Formal Volunteerism rate was 26.2% (2007)
Sources: Commissioner of Charities Annual Report 2007, "Individual Giving Survey" 2008, NVPC; and Giving USA Report 2008, "Volunteering in the US" (2008), Corporation for National & Community Service, US	

We should also encourage more volunteerism because giving should not just be about money. I do not think giving money is a trade-off to giving time. According to surveys done by the NVPC, volunteers give four times more than non-volunteers in donations. Giving is not just about saving money for the government. We should encourage private giving because there are limitations to what the state can do. Firstly, as I mentioned earlier, government policy cannot be too customised. Secondly, I think the people sector can do some things better than the government. People-sector organisations have the moral authority to address difficult social issues. A dollar given by a concerned neighbour is very different from a dollar given by your Community Development Council (CDC). People-sector organisa-tions can also be a rich source of innovation and experimentation that go beyond national policy and ideology. Thirdly, we need to cater to different and holistic needs. The government tends to focus on material and physical needs because it has a comparative advantage in doing large-scale wealth redistribution. However, a human being also needs social, emotional and spiritual support.

CONCLUSION

We need to show that as a society, we care. There are discussions about the need to build high social capital, engaged citizenry and active citizenry to build national pride and passion. A key test of a mature society is how one would treat the less fortunate. A happy society is one where people share and give. Individual happiness is the social fabric of the society and is something that we need to keep intact. For society to continue to progress, we cannot afford to have the divides between those who do well and those who struggle to just get by. We often talk a lot about the poor having an entitlement mentality. The wealthy can also have an entitlement mentality. They may believe that they deserve everything that they get, and everything that they earn. And I am especially concerned that younger Singaporeans who do well are a bit more ostentatious and less compassionate than older Singaporeans. The current financial crisis is a great opportunity for Singaporeans to show that they care. This is my last point and I am confident that many of us will step up to the plate just like we did in previous recessions. The year 2001 was a recession year but donations to IPCs went up by 17 percent from the previous year. The current recession is worse than the previous one, but I hope those who can afford to give will do so. If the government is drawing down on national reserves, we and our families should likewise consider giving more as well.

CHAPTER 4

Singaporean Rootedness: Taking Stock and Moving Forward

TAN ERN SER

INTRODUCTION: WHAT IS ROOTEDNESS?

Let us begin by exploring three different contexts in which we can apply the concept of rootedness. First, rootedness can be associated with living in a small town. Some years ago I managed to visit quite a number of small towns across America. There I witnessed a sense of community, of people who seemed to be quite happy and relaxed where they felt that they were living among friends and relatives. Second, rootedness is related to the sense of autobiography, or the place where one is raised. Personally, I was brought up in something akin to a slum area near the Subordinate Courts in the city, and while I have memories and some nostalgia relating to that place, it certainly is not where I would want to be rooted to. The third context relates to the famous example of the Jewish diaspora. The Jewish diaspora has spread out for the last 2,000 years to Europe and the United States and other parts of the world, but the Jews remain very much rooted to their homeland. The Jewish situation is also problematic in that the Palestinians claim the same piece of land in the Middle East. Both groups are just as rooted to this place but these are somewhat mutually exclusive sentiments.

What is rootedness? It is the quality or state of having roots, of being firmly established, settled or entrenched in a place. There is the sense that one is in tune with the socio-cultural world associated with a particular locality. It refers therefore to both the social world and the physical location. Rootedness provides the basis of a socio-psychological anchor, attachment and affiliation, and provides continuous nourishment towards that end. Like a tree, one receives nourishment from that source. Another point about rootedness is the connection to the past, present, and future of the people and place in which one is rooted. This provides the basis for the struggle for national survival and well-being. For our purpose here, I choose to think of this concept as rootedness to the nation with implications for national survival — the nation of Singapore, rather than a sense of affiliation to certain districts in Singapore like Queenstown or Toa Payoh.

Robert Bellah and his team explored some key characteristics of rootedness in their book titled *Habits of the Heart: Individualism and Commitment in American Life*[1]. Rootedness is about identity, a sense of belongingness and emotional attachment. A person's identity is formed in his or her growing years and by connecting with others. These definitions have been used quite a bit in Singapore. Another characteristic of rootedness relates to the place where one is willing to invest his or her ambition and future. Are we willing today, to invest our ambition and future in Singapore? That is a question of rootedness in Singapore. Further, when we say that one is rooted to a place, he or she would also be willing to link his or her self-interest to the public good of the community therein. Do we have a sense that we and our fellow citizens are actually in the same boat?

Rootedness also operates on the logic of community rather than the marketplace. Earlier in this conference, the speaker Mr Peter Ong had suggested that respondents to a survey on the "soul" of Singapore had suggested that their well-being would be most heavily influenced by their job. I disagree with that notion. There is a distinction between the utilitarian world of work and the expressive world of friendly community. Rootedness has to do with the expressive world of friendly community, where we should feel that we are among friends and people who care for us, and

---

[1] Bellah, Robert *et. al.* (1985). *Habits of the Heart: Individualism and Commitment in American Life*. Berkeley and Los Angeles, California: University of California Press.

amongst people whom we are willing to contribute to and invest in. Rootedness is also associated with a generosity of spirit where citizens are willing to engage in nurturing connectedness with others in the community. There is a sense of owing a debt, or debts, to society.

Rootedness has to do with community, connectedness, commitment, involvement and memory. This relates to a sense of engagement in the nation and a desire to bring about a better future for this nation. Rootedness is also about having a common purpose and a national life which transcends particular interests. Rootedness is not just about whether we get jobs, but whether there is a sense of common or national purpose. Rootedness can also manifest in exclusion or an "island" mentality, as can sometimes be seen in small towns. This may not seem like the best attitude in the age of globalisation, for even as we are rooted, even as we love this place and country, are we willing to allow others to share in what we have?

Rootedness is also about being tied to a place, even for the mobile, the cosmopolitan. I believe it is possible, even if you are cosmopolitan, working elsewhere, to feel rooted to Singapore. While we may not have the same history and culture as the Jews, there is nothing to say that we cannot be rooted to Singapore while we are overseas in places like Perth and Toronto.

WHAT BRINGS ABOUT ROOTEDNESS?

What brings about rootedness? Rootedness takes place when one moves from a self-interested position and mentality to that which prompts an interest in the common good of the larger community. I believe that people will be rooted if they feel a sense of security, comfort and can have a decent quality of life and well-being for themselves and their children. Most would not want to be in a place that does not even have the basic necessities. People also want to be in a place, a community which has an affirming and encouraging culture. In Singapore, we tend not to rejoice with those who succeed and are sometimes quite dismissive of small successes. Perhaps if we affirm one another more, we would feel more "together" and hopefully this would result in an increased sense of rootedness. Correspondingly, community support, a sense of membership in that one is not marginalised because of one's ethnicity or class and involvement also encourages rootedness and especially so in multi-ethnic, multicultural Singapore.

Rootedness could, on the other hand, result from shared negative experiences which lead to the need for self-preservation. The Jewish diaspora has the collective experience of discrimination and exclusion. The Jews and Palestinians can both relate to a collective sense of suffering injustice. In addition, contestation for a certain geographical terrain can increase the sense of rootedness within the related community of peoples where there was not much of a connection before.

WHAT ARE OUR EXPECTATIONS OF ROOTEDNESS?

I will address this question of "our expectations" from the perspective of the government, and what the government expects of Singaporeans in terms of rootedness. The Singapore 21 (S21) initiative, inaugurated in 1997, had five key ideas. First, the S21 vision proclaimed the principle that "Every Singaporean Matters". I believe that if we did abide by this, Singaporeans would be rooted, or at least we would be in the process of getting there. The second and third principles were that we need strong families and opportunities for all. The fourth is the Singapore Heartbeat, of feeling passionately about Singapore, because this is where we find our roots and our future; to think of Singapore as our home, a place worth living, fighting and dying for. Rootedness is much more than just money, benefits, or jobs and has to do with our whole sense of well-being and identity. The fifth principle set out the desire to inculcate active citizenship, or allowing citizens to make a difference to society. S21 had to do with thinking about Singapore as home.

In 2007, the Committee on National Education came up with the 3H framework aimed at strengthening "heartware" and rootedness. The three Hs are "Head, Heart and Hands". "Head" referred to developing an understanding of the challenges facing Singapore and what it meant to be a Singaporean. "Heart" referred to an emotional connection to the Singapore story and a love for the nation. "Hands" referred to giving back to society, and having a part to contribute to and create Singapore's future. The 3H framework was not very different from S21, but was couched in a way that was more accessible to students and teachers.

HOW ROOTED ARE WE?

How are we doing in terms of rootedness? A 2005 IPS Survey on Rootedness conducted by Brenda Yeoh, Gillian Koh and me defined rootedness in terms of five components. The first is a spatial or physical familiarity, or a certain fondness for a place. For instance, I understand that people who were raised in Tiong Bahru like Tiong Bahru for its nice, friendly and relaxed atmosphere. The second relates to socio-behavioural rootedness, which concerns integration into formal and informal social networks and the community. The third is an "autobiographical insideness", or a repository of memories, providing a sense of identity, continuation of one's life trajectory. This relates to the past, present and future. The fourth is a passive belonging, or an instrumental form of belonging relating to access to jobs, social entitlements and benefits. The fifth is governmental belonging, or ownership and control over national affairs and the nation's destiny in terms of citizens who get involved, engaged and contribute to society.

The overall score of Singaporeans on the rootedness scale in this survey was 74 out of a maximum of 100. While 74 appears to be quite a decent figure, there is no equivalent benchmark, and thus there is no means by which this result can be compared across countries apart from us conducting the survey again over time. In a comparison of the data across the different ethnic groups, 31 percent of Indians and 14 percent of Chinese had a high score for rootedness (see Table 1). 24 percent of seniors aged 60 to 64 had a high score for rootedness, but 14 percent and 18 percent respectively of the younger age groups of adults aged 30 to 44 and 15 to 29 had a high score for rootedness. A surprising finding was that 21 percent of Working Class respondents (skilled, semi-skilled and unskilled workers) and 13 percent of the Service Class (managers, professionals and associate professionals) scored well on rootedness. 21 percent of survey respondents thought that the government was doing a good job, while none (0 percent) thought that the government was doing badly. It appears that good government performance helps to bring about rootedness. 23 percent of respondents with a high degree of social capital (defined as the extent to which one could count on the support of, as well as be counted upon by one's social networks to provide support) scored high on the rootedness scale while only 16 percent of those with low degree of social capital scored highly on the rootedness scale. People who demonstrated a high degree of social capital tended to be very connected within their neighbourhood, and exhibited a high degree of trust and reciprocity amongst friends and family members.

Table 1   Selected subgroups in the IPS Survey on Rootedness

The numbers in parenthesis are the percentage of the subgroup that scored well in rootedness.

Overall Score = 74/100	
Indians (31%)	Chinese (14%)
Seniors 60–64 (24%)	Adults 30–44 (14%) Young 15–29 (18%)
Working Class (21%)	Service Class (13%)
High Evaluation of Governmental Performance (21%)	Low Evaluation of Governmental Performance (0%)
High Social Capital (23%)	Low Social Capital (16%)

HOW CAN WE DEVELOP ROOTEDNESS?

The following are some hypotheses on barriers and facilitators to the development of rootedness. First, the over-emphasis on meritocracy and self-reliance has sent out the message that Singaporeans need to depend on themselves. While there is some degree of welfarism in Singapore in the sense of government subsidies and cash hand-outs for the poorest, there is a greater sense that Singaporeans are on their own. This is not conducive for the cultivation of rootedness. Perhaps a more balanced approach is needed here.

Second, although it is said in the domain of public rhetoric that "Every Singaporean Matters", there is much emphasis on market relations in reality. This tends to convey the message that the economic value-add of Singaporeans matters more than their membership as citizens.

Third, which I have mentioned above, is the lack of a culture of affirmation and a broader definition of success and contribution. The way I see it, only qualifications, net worth, and being world-class matters in Singapore. In reality, only the top 5 percent to 10 percent of the population will qualify as world-class at most. What will then happen to the rest? Unfortunately this disparity does not stand at a 50-50 divide, but we are instead likely to see 90 percent of Singaporeans in the lower end, and 10 percent who qualify as world class. So I think we need a culture of affirmation and a broader definition of success and contribution.

Fourth, is Singapore more of an economy or a nation? We have to start thinking of ourselves as a nation and a community. Conceiving of ourselves as an economy is not conducive to the development of rootedness.

Fifth, is there a tolerance of differences, or the acceptance of people with different ideas, viewpoints and paradigms? My sense here in Singapore is that very often we cannot let our hair down, and always have to look over our shoulder. We would, if we are among friends and fellow members in the community, be able to relax and speak our minds freely.

Having said all this, all is not lost. The process of enhancing rootedness has already begun in earnest. The government has demonstrated through S21 and National Education that it has identified what needs to be done to encourage Singaporeans to think of Singapore as a nation, and we need to facilitate the process of Singaporeans thinking of Singapore as a nation.

WHERE ARE WE HEADING?

So where are we heading? Is globalisation a threat to rootedness? In my view, globalisation has nudged Singaporeans to make a choice of asking themselves "Is Singapore my home, wherever I may be?" Geographical mobility "forces" Singaporeans to make comparisons and hopefully with this, Singaporeans will decide that Singapore is still home where they find acceptance and security. On the issue of the influx of foreign talent, my feeling is that Singaporeans will demonstrate a generosity of spirit towards new citizens, PRs and foreigners if and when they feel secure, accepted, and affirmed in their own country.

5

Can Singapore Advance as a Regional Hub?

MANU BHASKARAN

I want to look at how Singapore has done as a global city, as a regional hub. The bottom-line for me is that we have done extremely well, but the challenges are proliferating, so we need to do a lot more to fill in the gaps if we are to continue succeeding in this area. Let me begin by looking at some global rankings, one of which Dr Tan Chin Nam has shown you, to take stock of where we stand and what drives that ranking. I want to look at the challenges that we are facing, the gaps that we need to fill, and in particular to focus on what is our key gap, which is the lack of scale and which might be our undoing in the future.

First of all, what am I talking of in terms of a "hub"? The global economy is increasingly a network economy that links different global cities all over the world. Each of these global cities is like a node that switches all kinds of flows, be it flows of people, capital, ideas, telecommunications or tourists. These are nodal points, and what is important is that they create a lot of value. People in such cities can generate a lot of income, and, therefore, welfare if a city succeeds in becoming and maintaining itself as a regional hub. That is what is in it for us.

WHERE SINGAPORE STANDS

Where does Singapore stand now? I want to present to you some of the results of the MasterCard Global Centers of Commerce Index, an exercise of which I was a small part. The Index was constructed to identify the 75 most influential cities around the world that drive the global economy. Essentially, these are the drivers which we think make a successful, effective and sustainable global city.

Seven evaluative dimensions were included in the consideration of what makes a worldwide centre of commerce. The first thing is that the legal and political framework must be there to give stability and certainty to businesses so that they would locate in the centre. It must be at least stable economically, otherwise if your currency is gyrating all over the place, or if you have high inflation, it is not a very attractive place at all. We need it increasingly to be a centre of knowledge-creation and also a place where information flows freely and easily. Businesses need information to make good, well-judged decisions.

We also looked at the World Bank's indices which measured the ease of doing business. How easy is it to set up a business? How easy is it — when it is painfully necessary — to retrench workers? Liveability: is it an attractive place where you want to bring a family to, is the air breathable, are the schools good, and is the crime rate low? And then there are two achievement indicators which tell you if you have already achieved 'it' as a global centre. First, have you actually generated the volume of financial activity: stock market, foreign exchange trading, bank syndication, private wealth management, *et cetera*? Second, are you generating flows of business activity? Are there operation headquarters based in your city? Are key business decisions for the region or for the world made where you are? This is what we think drives a global hub.

Singapore has done extremely well according to this metric. In the last exercise we did a few months ago, we ranked Singapore number four and as you can see (refer to Chart 1), very close to Tokyo, but well behind London or New York. If you look at the changes (refer to Table 1), we have actually been improving. We are one of the very few cities which went up in the rankings very rapidly compared to other cities.

One of the things that came out in our exercise was that the rankings are highly dynamic. We have made it as a global city, but there is no guarantee that we will remain highly-ranked forever. For instance, Amsterdam moved up a lot, and Shanghai has moved up a few notches from virtually nowhere in every year we have done this exercise. Moscow

Chart 1 Singapore does well in the 2008 MasterCard Worldwide Centers of Commerce Index

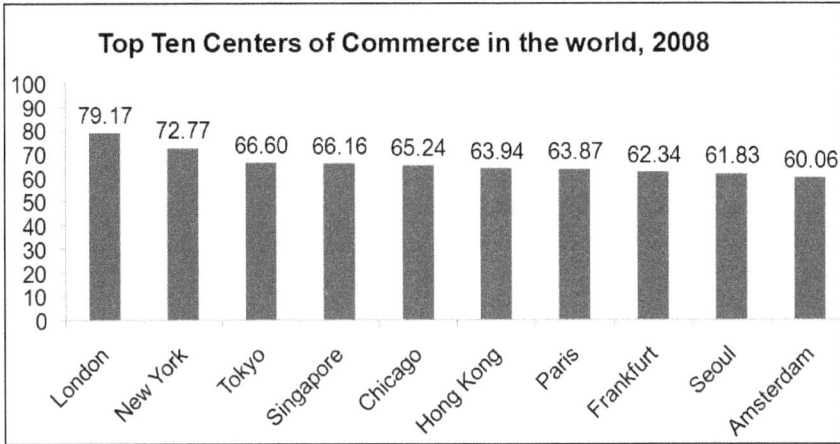

Top Ten Centers of Commerce in the world, 2008

Table 2 In the 2008 ranking exercise, Singapore moved up the list by two places

Top Ten Centers of Commerce in the world, 2008

	City	WCOC Index 2008 (out of a possible 100)	Change
1	London	79.17	0
2	New York	72.77	0
3	Tokyo	66.60	0
4	Singapore	66.16	+2
5	Chicago	65.24	-1
6	Hong Kong	63.94	-1
7	Paris	63.87	+1
8	Frankfurt	62.34	-1
9	Seoul	61.83	0
10	Amsterdam	60.06	+1

and Dubai are also making their marks in their respective regions. One thing that I noticed in these changes: cities that are rising rapidly are benefiting from a surge in activity in their particular regional hinterlands. The scale of activity is clearly very important.

What else determines changes in ranking? One thing should be said from the onset: it is very difficult to dislodge the top two cities, which are London and New York. Legacy is important, and it is easy to understand why. Once critical mass assembles in a global city, the lawyers are there because the investment banks are there; the investment banks are there because the wealth is there; the wealth is there because the lawyers and all the other services are there. Everything interlocks. No single part of this interlocking system can leave without damaging its own business potential. Once you create critical mass, it is very difficult to dislodge it.

An example of that is Beirut, which amazingly continued for quite a while — into the Lebanese civil war — to be the heart of commerce in the Middle East. It was well into the civil war before Beirut lost its status as a regional hub. Critical mass, once created, is difficult to dislodge. But what we see below the top two is constant change, and therefore Singapore is at risk. We are rising now, but the challenges are clearly increasing as you can see with Shanghai and Dubai coming up. I will talk about these challenges, and then about how we can deal with them.

WINNERS AND LOSERS

First of all, there is a great opportunity because in 2007, we had a very important historical turning point. For the first time in human history, more people lived in towns than in rural areas. Urbanisation is an important trend and clearly benefits nodal points like Singapore. Another trend is that activity is increasingly concentrated, and there are winners and losers in this trend. New York and London have clearly been the winners in the last 10 years. On the other hand, Paris, Frankfurt and Boston are still very important cities but, in the case of Frankfurt, the city has lost operational headquarters and key elements of the financial sector to London despite very hard work on the part of the Frankfurt authorities. We are in a world where more and more activity tends to gravitate towards the winners. There is room only for a truly few global cities in this new economy.

So, what do we have to face in Singapore? Clearly, the rise of the Asian giants is both an opportunity as well as a risk. The risk to us is that China and India each have the sheer scale. As they start growing, their cities can gain in scale very quickly and emerge as challengers to established global hubs like Singapore. What is also interesting is that both these countries are based on civilisations going back thousands of years, and these are countries which are very proud of their heritage, and which feel that they have lost out in the last 200 years and are hence trying to make up for lost time. They have the ambition to become top again; they see it as their natural historical role. Both are liberalising (clearly China is ahead of India); both are building infrastructure (China is well ahead of India there); both are building multinational companies on their own, and as you can see, multinational companies generate huge amounts of activity and where they locate their headquarters, can help drive a particular city's growth and prospects. And unlike the rise of the previous set of challengers for us such as Korea and Taiwan, China and India have that scale that can really cause a challenge to us.

In addition to that, you have the growth of the sub-regional economic areas close at hand. One is the Greater Mekong sub-region. The Asian Development Bank (ADB) has done excellent work to promote this sub-region, encompassing Vietnam, Laos, Cambodia, Thailand and eventually Myanmar, as well as Yunnan Province in the southern part of China. There has been a rapid growth in transport links and a huge amount of deregulation that has improved customs flows among other things. This is going to benefit Bangkok as a regional hub. Bangkok is already almost as important as Singapore in terms of being an aviation hub. It is also a very important manufacturing hub in the sense that a lot of multinational companies locate the manufacturing part of their regional headquarters in Bangkok. In China, with the improved relationship between Taiwan and the mainland and increasingly economic agreements between Hong Kong and Macau on one side and China on the other side, there is an increasing integration of the Chinese economy. With Taiwan now going to encourage liberalisation, Taipei could become more of a challenge as a regional hub.

And what about our own hinterland? In a sense, I think ASEAN (the Association of Southeast Asian Nations) has been losing out. Clearly, in the wake of the 1998 economic crisis, ASEAN has been losing out. The integration of ASEAN could have created the scale of the economy that could have benefited us. Real integration, rather than rhetorical gestures, has not really come through. We have not had the level of integration that would allow ASEAN governments to scale up, and to allow goods made in one ASEAN country to be easily sold and marketed in another. We have not had the level of integration that would allow a country registered in one ASEAN country to operate easily in another. This would have benefited Singapore.

So if you look within the region, Singapore is doing extremely well now. However, the cities I have highlighted, such as Bangkok, Shanghai and Dubai are already important challengers. I think Taipei, which has not yet deregulated or liberalised its services sector, is poised to join Shanghai to become a serious challenger in the next 10 years. Mumbai has its share of problems as we have seen with the recent terror attack and with the horrendous infrastructure that you have seen, but I guarantee you, in five years' time, they will get their act together, and the infrastructure and policy regime in Mumbai will improve significantly. By which time, the scale of activity in Mumbai will be huge. So we have a lot of challenges ahead.

If we drill down to the nitty-gritty of the MasterCard Index, what are the strengths and weaknesses? (Refer to Table 2) Clearly, in terms of strengths, we are a fantastic place to do business in. The government goes all out to make it very easy to register a business and close a business. The political and legal framework, stability, legal certainty, independence of

Table 2 Singapore's strengths and weaknesses as a global city

SINGAPORE'S RANKING: PLUSES AND MINUSES

STRENGTHS	WEAKNESSES
Ease of doing business: # 1	Financial Flows: # 11
Legal/Political: # 2	Knowledge Creation & Information Flows: # 14
Business Center: # 3	Economic Volatility: # 19
	Liveability: # 40

the judiciary, commercial cases: excellent. As a business centre, in terms of the volumes of activity that gives you critical mass: again, Singapore does very, very well.

What about weaknesses? Surprisingly, in terms of financial flows, we are not ranked all that highly and I suspect that over time, our relative ranking is going to slip. In terms of the ability to create knowledge and allowing information to flow freely, which is very important if you want to go to the next level of being a global hub, we are quite weak. In terms of economic volatility, we are rather weak, surprisingly, compared to some of the other cities. In terms of liveability, of course Singapore is a very liveable city, but all things are relative, and according to various surveys we actually do not rank all that highly in this area.

If you drill down even further, what we do well in as a regional hub is in the process areas, where the government and civil servants can manage the process and regulation. We have done very well. Trouble is, we have maxed out what we can do there. There is still intensifying competition in these areas and I think it is really in the area of the hinterland that you need critical mass and so on, where things like our port, airport, and regional business capital will face more challengers. We have performed less well in financial flows, knowledge-creation and liveability as I have said. If you look more clearly, the reason for the weakness in financial flows is, the insufficient critical mass or savings actually being managed here by domestic institutions unlike in other cities. In terms of liveability, we scored very poorly on personal freedom and the quality of life is not as good as we think it might be.

So basically, the bottom-line is: we have not really made it yet. We have been lucky, I think, and in the global context of increased competition, Hong Kong, Shanghai, Mumbai and maybe Bangkok will pose a serious problem for us. In this context, there is a lot that I think we need to do, but one of the things that strike me as being very important from a policy perspective is the need to create scale. That means real regional integration so that we have the scale to generate the kind of flows that attract people to base themselves in Singapore as a hub.

I can think of a lot of things that we have to do. Clearly, the government has been doing a lot. We have been restructuring, brought in the IRs (Integrated Resorts) which have been a taboo before, and reduced taxes. We have been giving incentives; we have allowed inward migration on a scale that few other countries allow; we have attracted a lot of new manufacturing plants which are highly value-added. We have done a lot. But clearly, we are coming to a point where we are facing a capacity constraint. That showed up in the previous economic boom, in the overheating that accompanied the growth we enjoyed. Inflation rose, and costs rose. We are hitting at the constraints of growth.

When we come down to ask the question of whether we can really make it in the future as a global hub, there are a few points that emerge. For instance, most other global cities that we compete against have two airports, a major airport and a secondary airport. In fact, London has four, New York has three, and Tokyo has two. In terms of the port, we cannot just keep growing a port. There is a physical limit to the coastline and the anchorage space that we have. If we want to move beyond to the level of global cities, we need to have a much larger population. But talented people who drive a global city demand a high quality of life. However, in Singapore we do not have that option. We are very densely-packed with no real hinterland, unlike Manhattan where one could always drive to Connecticut for commuting and leisure purposes.

A PROPOSAL

I could go on and on about what we need to do, but I want to focus on the Iskandar Region, because to me, here you have, ready-made for you, what I think would be very, very good for Singapore as well as Malaysia. I think the Iskandar Region, which the Malaysians are actively pursuing, is a great opportunity for us to scale up. It is a region that wants to do business with Singapore, a region that cannot succeed — I think — without Singapore's active help, and yet will allow us to grow beyond the limits placed on our own area. Here are some data points (refer to Table 3) to make my point more convincing.

Some people worry about Iskandar being a competitor to Singapore. I do not worry about that. Without downplaying the importance of competition, the fact is in terms of the key factors of production such as land and labour, we are complementary and do not compete. In terms of the critical mass that we need, Singapore has and can offer it to the

Iskandar Region. In terms of entrepreneurship, the Malaysians have it, and Singapore has it to some extent. I think we complement each other quite well.

Table 3 Integration with Johor: The Iskandar Region and
Singapore compared

Iskandar Region: Opportunity for Singapore

	Singapore	Malaysia/IR
Area (square kilometres)	692.7	2,216.3
Population	4.5m	1.353m
GDP (USD bn)	136.9	20
Population per sq km	6,376	631.8
GDP per sq km (USD)	197.6 million	9 million
GDP per head (USD)	30,422	14,790

Essentially, what am I saying? I am saying that although we have done extremely well, we cannot rest on our laurels. If we want to go on growing with this particular strategy, I think we need to think out of the box and we need to expand the economy beyond the confines of our geographic constraints. That, to me, means seizing the opportunity of the Iskandar Region and moving more actively with Iskandar, which can then join Singapore in success.

CHAPTER 6

The Third Phase of Singapore's Multiculturalism

DANIEL P S GOH

In 2003, Minister Yaacob Ibrahim made a landmark speech envisioning the third phase of Singapore's multiculturalism as combining and going beyond the melting pot and mosaic approaches of the first two phases. Starting from the attainment of self-government in the 1950s, the first phase involved the nation-building promotion of multiracial harmony and construction of a Singaporean identity through the enlargement of the area where Chinese, Malay, Indian and other cultural beliefs and practices overlapped. In the 1980s, as the effects of Westernisation were felt with successful capitalist development, emphasis was shifted to the construction of hyphenated Chinese-Singaporean, Malay-Singaporean, Indian-Singaporean identities to encourage the retention of ethnic culture. In the current third phase, as globalisation brings with it cultural diversity, cross-cultural understanding and dialogue are encouraged to foster hybrid Singaporean identities that would bind Singaporeans in a lattice of shared cultural links, grounded in the heartland and spreading out into the cosmopolitan world.

It is not an easy task to combine the melting-pot and mosaic approaches and yet foster hybrid identities. In principle, the promotion of racial and religious harmony can complement ethnic heritage preservation. One can develop a deep appreciation and actively practise one's own cultural heritage while exercising tolerance of other cultures. Indeed, sociologists have demonstrated that the individual who preserves his or her own cultural heritage is better equipped to appreciate, understand and adopt other cultures. If hybridity involves the fusion of two cultures to create unique shared cultures, then it makes sense that one must have a culture to share and fuse with other cultures to begin with. Institutionally, in Singapore, the same individual can be involved in the cultural exchange programs at the local community centre, volunteer to help his or her own cultural kin at the self-help groups Mendaki, the Chinese Development Assistance Council (CDAC) or the Singapore Indian Development Association (SINDA) and participate in cross-cultural dialogues in an Inter-Racial and Religious Confidence Circle (IRCC) without feeling torn or conflicted. The problem does not lie at the level of individuals or the institutions themselves, but at the level of the public sphere. The public sphere lies between individuals and the state. It is the civic space where individuals interact with each other and produce public opinions, shared cultural values and the social practices of citizenship. This is the space where society is created and trust, the glue that binds society together, is cultivated. Multiculturalism describes the principles and norms of intercultural interaction that have been established in the public sphere. Individuals form associations and organisations to act as a group in the public sphere, creating what we call civil society.

In Singapore, the state has intervened heavily in the public sphere and influenced its multiculturalism through state institutions such as community centres, ethnic self-help groups and confidence circles for good reason. Colonial civil society was largely commercially- and philanthropy-oriented, with only a few associations geared towards cultural modernisation. New multicultural institutions were urgently needed in the 1950s to replace the vicious colonial circle of racial divide-and-rule with a nation-building one. In the 1980s, another set of institutions was called for to substitute the virtuous circle of heritage preservation with the capitalist circle of consumerist individualism. We have been relatively successful, but the unintended consequence has been the creation of a new vicious circle that undermines the multicultural dialogues and hybrid identities that are needed to maintain social cohesion in the age of globalisation. To make my case, I will use examples from my observations of the Racial and Religious Harmony Carnivals in Punggol town, my experiences teaching the sociology of race relations to undergraduates and my observations of recent events concerning race and religious relations in Singapore. I do this without prejudice to the local grassroots volunteers and Member of Parliament in Punggol, my students and other individuals. The problem cannot be tackled on the level of the individual, but must be a concerted effort at the level of the public sphere. I conclude by proposing eight principles that could be followed to break this new vicious circle and realise genuine multicultural dialogues.[1]

MAKING VIRTUOSITY OF COLONIAL RACIALISM

In the early 1950s, in the midst of the propaganda war against the communists during the Emergency, the Malayan Director of Information Services outlined his approach to citizenship education: to teach the new citizens of a nascent Malaya to understand "how the wheel goes round, who keeps it in motion, and the part played by Ahmad, Ah Seng and Ramasamy in its revolution". The how and who, of course, refer to the colonial state. The three characters were caricatures emblematic of British colonial racialism in Malaya and were predecessors of the Chinese, Malay and Indian figures that dominate our multicultural imagination today. Colonial rule was built on the hard racial divisions institutionalised in politics and the economy. Racial segregation and pluralism were the order of the day, allowing for a handful of white colonialists to rule over a large native population. In British Malaya, the Chinese, viewed as apolitical economic animals and long treated as aliens in a country they were increasingly calling their own, were kept out of the bureaucracy and the military. The Malays were treated as a highly conservative people protective of their traditions, so many were therefore kept in their fields and cajoled and coerced to plant only rice and vegetables, while the Malays of noble birth were inducted by

---

[1] For smoother reading, I have decided not to pepper this article with notes and academic references. For fuller academic expositions of my arguments with proper referencing of the academic literature, please see Daniel PS Goh, "Colonial Pluralism, Nationalism and Postcolonial Multiculturalism: Race and the Question of Cultural Diversity in Malaysia and Singapore," *Sociology Compass*, 2008, vol. 2, no. 1, pp. 232–52; "Multiculturalism and the Problem of Solidarity in Singapore," in Terence Chong (ed.), *Singapore: Management of Success Revisited*, Singapore: Institute of Southeast Asian Studies, 2010, forthcoming, and with Philip Holden, "Introduction: Postcoloniality, Race and Multiculturalism," in Goh *et al.* (eds.), *Race and Multiculturalism in Malaysia and Singapore*, London: Routledge, 2009, pp. 1–16.

the British into the bureaucracy and the military because they identified with fellow aristocrats. Indian migrants were specially "imported" into two classes — the supposedly docile Tamils as plantation workers and manual labourers and the well-schooled Indians as white-collar clerks.

Caught up in the institutionalised segregation, the socialised behaviour of the different races easily became racial stereotypes and these were taken as natural inborn attributes. The Malays who preferred planting to hard mining labour were said to be lazy sons of the soil. The Chinese, seeking every opportunity to earn a living, were said to be irredeemably greedy, scheming and untrustworthy. The Tamils suffering in the isolated plantations under powerful European masters were said to be uncivilised, childlike and naïve. The British officials wrote extensively of these attributes as justifications for colonial racial policy. Hence, the caricatures of Ahmad, Ah Seng and Ramasamy also represent the colonial racial stereotypes that still thrive today in the undercurrent of prejudices beneath the calm surface of racial harmony.

The Vicious Circle of Colonial Racialism

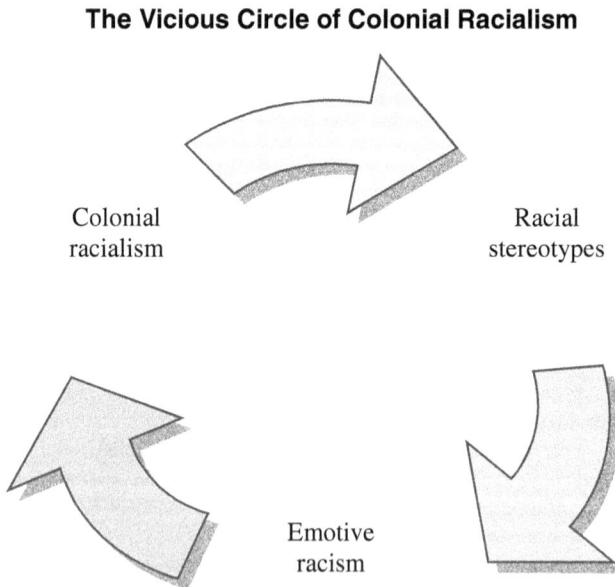

Colonial racialism

Racial stereotypes

Emotive racism

Figure 1 Vicious circles are also often self-fulfilling prophecies

These prejudices have erupted three times as racial riots — in 1950, 1964 and 1969. There is no need for me to repeat the well-trodden history of the riots, except to say that the racial stereotypes offered a dangerously rich pool of emotions and symbolisms for unscrupulous politicians to exploit and turn into emotionally charged racist acts for their own gain. The strife was also underpinned by the economic competition between the races, with the stereotypes playing a key role in overt and covert discrimination, thus adding emotional fuel to racism. In turn, this emotional racism affirmed the "truth" of colonial racialism — that race is a "primordial" fact and races should be kept apart and race relations managed by strong government.

The first phase of multiculturalism attempted to transform the vicious circle into a virtuous one. The melting pot multiculturalism envisioned by then-Minister of Culture S. Rajaratnam accepted the colonial racial divisions as hard facts. Thus, Chinese, Malay, Indian and the residual category of Others (CMIO) were said to be constituent races of Singapore and were represented by discrete, closed circles. Rajaratnam's ingenious adaptation was to make these self-contained circles overlap by arguing that there was a common shared cultural space between all of them. The enlargement of this space through government-sponsored campaigns and institutions would therefore bring about a unifying Singaporean national culture. In this sense, the terms of colonial racialism were accepted but transformed into postcolonial multiracialism. It was a pragmatic solution, as colonial racialism was already deeply embedded in the population, in institutionalised economic practices, in people's minds as stereotypes and in people's hearts as emotional prejudices.

Today, postcolonial multiracialism continues to be a major cue in organising the grassroots activities in the public sphere. Each year, on the weekend close to Racial Harmony Day, the informational flyer advertising the Racial and Religious Harmony Carnival in Punggol shows children, decked out in ethnic costumes representing the CMIO races, posing with government ministers and Members of Parliament. Carnival activities follow the CMIO representation. Residents visiting the exhibition on cultural heritage will find themselves learning about Chinese, Malay, Indian and Eurasian or Peranakan customs and can take part in a quiz to earn prizes. Educational stalls set up by invited religious groups will definitely include a

Buddhist or Taoist temple, a mosque, a Hindu temple and a church in the area. Food stalls offer free *halal*-certified CMIO cuisines for all to sample and share. The carnival parade itself is also structured as such, with different schools offering a menu of traditional Chinese, Malay, Indian and Eurasian cuisines and modern dances choreographed in different combinations.

Overall, the activities offer positive cultural stereotypes to replace the negative stereotypes of colonial racialism. For example, Indians are associated with saris, Bollywood music, tandoori chicken, henna hand-painting and Hinduism. And the primary mode of interaction here is cultural exchange. Thus, we find Chinese and Malay children getting their hands painted and sampling tandoori chicken. The result is a sense of emotional bonding through cultural exchange, which replaces the racist emotions of colonial racialism. In this way, the shared cultural space is gradually enlarged and postcolonial multiracialism realised.

The Virtuous Circle of Postcolonial Multiracialism

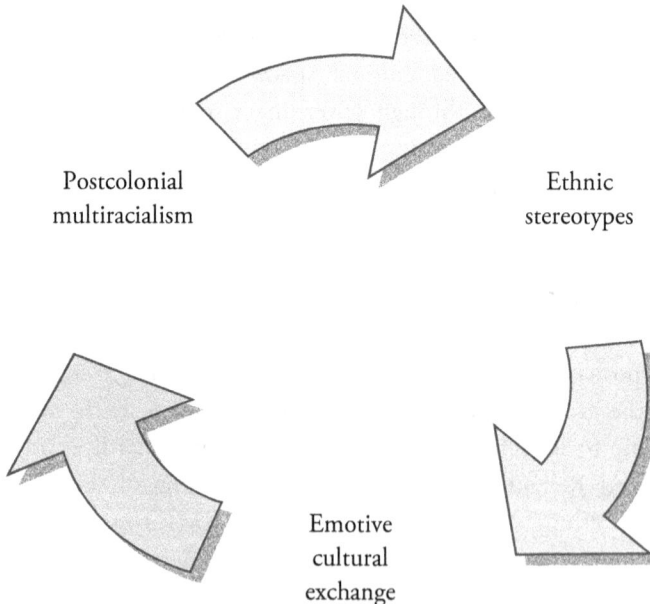

Postcolonial multiracialism

Ethnic stereotypes

Emotive cultural exchange

Figure 2 The virtuous circle of postcolonial multiracialism may be realised by gradually enlarging the shared cultural space

MAKING VIRTUOSITY OF CONSUMER CAPITALISM

By the end of the 1970s, with successful industrialisation and Singapore well on its way to becoming a fasting-developing "Asian Tiger", another set of problems presented itself. Because of Singapore's open economy and close economic linkages with the West, particularly the United States, capitalism came with strong cultural baggage. Before economic modernisation, consumption cultures were limited to the "leisure classes" — the propertied and capitalist classes who displayed their status through luxury lifestyles and conspicuous mass consumption invented in early twentieth-century America and accelerated in the postwar era. Consumer capitalism promised the common folk a wide range of cheap goods and comfortable materialist living. Every hardworking American could get easy credit, own a suburban home, buy a car, drive to shop at the neighbourhood supermarket and departmental stores filled with goods from all over the world and take a vacation every summer holiday. American mass consumption supported the global capitalist economy but also promoted and universalised this American Dream.

Today, we do not think much of the American Dream because we have our own version of the Singapore Dream — the 5Cs, representing condominium, car, country club, credit card and cash. Today, consumerism has become a basic aspect of Singaporean culture and the national pastime is quite obviously shopping. But, it must have been a strange thing taking root in Singapore in the 1970s. While the Singapore government's home ownership scheme allowed the majority of Singaporeans to own their own homes, like Americans, the Singapore scheme was and is a public housing programme with socialist underpinnings. As an export-oriented economy, consumerism was seen as irrelevant at best and a distraction that detracted from productivity and reduced the savings rate at worst. The worry was that a consumption culture, once taken root, would pave the way for excessive runaway consumerism that would undermine the newly built economic success of the country. Very quickly, a situation arose that sociologists call "moral panic": the fear that political, economic and social change would spell the collapse of morality, civilisation and society itself. Excessive consumerism, it was feared, would encourage selfish individualism and destroy the nuclear family household that had been the basis of governmental social policy. It was believed that the nuclear family performed the function of transmitting moral values to the next generation and it was feared that the traditional Chinese family, in particular, was under threat. The precedent for this moral panic could be found in the anti-"yellow culture" campaigns advocated in the 1960s by the Chinese-speaking intelligentsia who associated bourgeois decadence with Western individualism.

The Vicious Circle of Consumer Capitalism

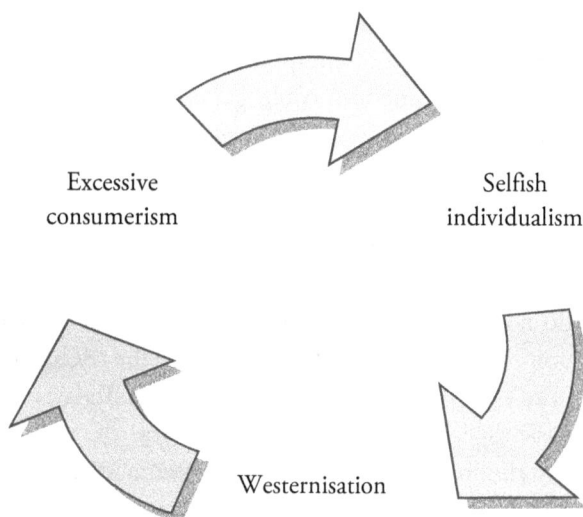

Excessive consumerism

Selfish individualism

Westernisation

Figure 3 In the 1970s, the vicious circle of excessive consumerism, selfish individualism and Westernisation threatened not only the industrialising economy and moral society, but also the nascent nation

To make matters worse, individualism had taken on a more sinister shade in the late 1970s because its association with Westernisation portended the erosion of the values of the CMIO cultures that had been the building blocks of postcolonial multiracialism. It was feared that, released from the moorings of ethnic culture, the nation-building project would collapse and racial and religious strife would return. Intensifying economic competition was also leading to unequal outcomes for the races and it became apparent that Malay and Indian children were disproportionately over-represented among the underachievers in school. Therefore, for government leaders then, the vicious circle of excessive consumerism, selfish individualism and Westernisation threatened not only the industrialising economy and moral society, but also the very nation that was just being born.

The 1980s saw the creation of many institutional innovations aimed at shoring up ethnic culture and tackling the consequences of successful capitalist development. Goh Keng Swee, then-Deputy Prime Minister, introduced moral and religious education in schools. The Prime Minister, Lee Kuan Yew, launched the Speak Mandarin Campaign by switching from Hokkien to Mandarin in his National Day Rally speech. The Special Assistance Plan (SAP) program converted some elite schools into specialised schools for Chinese language and cultural education. Confucian ethics were promoted and academic specialists were invited to write textbooks and set up a research institute on the subject. The Malay self-help group Mendaki was established and became the template for other ethnic self-help groups to follow. The Ethnic Integration Policy and the Group Representation Constituency were set up to ensure proportional ethnic mixing in public housing estates and proportional ethnic representation in Parliament respectively. Parliament enshrined a set of shared Asian values in the National Ideology.

These institutional innovations replaced individualism with communitarianism and Westernisation with "Asianisation". As a result, excessive consumerism and conspicuous consumption were soon frowned upon as unbecoming of an Asian society and immoral, while community service and the development of the philanthropic spirit were encouraged. Consumerism was not eradicated; it cannot be in an open capitalist economy. Consumerism was instead moderated and Asianised, and as such, deployed in the service of multiracialism.

The Punggol Racial and Religious Harmony Carnival is immersed in the trappings of consumption culture. On top of publicity materials on community service work, most of the religious educational stalls offer suitably ethnic free food, drinks and gifts. One can get Indian sweets at the Hindu temple booth, soya bean milk and grass jelly drink at the Taoist temple booth, vegetarian vermicelli and spring rolls at the Buddhist temple booth, and fruit chocolate fondue and balloon sculptures at a Christian church booth. The parade seems almost like a sideshow alongside the food and funfair, but the manning of the stalls by grassroots volunteers who fairly apportion the free food affirm both communitarian spirit and moderated consumerism. Even McDonald's, the epitome of Western consumerism, which gives out free drinks and burgers, takes on a communitarian and Asian flavour here. At its booth, an exhibition panel features a cast of multiracial employees, highlighting McDonald's as a community-oriented, family-like and equal-opportunity employer.

The Virtuous Circle of Communitarian Capitalism

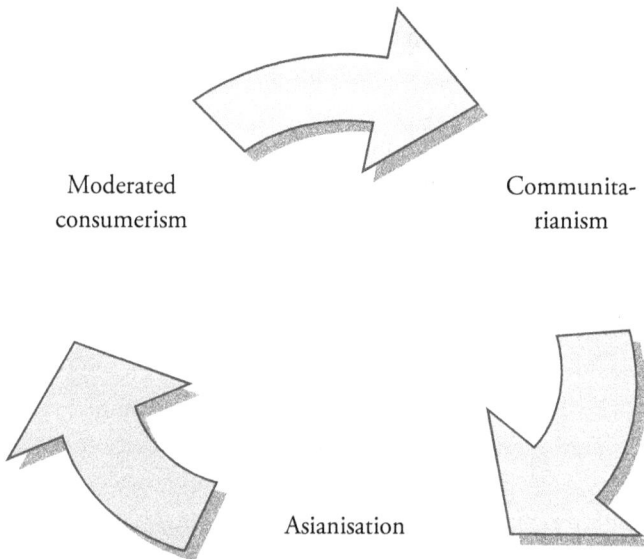

Moderated consumerism

Communita-rianism

Asianisation

Figure 4 Individualism, Westernisation and excessive consumerism were countered by an attempt at Asianisation, moderated consumerism and communitarianism

DIALOGUE VERSES THE VICIOUS CIRCLE OF FEAR

Compared to the first phase and its emphasis on shared common space, the second phase of multiculturalism brought racial and religious differences to the foreground of the public sphere and into the calculations of governmental policies and social interactions alike. As such, the institutional innovations opened up a Pandora's Box of heightened racial and religious consciousness in the public sphere. This is not necessarily a bad thing, as the search for commonalities can only be achieved through frank discussions and debates about differences. However, the government eventually closed the Box by enacting the Maintenance of Religious Harmony Act and began to define hard "out-of-bounds markers" for the public discussion of racial and religious issues. This has led to hypersensitivity and much self-censorship in the public sphere.

When I discuss issues of racial prejudice, stereotypes and institutional racism and give Singaporean examples in lectures, students are often visibly uncomfortable with me openly talking about a subject they think is highly sensitive. Once, after a lecture, a Chinese–Singaporean student emailed me at length to tell me that I should be more sensitive to the Malays in class and not try to explain sociologically why Malays are disproportionately underachieving in school. She spoke for Malay classmates that she did not know and claimed that they were upset without finding out whether they actually were. She informed me that she interned with a newspaper and implied that she could report this if she wanted. Another time, I had to intervene after Chinese–Singaporean students emailed to complain about their Malay tutor bringing up hard questions about racial prejudices and discrimination in Singapore and threatened to make a complaint in the press and to the authorities. Even in smaller tutorial classes, it is much more difficult to get students to talk about racial and religious issues than about other issues.

These are university students who should be open in their thinking and challenging conventional understandings in the scientific search for truth. Yet, many have proven to be unable to overcome their conditioning to be hypersensitive. They would rather not discuss racial or religious issues because they are afraid of offending someone, as they are hypersensitive and will take offence themselves. Because they do not discuss racial or religious issues, over time, they will lose their capacity to talk and use their reasoning to disentangle the issues. Postcolonial multiracialism and Asianisation do not help either. Students conditioned by activities such as the Punggol carnival remain stuck within the CMIO framework and cannot imagine multicultural possibilities beyond it. Emotional cultural exchange encourages them to trade superficial details about customs that many do not even practise anymore, and the emotional component further encourages hypersensitivity. For them, multiculturalism refers to the consumption of other Asian cuisines, the moderated consumerism of the second phase. It is significant that Minister Yaacob used the example of people of different races eating vegetarian food at Komala Vilas in Little India to exemplify hybridity in his 2003 speech.

What disturbs me most is the patronising attitude that some of my Chinese students adopt towards their non-Chinese classmates. They do not check with their classmates on how they are feeling before purporting to know that they are uncomfortable and arrogantly speaking on their behalf. They assume that their non-Chinese classmates are narrow-minded and hypersensitive and have not considered that they may have projected their own discomfort on their classmates. In the case of the complaint against my tutor, I surveyed the rest of the students in the class. Most told me that they had appreciated the discussion although they had felt uncomfortable while

The Vicious Circle of Fear and Self-censorship

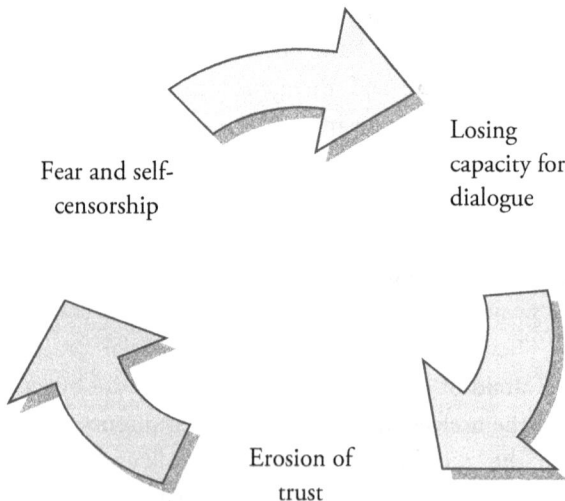

Fear and self-censorship

Losing capacity for dialogue

Erosion of trust

Figure 5 The vicious circle, if allowed to spiral, will undermine the racial and religious dialogue that is being promoted in the third phase of multiculturalism

the rest were angered by the patronising attitude of the complaining students. This is highly disturbing because it shows the erosion of trust among Singaporeans, to the extent that the leading members of the Chinese majority feel an obligation to represent the non-Chinese minorities and protect them paternalistically against "sensitive" comments by reporting matters to the authorities. They cannot even trust themselves or their fellow Singaporeans to talk about the matter as reasonable individuals. If this process continues, the racial and religious dialogue that is being promoted in the third phase of multiculturalism will be short-circuited.

Two recent events show clearly the operation of this vicious circle of fear and self-censorship. Early this year, McDonald's launched its Chinese Zodiac Doraemon doll series. However, the company replaced the pig doll with a Cupid doll, explaining to customers that it could not sell pig dolls because it was a *halal*-certified restaurant. The move backfired when some Chinese customers protested and even blamed Muslims for being oversensitive and intolerant of Chinese culture. The company then tried to fudge the issue by claiming that the series was not a Chinese Zodiac series after all, despite the fact that, with the pig reinstated, it would have contained all 12 animals of the Chinese Zodiac. Also, Singaporeans soon realised that McDonald's was selling a complete set in Hong Kong, with the pig. This led to more protests and the incident quickly became a media event. The company eventually apologised and brought back the pig into the series.

This incident not only shows a general lack of cross-cultural understanding, but also the lack of capacity for dialogue, both of which have important consequences in a globalised Singapore. McDonald's could have avoided the whole fiasco if the company had consulted Muslim leaders and scholars, who would have told the company that Muslims do not mind pig toys and would even buy them for their kids to play with. Instead, it chose to go the route of hypersensitivity and self-censorship and, even when questioned, was not capable of engaging in dialogue with the public, acting instead in a seemingly patronising manner towards Muslims and non-Muslims alike. The company eventually made a graceful public apology to end the saga. But the damage had been done as the incident made Muslims look insensitive and the Chinese too defensive of their customs, thus further eroding the trust quotient of society.

Very recently, the Internal Security Department called up and warned Pastor Rony Tan of a large Christian mega-church to be mindful of religious sensitivity. Tan had ridiculed and belittled Buddhism at length during a Sunday service and a video clip was posted on the church website which spread quickly and created a huge uproar on the Internet. At the time of writing, the event is still being played out, but the response to Tan's grave mistake is already telling. While many wrote to Pastor Tan to communicate their disagreement and disapproval in the proper spirit of multicultural dialogue, enough citizens complained to the authorities and made police reports, causing the Department to act in a public manner to calm things down. Tan made a public apology and a personal apology to Buddhist leaders and promised that he would get involved in inter-religious dialogue after the governmental warning. But the element of fear and self-censorship still hangs over the event. It would have been more reassuring if he had apologised because a multi-religious group of community leaders went to talk to him. Or perhaps the Inter-Racial and Religious Confidence Circles could have made Pastor Tan see that he was wrong, thereby restoring public confidence in our multicultural system. Using a sledgehammer to crack a nut is counterproductive. Thus, despite Tan's apology, some citizens are still calling for him to be arrested and a few religious leaders want the authorities to ensure that this will not happen again. This erosion of social trust means the government has to constantly be on guard to police racial and religious relations and step in with the threat of force to resolve disputes, which in turn reinforces a climate of fear and hypersensitivity and reduces dialogue to a minimum.

BUILDING MULTICULTURAL CAPACITY

There is a glimmer of hope yet for the third phase. The international World Values Survey shows that Singapore ranks very poorly among Asian countries in terms of social trust and participation in political discussions. Yet, when asked what the country should prioritise, other than economic development, a larger percentage of Singaporeans want the government to give them more say, compared to citizens in other countries and other priorities.

Social Trust in Selected Asia-Pacific Countries

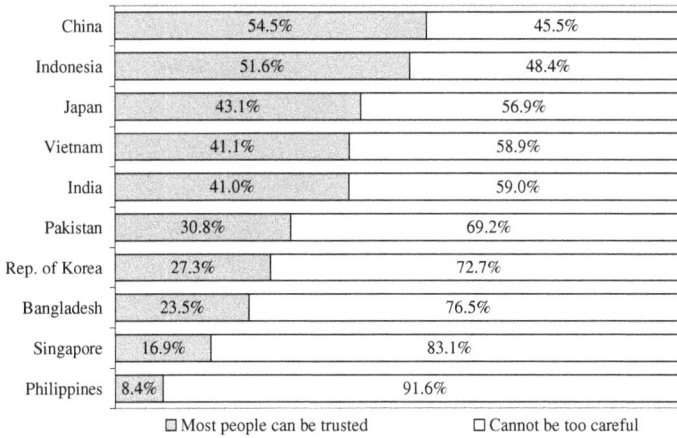

Country	Most people can be trusted	Cannot be too careful
China	54.5%	45.5%
Indonesia	51.6%	48.4%
Japan	43.1%	56.9%
Vietnam	41.1%	58.9%
India	41.0%	59.0%
Pakistan	30.8%	69.2%
Rep. of Korea	27.3%	72.7%
Bangladesh	23.5%	76.5%
Singapore	16.9%	83.1%
Philippines	8.4%	91.6%

☐ Most people can be trusted   ☐ Cannot be too careful

Figure 6 The 2000–2002 World Values Survey shows that among selected Asia-Pacific countries, Singapore society exhibits a relatively lower level of social trust
Source: World Values Survey, 2000–2002

Frequency of Discussion of Political Matters with Friends, Selected Asia-Pacific Countries

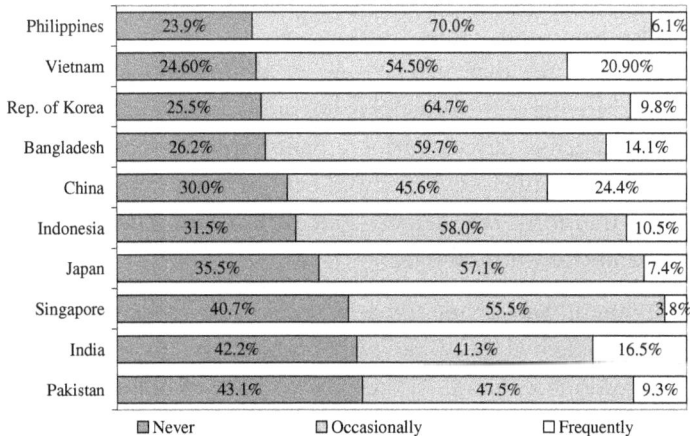

Country	Never	Occasionally	Frequently
Philippines	23.9%	70.0%	6.1%
Vietnam	24.60%	54.50%	20.90%
Rep. of Korea	25.5%	64.7%	9.8%
Bangladesh	26.2%	59.7%	14.1%
China	30.0%	45.6%	24.4%
Indonesia	31.5%	58.0%	10.5%
Japan	35.5%	57.1%	7.4%
Singapore	40.7%	55.5%	3.8%
India	42.2%	41.3%	16.5%
Pakistan	43.1%	47.5%	9.3%

■ Never   ☐ Occasionally   ☐ Frequently

Figure 7 Singapore also fares poorly in terms of how frequently they engage in discussions involving political issues with their friends
Source: World Values Survey, 2000–2002

Prioritise Democratic Development or Social Order?

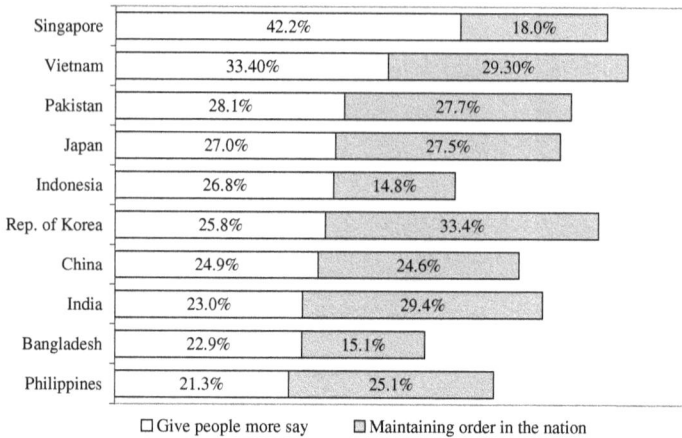

Country	Give people more say	Maintaining order in the nation
Singapore	42.2%	18.0%
Vietnam	33.40%	29.30%
Pakistan	28.1%	27.7%
Japan	27.0%	27.5%
Indonesia	26.8%	14.8%
Rep. of Korea	25.8%	33.4%
China	24.9%	24.6%
India	23.0%	29.4%
Bangladesh	22.9%	15.1%
Philippines	21.3%	25.1%

☐ Give people more say   ☐ Maintaining order in the nation

Figure 8 Compared to some other countries surveyed, when asked to choose between the two, more Singaporeans favoured democratic development over the social order
Source: World Values Survey, 2000–2002

Just as we did in the first two phases of multiculturalism, we need to confront and transform the vicious circle that is now obstructing cross-cultural dialogue and, thus, preventing us from achieving hybrid Singaporean identities that preserve our social unity in a globalised world. I conclude by offering eight principles for public sphere participation that I draw from academic discussions on deliberative democracy and public spheres. These are principles that could help us build multicultural capacity and help us transform the vicious circle of fear and self-censorship into a virtuous one of dialogue and trust.

- **Facilitate, not frame**: leaders should act as facilitators of honest open-ended discussions rather than try to frame and limit discussions with political agendas and out-of-bounds markers.
- **Use understanding, not therapy**: participants in multicultural dialogue should use reasoning to seek the understanding of others and empathy to understand others, rather than resort to emotional outpourings and sympathy.

- **Be sensitive, not patronising**: participants should be sensitive in their phrasing but not so sensitive that they adopt a patronising attitude towards others.
- **Ethnicise, not racialise**: participants should focus on culture and recognise the possibility of creative cultural change and adoption rather than reduce behaviour to unchanging biological instincts.
- **Be relational, not communal**: participants should relate to each other as individuals with experiences and opinions to share rather than as communal or self-appointed representatives exercising authority.
- **Act, not react**: participants should be actively and continuously engaging in multicultural dialogue, rather than speaking up only in offensive or defensive reaction to an incident.
- **Consensus, not suppression**: participants should seek genuine consensus on views and norms, and working consensus on norms for tolerance and coexistence when differences are irreconcilable, rather than suppress differences.
- **Evaluate, not judge**: participants should evaluate cultural beliefs and practices using shared moral standards and should not judge and belittle them using their own ethnic or religious standards.

CHAPTER 7

Between Nation-State and Global City

DEREK DA CUNHA

This paper will examine the following themes:

- Between nation-state and global city
- Monaco of the East?
- The bet on casinos
- A diversified economy
- Opinions and practices in a global city

BETWEEN NATION-STATE AND GLOBAL CITY

The concept of the global city is often viewed in economic terms. Its simple definition is that it is a city that is an important nodal point in the global economic system. To that extent, there are several international surveys that rank many cities or countries in terms of their levels of globalisation. These rankings are based largely on economic, political, cultural, and infrastructural characteristics.

The global management consultancy, A. T. Kearney, in its 2006 rankings, rated Singapore the most globalised country in the world.[1] Note the word "country," not "city." This is the main problem with these surveys. They may not compare like with like. The same survey ranked the United States third. So, here you have one of the smallest countries as

---

[1] See Global City, Wikipedia. <http://en.wikipedia.org/wiki/Global_city>.

No. 1, and one of the largest as No. 3. This is one reason why such surveys should be taken with a grain of salt.

Singapore is both a city and a nation-state. This complicates matters. Most foreigners think of Singapore simply as a city. But most Singaporeans think of Singapore in national terms. The government's stand lies in between these two views, although in recent times the Singapore government appears to have placed far greater emphasis on Singapore as a global city — at least that is the perception. This, by default, has had the unintended side effect of causing some fissures in the national fabric. It is possible to be both a global city and a nation-state. But it could be argued that the global city project pursued by Singapore has come at a heavy price for the nation-building project.

To establish a critical mass in population, so as to create what is known as "buzz," Singapore's doors have been thrown wide open to foreign nationals. No other country in recent times has seen an influx of foreign nationals of a similar magnitude. This has put pressure on infrastructure, such as housing and transport. And, while foreign nationals in other countries are only allowed to fill job vacancies that locals cannot fill, they are allowed here to compete directly with Singaporeans for existing jobs. With all things being equal, businesses will hire the person at the lowest cost.

The Singapore "grapevine" is rife with stories about how employers hire foreign workers on a specific grade of employment pass issued by the immigration authorities, declaring the minimum salary level stipulated by the pass and then circumventing that minimum salary level by making "deductions" for training, under-time, uniform and other gear, and so on. For example, an "S" pass holder with a minimum salary requirement of S$1,800 (which was raised to S$2,000 in 2011) could be paid between only S$1,200 and S$1,400 after all the deductions.[2]

In a society with a relatively high cost of living, there is a segment of Singaporeans who are not able to make ends meet with such salary levels.

---

[2] Ng, Esther and S Ramesh (2007). EP, S pass salary thresholds to be raised, *Today*, 10 March 2011. And Sim, Melissa (2007). Work pass: More bosses caught cheating, 7 October 2007. <http://www.asiaone.com/Business/News/Office/Story/A1Story20071011-29453.html>

But the world is filled with hundreds of millions of highly skilled individuals who are prepared to do jobs with a pittance of a salary, including S$1,200. Significant numbers have already migrated to Singapore and have displaced some Singaporeans from existing jobs. To that extent, there are increasing numbers of Singaporeans who feel uncertain about their place in their own country.

MONACO OF THE EAST

Expanding the scope of the service sector in Singapore's economy has been one of the ways of building up its global city status. Two of the most visible manifestations of this in recent years are the decision to hold an annual Formula One (F1) Singapore Night Race, and the introduction of casinos, which the Singapore government calls "integrated resorts (IR)." (The IR did not exist before 2004, which was when the Singapore government came up with the concept of introducing of casinos as part of sprawling entertainment resorts that would include high-end shopping, eateries, museums, and the like.)

The introduction of the F1 race and casinos prompted descriptions of Singapore as the "Monaco of the East," a phrase coined by Minister Mentor Lee Kuan Yew in 2005.[3]

The actual Monaco is typically described as a playground for the fabulously wealthy and famous. One website provides this description of Monaco: "A favourite of European royalty, Arab sheikhs, and opulently wealthy Americans who dock their mobile playground yachts in the marina."[4] Those who have visited both of the casinos in Singapore are likely to agree that the Singapore version of Monaco appears to fall far short of such descriptions. Discounting patrons in the VIP rooms, casino visitors — up to 40% of whom are Singaporeans — who traipse through the two gaming halls in Singapore are largely people who are least able to afford splurging on gambling sprees. Research has shown that Singaporeans are possibly some of the most avid gamblers in the world.[5] As to why this is the

---

[3] Burton, Jack (2009). Secrets of Success, *Financial Times*, 27 March 2009.
[4] Monaco Casino Royale. < http://www.onlinecasinojoy.com/monaco-casino-royale.html>
[5] Arnold, Wayne (2006). International Business; The Nanny State Places a Bet, *The New York Times*, 23 May 2006.

case, one conclusion is that Singaporeans live in such a compact and competitive society, where the punishment for poverty is of such frightening proportions, that it rewards greed and skews many Singaporeans' values towards material gain.

Just as was the case with another slogan — "Renaissance City of Asia" — which had been coined in 1998 to denote Singapore as a vibrant artistic and cultural hub, the slogan "Monaco of the East" also seems fated for eventual obscurity. A global city has to be global in all its dimensions, not just in its economic and infrastructural characteristics. And it cannot be a derivative of other cities. It has to be unique in a number of ways, so as to give it a competitive edge internationally.

THE BET ON CASINOS

On the surface at least, Singapore's IRs give it a sheen of sophistication. In reality, however, the resorts are just like the resorts in Macau — which are completely dependent on their casinos. The high-end retail outlets at Marina Bay Sands, for example, are largely spurned by visitors to the IR, as a 2010 *Today* article reported.[6] It seems that visitors have money to gamble away at the gaming tables, but not the money to spend on luxury merchandise.

However, all that may be immaterial as the revenues and profits of both casinos during their first incomplete calendar year of operations in 2010 exceeded even the most optimistic projections, generating hundreds of millions of dollars in profits within a matter of months.

The casinos and other facilities offered at the IR's have also created many new jobs, even if a significant number may have gone to foreigners.[7]

Moreover, the resorts have also had a positive spill-over effect on the wider economy. The combination of entry levies on Singaporeans and permanent residents and taxes on gaming profits now form a new and important revenue stream for the government.

---

[6] Yng, Ng Jing and Chin, Neo Chai (2010). MBS retail scene not as hot as expected, *Today*, 17 December 2010.
[7] Singapore Casino Jobs and Gaming-Related Careers.
<http://www.worldcasinojobs.com/singapore>

While there is a general consensus that these facts constitute a successful dimension to the IR project, there is a disinclination to recognise that the negative social impact of the casinos may have exceeded even the most pessimistic expectations.

Throughout 2010, the Singapore government repeatedly said that it was too early to determine the casinos' social impact, even as figures showed that by the end of December 2010, around 300 families had secured family exclusion orders to exclude a family member from the casinos. For every such order, it is likely that there were prior unsuccessful applications when the family member in question resisted attempts to be placed under such orders.

The same rule-of-thumb would apply to the reports of gamblers who were engaged in theft to fuel their binges at the casino. In a breakfast talk on the social and economic impact of the casinos, which I gave in August 2010 to some 30 KPMG auditors and accountants, I urged them to refresh their skills in the specialised area of forensic auditing. This was because I expected cases of fraud and theft in the months ahead, committed by gamblers siphoning money from their employers in order to fuel their casino visits. From the experience of other jurisdictions, it can take years for such white-collar crimes to come to light.

One of the consequences of having a casino industry in Singapore, despite all of its positive economic benefits, is that it would entrench an underclass and lead to social divisions. These are already significant in Singapore, and could get worse. Given Singapore's small size and population density, these divisions tend to be perceptually magnified many times over.

A DIVERSIFIED ECONOMY

Widening social divisions have become evident even as Singapore's economy has become more diversified and resilient. The influx of immigrants has helped in that process of diversification. Building up the population base with added foreign talent also ensures that Singapore will have a springboard for seizing new economic opportunities when they arise.

The issue at hand, however, is whether there is a disproportionate reliance on a small segment of the local population — 20% to 25% — to generate the vast bulk of economic growth.[8] In such a situation, spectacular headline numbers of economic growth come across as purely statistical in nature to the vast majority of the population. They may be impacted only marginally, in the form of nominal salary increments and bonuses.

Of course, significant economic growth also leads to rising property prices. That might be very material in many other countries, where people can draw what is known as equity from their residential property. But this generally does not apply in Singapore because some 86% of residential property comprises public housing and the rules governing Housing and Development Board (HDB) flats are such that owners are not allowed to pledge their flats as collateral for loans.

An economic strategy which results in a substantial and widening social and income gap between the top one-quarter of the population and the bottom three-quarters can only be sustained for a period of time — but not over the long haul, and clearly not indefinitely. For democratic entities, in the long run, this strategy will have inevitable political repercussions.

OPINIONS AND PRACTICES IN A GLOBAL CITY

In a global city, the opinions of the native-born and the immigrant population are given equal weight. This is what makes for the success of a global city — the acceptance of any number of opinions, whatever their origin. Another thing that is essential to a global city is that it subscribes to best international practices. This means more transparency and accountability. Policies can still be made by a small number of individuals, but these policies have to be explained so as to avoid speculation and second-guessing.

However, when a global city is also a nation-state, a portion of the local population may be less tolerant about accepting the opinions of non-citizens when it comes to sensitive national issues. This is where a global city and nation-state come into contention.

---

[8] Those who live in public housing are provided various social and financial assistance. The government terms this as "targeted assistance." Those who live in private housing receive very little, if anything. The 2010 figure of HDB dwellers are 76.3% of all stock of residential housing, hence estimated figure of 20% to 25% of private housing dwellers. Section 1.9 on *Residential Dwellings of the Department of Statistics 2011 Yearbook.* <http://www.singstat.gov.sg/pubn/reference/yos11/yos2011.pdf>

The Singapore press regularly features commentaries by foreign nationals either living in or visiting Singapore, who offer high praise for the country and its government. For those who may not understand why such praise comes across as contentious, the reason can be summed up in a single word — condescension.

However, not everyone thinks so. In fact, there are those who feel that the regular evidence in the national dailies of how much non-citizens seem to love Singapore provides reassurance and vindication. Here, a distinction can be drawn with the attitude in truly First World societies. For instance, American author Kenneth Pyle, in his book *Japan Rising*, wrote that more than 100 years ago "the Japanese had no time for Japanophiles and took no pleasure in the patronising compliments of foreign visitors… The British poet Sir Edwin Arnold on a visit to Japan in 1891 was rebuked by the Japanese when he lavished praise on their traditional aesthetics."[9]

The same theme recurs in many other First World countries. For instance, a web posting on American culture for foreigners states: "The average American will not take kindly to bullying, condescension, line-jumping, or downright pushiness."[10]

The contention between the imperatives of being a nation-state and a global city will continue to play out in Singapore. At the time of writing (March 2011), Singapore was gearing up for a general election, whose results would provide an indication of where voter sentiments lie on this major issue. The 2011 election will be the most crucial in a generation. Its results will either give renewed vigour to Singapore's global city project, or it will decelerate that process.

---

[9] Pyle, Kenneth (2007). *Japan Rising*, New York: Public Affairs, p. 103.
[10] American Culture for Foreigners. < http://www.essortment.com/american-culture-foreigners-63697.html>

CHAPTER 8

Singapore as a Global City: A Balancing Act

SYLVIA LIM

One of the "Key Goals" recommended by the Economic Strategies Committee (ESC) Report 2010 is to further Singapore's position as a "Global City."

This goal was articulated to mean Singapore should be "vibrant and distinctive," "open and diverse," and "a home that provides an outstanding quality of life for our people" (Shanmugaratnam *et al.*, 2010).

While there is no doubt that Singapore needs to be plugged into the world outside its borders, it is submitted that Singapore faces certain inherent limitations in its quest to become a hub for creativity and innovation. These limitations must be addressed if it is to realise its full potential.

For example, Singapore is often seen as a sterile cultural desert with inadequate cultural activities to attract workers who are talented and highly skilled (Ooi, 2008). It is further submitted that enhancing Singapore's appeal as "home" must go beyond infrastructural spectacles and requires concrete measures to give Singaporeans a sense of empowerment and of being cared for within its porous borders.

HOW FAR CAN SINGAPORE BE A HUB FOR CREATIVITY AND INNOVATION IF IT MAINTAINS AN ILLIBERAL CLIMATE?

In its ranking of liveable cities in 2010, the Economist Intelligence Unit placed Singapore 53rd out of 140 cities (*The Straits Times*, 13 February

2010). Singapore's ranking was pulled down partly because of a low score for culture and environment.

This assessment exposes some challenges facing efforts to develop Singapore as an arts and creative capital, where "talented people....see this as a place where they can develop skills, expertise and creative imagination, achieve their aspirations, and contribute meaningfully to a society that is on the move," as advocated by the ESC Report.

Creativity typically thrives in free environments, which foster spontaneity, encourage the exploration of unconventional thought, encourage challenges to the status quo, and provide safety nets for failure. One dictionary meaning of "create" is to "bring into being out of nothing or by force of imagination." The micro-management of Singaporeans' everyday lives may not be the most conducive environment to nurture creativity and innovation.

As far as free expression is concerned, Singapore is not the most liberal of regimes. While the government may welcome commercial creativity and artistic activities that bring commercial benefits, it has been wary of activities which challenge the official social discourse.

Censorship is still a reality. Even a collaboration between Singaporeans and foreigners for Singaporeans to sing about their pet peeves as a "Complaints Choir" encountered problems when applying for a performing licence (Hansard, 15 February 2008). If this situation does not change, can Singapore ever claim to be an arts capital?

As for innovation in the commercial sector, there has been much government investment and many incentives to encourage research and development. Our potential in this area was addressed in the first Singapore Competitiveness Report in 2009 (Ketels, 2009). While noting Singapore's strong infrastructure, concerns were raised by industry players that the controlled nature of Singaporean society might inhibit "creative" activities that tend to thrive in less-structured environments.

Reasons why Singapore society has developed this way include decades of emphasis on "practical" knowledge in the education system and pragmatism as part of the work ethic. By and large, parents tend to encourage their children to take on "safe" jobs with established companies, rather than go into the creative industries or entrepreneurship. In addition, jobs in the elite administrative service are sought after as a fast route to success. A resident in his 30s, now successful in marketing, recently shared with the author that he did poorly in school as he was often faulted for being a "dreamer," which goes against the ethos of pragmatism preached by the state.

Why is the level of entrepreneurship in Singapore lower compared to many other countries? Some of the contributing factors, in my view, are an education system and culture that reward conformity and obedience, the fear of failure and the drastic consequences of failure. Being an undischarged bankrupt in Singapore, for instance, carries many disabilities and may not be worth the risk to many potential entrepreneurs.

One notable concern of the government is that talented people, including Singaporeans living overseas, must see Singapore as a place where they can make meaningful contributions. Indeed, the articulated aims of Singapore as a global city include making it a centre for leadership and ideas. People may have different ideas about how to contribute meaningfully, which may include becoming a pressure point for the government. Is the government prepared to embrace that?

THERE HAS BEEN A PALPABLE SENSE OF LOSS OF IDENTITY AND NATION IN VIEW OF THE RAPID PACE OF CHANGE IN THE LAST FEW YEARS

Although "Global City" and "Endearing Home" were articulated as twin aims in the government agenda, the writer's view is that there is an inherent contradiction between the two.

A simplistic illustration is Singapore's hosting of major meetings such as the International Monetary Fund and World Bank meetings in 2006. The tagline used then was the "Land of Four Million Smiles," which presumably intended to get the whole population smiling at the visitors.

However, due to the high security and traffic diversions, many people were inconvenienced and avoided the meeting area like plague, causing retailers in Suntec City to suffer significant business losses. It is doubtful that many locals were smiling during these meetings!

The concept of "Home" is an emotional one, which has nothing to do with more museums, new civic centres or being open to the world. Instead, the ordinary understanding of "Home" connotes familiarity and a sense of belonging.

An influx of foreigners over the last few years has resulted in a palpable sense of loss of identity and nationhood among Singaporeans.

There has been a drastic increase in the size of the population, from three million in 1990, to four million in 2000, and five million in 2010. Those who feel uncomfortable about this should note that the government has announced that it is using a population size of six and a half million as a planning parameter. These numbers, in an island of 700 square kilometres, are unimaginable to most of us.

Besides population density, the citizen to non-citizen mix has also changed. In 1990, 86% of the population comprised Singapore citizens. By 2010, this had fallen to 63%. This means that nearly four in ten here are non-citizens. This displacement affects the whole country, as Singapore has no hinterland. Unlike the residents of major cities like London or New York, locals here cannot move out of the city in order to seek refuge. Even in "heartland" areas like Tampines, one can close one's eyes at a traffic junction, listen to the surrounding conversations and imagine oneself to be in another country. Many Singaporeans feel that Singapore is "not recognisable anymore" and they are strangers in their own country.

The reaction from "the ground" has, naturally, not been good. Every day, the strains on infrastructure such as transport systems and other public amenities are keenly felt. During a recent personal encounter, a Singaporean told the writer that he disagreed with the government's exhortations to see foreigners as a form of healthy competition. In his view, the competition had reached unhealthy levels and is adversely affecting Singaporeans' quality of life.

In the face of these developments, how can Singaporeans feel more assured that they belong to Singapore rather than some other place? It is submitted that two important factors to address are empowering Singaporeans and showing them more care in our policies.

WE CAN RECLAIM SOME IDENTITY AND SOCIAL COHESION THROUGH EMPOWERMENT AND MUTUAL SUPPORT

Singaporeans must feel empowered at home.

To this end, it is felt that the government should retreat from spheres of life that are not central to government functions, and allow authentic leadership to grow organically. Examples of such spheres include sports associations, consumer groups and grassroots organisations. By facilitating the evolution of natural leaders, Singaporeans can "own" their pet causes and feel that they have a stake in Singapore's evolving society.

Political diversity should also be celebrated as an important means of keeping Singaporeans engaged in the country's direction and future. Not valuing such diversity creates the risk of apathy and cynicism towards "top-down" initiatives. Empowerment at home must include having diverse voices competing for public opinion, so that the public will be engaged in making choices that determine the country's directions.

Indeed, in the context of influx of foreigners into this country, the importance of the General Election as a reinforcement of the essence of Singapore citizenship cannot be under-estimated (Ting, 2010).

As for policies, it is time for Singaporeans to feel that they have intrinsic value and that the country will not fail them, especially when they are frail or old.

Hitherto, the official discourse has characterised welfare as a dirty word. Yet, Singapore is becoming an increasingly polarised society, with a widening income and wealth gap. Instead of embracing the future, many people find life worrying due to rising costs and issues facing the elderly.

The government policies regarding social protections are generally predicated on the principles of self-reliance and family support. How fair is this in practice?

The whole debate concerning the Central Provident Fund (CPF) Life initiative in 2007 was instructive. Reforms were made to the existing mandatory savings scheme, the CPF, to ensure that Singaporeans purchased annuities to provide monthly payments for life. This reform illustrated the government's worry that citizens would seek public financial assistance in their old age. Despite its strong financial position, the government would not countenance any suggestion of setting aside some funds in order to grow income to support seniors in their 80s (Hansard, 18 September 2007).

Medical costs are another area of concern. It is typical to come across sick senior citizens who are denied permission to draw on their compulsory medical savings accounts (Medisave) for various treatments, and who are instead forced to ask for money from their children to pay for medical bills.

A case in point is an elderly gentleman with a chronic illness, whom the author met recently. He had to regularly ask his son for cash for outpatient treatments, as his bills did not meet the Medisave withdrawal requirements. After his son got married and had a child, the son was saddled with his own family's medical bills, as well as other expenses. He then asked his father to move out to live with another child who, presumably, would take over the cash payments. Such tensions do not affect the wealthy, but rather the working and sandwiched classes. By requiring the elderly to exhaust their family resources, is this not tantamount to pass the buck to future generations, which the government has always warned against?

Each year, around 5,000 Singaporeans apply to the police for the Certificate of No Criminal Conviction, with 68% using it for permanent residency applications in other countries (Hansard, 25 August and 20 October 2008). It was reported in the press recently that some Singaporeans choose to immigrate to other countries because these had better social services. If Singaporeans are indeed immigrating to other countries because they believe other governments will take better care of them as permanent residents, it is high time to examine closely how well Singapore is caring for its own citizens.

REFERENCES

Ooi, Can–Seng (2008). *Credibility of a Creative Image: The Singaporean Approach*, Creative Encounters Working papers # 7, Copenhagen Business School.

Ketels, Christian *et al.* (2009). *Singapore Competitiveness Report*. Singapore: Asia Competitiveness Institute, Lee Kuan Yew School of Public Policy.

Hansard. Singapore Parliamentary Reports. Available online at http://www.parliament.gov.sg, accessed 13 January 2011.

Shanmugaratnam, Tharman. *et al* (2010). Economic Strategies Committee Report. Singapore. Available online at http://www.ecdl.org/media/Singapore%20Economic%20Committe_2010.pdf, accessed 5 December 2010.

Ting, Ming Hwa (2010). Ritual and identity: elections and voting in Singapore. *Taiwan Journal of Democracy* Vol 6, No. 2, pp. 101–124 (Dec 2010).

CHAPTER 9

Including the Disadvantaged in a Meritocratic Singapore: Past, Present and Future

DENISE PHUA

INTRODUCTION

Good morning, your Excellencies, Ladies, and Gentlemen. Thank you for giving me the opportunity to share my perspective at this Technology Entertainment and Design (TED)-like platform.[1]

The path of forging a more inclusive Singapore society is one of no return. As expectations rise in an increasingly progressive and affluent Singapore, the voices of different interest groups will only grow louder.

When I shared on Facebook that I would be speaking at this seminar, a passionate animal rights advocate reminded me to lobby for the interests of animals and ensure that evil animal abusers, including any relevant government agencies, would be taken to task.

One only has to scan the Internet to hear the voices of many groups who seek inclusion, state's attention and resources. These include the low-income earners, the disabled, human rights activists, animal rights activists,

---

[1] Online talks by interesting people <http://www.ted.com/>

the elderly, same-sex couples, religious groups, atheists, performance artists, as well as political parties. There is also the notion of an "e-inclusive society," where everybody is able to reap the benefits brought about by information and communications technologies. Advocates for this ideology want technology to be accessible and affordable for all, regardless of age, language, social background or ability.

But *who* should be prioritized for inclusion and provision, in the face of finite time and resources, especially if each group feels they deserve priority? We may never agree on the answer. But most of us will agree that the real wealth of a nation is reflected not only by the size of its coffers, but also in the way it includes and cares for those who are vulnerable and disadvantaged. For what shall it profit a man, if he shall gain the whole world, and lose his own soul?

In the interest of time, I will focus primarily on two groups of vulnerable Singaporeans who are at risk of being left behind. They are those in the lower economic strata of Singapore, and the disabled - young and elderly. The State is constantly under pressure to cater for members of these groups, in order to prevent a serious loss of social bonding, disunity and instability.

ON ENABLING AND INCLUDING THE DISABLED

Since Prime Minister Lee Hsien Loong announced the vision to create a more inclusive society during his 2004 inauguration, there has been much progress, especially for people with special needs in Singapore. In 2007, the Government commissioned the drafting of a new five year Enabling Masterplan by key community leaders and boldly accepted almost all their recommendations. Even politicians from opposition parties admitted that "for many years, prior to the birth of (this) Enabling Masterplan, "disadvantaged" Singaporeans [were] virtually an invisible group of citizens in our society."[2]

Indeed, when it comes to including the disabled, significant progress had been made over the last five years. This progress is the result of a caring community comprising the Government and agencies such as the National

---

[2] The Excluded in an Inclusive Society, 31 January 2008, the Workers' Party website, <http://wp.sg/2008/01/the-excluded-in-an-inclusive-society/>

Council of Social Services (NCSS) and Voluntary Welfare Organisations (VWOs) that champion and advocate for inclusion and resources.

Some areas of progress include the following:

(a) The number of Early Intervention Programme for Infants and Children (EIPIC) centres increased from three in 2003 to 11 in 2010;

(b) Although Early Intervention, like most other social service programmes, is means-tested, a new fixed subsidy of $300 per citizen child was introduced, making the costly EIPIC programme far more affordable to all Singaporeans;

(c) A Special Needs Trust Company and a revamped Centre for Enabling Living to serve both the disabled and the elderly-in-need have been set up;

(d) The Ministry of Education, which formerly took an arms-length approach to the education of special-needs students, has stepped up very actively to improve the effectiveness and quality of special schools; and

(e) Efforts to include adults with disabilities and to ensure they have access to employment support and community integration are underway, although there is still a general dearth of these services.

There is still much to do in terms of raising the bar for essential services to the disabled community. This has hitherto been left to the care of the charity sector, but there is now a light at the end of the tunnel for those in need.

ON INCLUDING THE POOR AND LOW-SKILLED

As for the poor and low-wage, low-skilled population, last week's robust Parliamentary debate on inclusive growth has highlighted their plight and re-affirmed Singapore's conviction that they should not be left behind.

Whilst globalisation has fuelled Singapore's economic growth, not all have benefited equally from this growth. Singapore's highly educated and skilled workers are sought locally and overseas, leading to an inevitable hike in their income. On the other hand, many low-skilled workers, especially those in low-end production jobs, face the daily risk of losing their jobs to countries of lower cost.

Unless they upgrade their skills in time, they will become either permanently redundant or chronic low-wage workers, stuck in what I call the "3-L" (low pay, low status, and long hours) industries that cannot be relocated overseas. These are the cleaning, food and beverage, laundry and other service industries. Ensuring these low-skilled workers are not left behind in the wake of Singapore's economic growth is important.

Schemes such as the Workfare Income Supplement scheme anchors inclusive growth. Introduced in 2007, some 400,000 low-wage workers with gross monthly incomes of up to $1,700 per month saw a total top-up of $400 million to date. There is also the Workfare Training Support scheme and a national Workforce Skills Qualifications (WSQ) framework to certify skills and lay the pathways for Continued Education and Training. There are Productivity and Innovation Initiatives, the latest being the National Trades Union Congress (NTUC) Employment and Employability Institute's $40 million Inclusive Growth Programme. Other schemes include the restriction of foreign labour in order to encourage local hiring.

In addition, the poor in our country benefit from a slew of social assistance programmes if they qualify under means-testing. These include:

(a) Home Ownership and Upkeep, which includes the Rent and Utilities Assistance Scheme; Home Ownership Plus Education Scheme;

(b) Healthcare – Medisave, Medishield, Medifund;

(c) Education — Kindergarten Financial Assistance Scheme; Student Care Free Assistance Scheme Centre-based Financial Assistance Scheme for Child Care;

(d) Compulsory Savings such as the Central Provident Fund (CPF), Singapore's version of Social Security; and

(e) Transfers such as the Goods and Service Tax (GST) credits, utilities and rental rebates and public assistance for some 2,000 elderly citizens with no family support.

However, these measures are not always perfect. As the cost of living escalates, there is a need to constantly tweak the configuration of these help schemes to take care of those who are at risk of becoming chronic low-wage or even no-wage workers, due to their inability to learn or catch up. Suggestions to increase workfare, a government-paid income top-up scheme; increase the cash portion of the payout; and escalate efforts to transform low-productivity jobs have been tabled and are now under consideration.

I have also requested that the public sector identifies and awards contracts or jobs to workers who cannot benefit from further training due to their advanced age and/or lower learning abilities. Many of these workers are the last to be hired and first to be fired. I hope that my proposal is heeded.

PRINCIPLES UNDERPINNING SINGAPORE'S SOCIAL SAFETY NET

The three basic principles underlying the social safety net are:

(a) Self-reliance, or work before welfare
(b) Family as the first line of defence
(c) Many Helping Hands.

PRINCIPLE ONE: SELF-RELIANCE, WORK BEFORE WELFARE

The principle of self-reliance underlines the support schemes for Singapore's poor, which encourages individuals to work before seeking welfare. This is the path that is uniquely Singaporean, and one that is less travelled than the path of welfarism.

It is telling that this supplement is paid out in the form of work incentives to encourage work, rather than in the form of unemployment benefits for those with no work.

In the face of data that the average Singaporean can live into his or her 80s, measures have been put in place to encourage Singaporeans to be in the workforce for a longer period of time; to build a bigger nest egg; and to take up annuity schemes such as CPF Life, so as to enhance the financial security of the elderly. Active ageing programmes have also been put in place so that senior citizens can enjoy a good quality of life during their golden years.

The implementation of these measures is not without challenges:

(a) There is the constant appeal of the more universally applied Minimum Wage Policy versus the unique Singaporean Workfare Income Supplement scheme, where pay is topped-up by the Government;

(b) Even as Members of Parliament (MPs) urge the raising of the Workfare Income Supplement in order to top up the pay of low-wage workers, there is fear of whether this would reduce the motivation of these workers to train or upgrade their skills for a potential rise in income; and

(c) While research has shown that a significant number of Singaporeans are financially ill-prepared for retirement, many remain resistant to the raising of the retirement and CPF withdrawal age. "Stop treating me like a child. Give me my money. I will cross the bridge when it comes if I do not have sufficient resources to live on for the latter part of my life." Such are the tensions behind the principle of self-reliance. Alas, not everyone agrees with the principle of self-reliance except the likes of poet Ralph Waldo Emerson, who said this of self-reliance and the beauty of work: "There is a time in every man's education when he arrives at the conviction that envy is ignorance; that imitation is suicide; that he must take himself for better, for worse, as his portion; that though the wide universe is full of good, no kernel of nourishing corn can come to him but through his toil bestowed on that plot of ground which is given to him to till."

PRINCIPLE TWO: FAMILY — THE FIRST LINE OF DEFENCE

The second principle underlying Singapore's social safety net is that the family is the first port of call in times of difficulty, failing which the community and the Government will step in.

Family members are encouraged to care for one another, with the support of Government-initiated legislative and administrative measures:

(a) The CPF Minimum Sum Topping-Up Scheme, for instance, encourages children to voluntarily top up their parents' accounts. Tax relief is given for these top-ups;

(b) Tax incentive in the form of parent relief is also extended to Singaporeans who look after the elderly;

(c) One can use Medisave for the medical care of family members.

The Maintenance of Parents Act states the floor or minimum standard of parental care expected of an adult child and the consequences he will face if he disregards the call to feed and clothe his own parents when he is able to afford it. Recent amendments to the Act have created more space for conciliation before a formal submission of a claim, in order to preserve family relationships.

But what happens if the family does not want to be the first port of call in the event of difficulties? What happens when parties claim that issues such as providing for one's parents are personal choices and *filial piety* cannot be reduced to financial maintenance? They may assert that if children will not take care of their parents even though they can afford to, then the State or the rest of society should foot the bill.

Such are the tensions behind this second principle.

PRINCIPLE THREE: MANY HELPING HANDS

The third principle underpinning Singapore's social safety net is Many Helping Hands. It is the Government's long-standing belief that "in helping the disadvantaged, everyone has the responsibility and an important aim is to foster a caring and compassionate society to encourage those who are more able to help those who are less able."[3]

Increasingly, service delivery and monitoring roles are outsourced to agencies like NCSS, family services centres and VWOs. The state has taken on the role of planner, policy-maker, and regulator, and also funds developmental and partial operating costs of selected service providers.

Many useful projects and initiatives have resulted from the "Many Helping Hands" approach. But this approach has often been challenged — not in terms of its spirit, but in terms of its effectiveness.

In my maiden parliament speech in November 2006, I expressed the need for this sacred cow to be sent for examination, to see if it ought to be

---

[3] Yap Mui Teng, Senior Research Fellow Institute of Policy Studies, Singapore, powerpoints, 2004.

slaughtered — or if it was at least due for a makeover, particularly in the area of the delivery of essential services to the disadvantaged. At the time, I was frustrated that services such as the education of special-needs students and the running of healthcare organisations such as the step-down community hospitals were led by charity organisations instead of the relevant government ministries.

I did not think that it was appropriate to leave the delivery of such essential services to charities whose board members were often too busy and distracted to focus on running these organisations. These charities, in turn, often had difficulty attracting qualified staff.

I also see a lack of co-ordination that has led to less than robust case management and co-ordination. Some clients are over-served, with multiple avenues for seeking help, while others are under-served. Some are not served at all, and fall through the cracks. I have observed that there is an inconsistent standard of service provisions. The prognoses of clients, young and old, is largely dependent on the varying degrees of commitment, competence and aspiration of each charity.

At the 2009 Committee of Supply debates, MPs expressed that the "Many Helping Hands" approach needed a "central mind to co-ordinate the efforts of different agencies," a database, and thorough case management to follow through on chronic cases.

Going forward with increasing pressure for results rather than schemes and activities, it is likely that the Many Helping Hands approach will be closely examined. Hopefully, the right hands would be deployed more effectively.

WHOSE JOB IS IT ANYWAY TO CREATE A CARING SOCIETY?

Whose job it is to create an inclusive and caring society and to ensure the disadvantaged are not left behind in meritocratic Singapore? If we conduct a straw poll among typical Singaporeans, the answer is likely to be: the Government.

GOVERNMENT

Indeed, the State has to play a leading role so that all individuals and groups, including those in the most marginalised communities, have equal access to the collective goods that are the citizen's basic social entitlement. It must be the role of the Government to strengthen the social safety net and to ensure that every citizen — not just those who are able and talented — partakes in the fruits of our country's growth. We are as good as our weakest link. If we do not commit to taking care of the weakest members of our society, fewer and fewer citizens will heed the call to procreate, lest they give birth to less than perfect children; or because their hope of getting out of the poverty cycle grows dimmer by the year.

At Government level, I believe in the need for a deeper study of our country's social safety net, particularly the principles behind who the safety net should catch and how it is cast. We should also identify the holes in the net and mend the gaping holes so that fewer people will fall through the holes.

In addition, the State must actively engage its citizens in developing and communicating the terms of the social contract, so that most citizens will enter and abide by it. There must be a better understanding and acceptance of the key principles that are good for the long-term survival of Singapore as a society; and what privileges should be considered basic rights of citizens without turning to unreasonable or unhealthy entitlement claims. As Dwight Eisenhower, the 34th President of the United States, once warned: "A people that values its privileges above its principles soon loses both."

But beyond the Government, each of us can do much more to make a difference in cultivating an inclusive and caring society. I believe that the real wealth of a country is when all stakeholders, not just politicians, businessmen and employers, take our place and play a role in developing a more caring society in everyday life.

ADVOCATES

Those of us who are advocates for our people or animals whose interests we passionately represent must first seek to understand. Only then we would stand a better chance of being heard and responded to. Only then there would be a higher probability that in the case of a stalemate, a creative third alternative can emerge.

In a neighbourhood where pigeons often congregate, residents who fear bird-related diseases insist that the pigeons be culled. Bird-lovers, on the other hand, continue to feed them and object to them being killed. Government agencies, wary of both parties, refrain from taking any action lest they become the ant on which the elephants trample.

Before coming to this conference, I received a very demanding and angry note from a disabled citizen, who insisted that Government is completely at fault for the current state of affairs in his life and community.

To be effective advocates, we need to understand the fine balance between courage and consideration. We must have the courage to identify the gaps, advocate for improvements, and shape services. However, we must also be wise and considerate, and learn to cite compelling cases so that others will want to support us. We must not only demand services, but, in most instances, be willing to become part of the solution. Some of the causes we fight for are at the initial stage of progress and others are at a more mature state. Some of our ideas may be ahead of times, so we need to be more patient and persuasive. Only then, our chances of being heard would increase and the solutions we propose would be supported and sustained beyond us.

INDIVIDUALS

As for the rest of Singaporeans, who are neither policy-makers, advocates nor the disadvantaged, I urge you to join in the journey to make our country a more inclusive and caring one. As Mahatma Gandhi put it, "We need to be the change that we want in the world."

"Treat others the way you expect to be treated"; "Love thy neighbour as thyself"; "Do unto others as you would have others do unto you" — so the wise sayings go.

Stop asking "what is in it for me?" But rather "how can I help?" Does not just rely on bashing others when things go wrong. Everyone can identify a problem — the real significance is how we can try to be part of the solution.

Each year, Singapore students with their Community Involvement Programmes (CIP) and Service Learning Plans hunt VWOs down with their favourite plans, telling others what they want to do and mostly forgetting to ask what their beneficiaries really need.

We have heard of the long queues for heavily subsidised Housing and Development Board (HDB) flats and desperate and angry applicants waiting their turns. It is, of course, the duty of the Government to meet the urgent needs of the homeless. At the same time, there are tenants who are no longer poor but insist they continue to stay in these subsidised flats because of their need for privacy or because they cannot bring themselves to give up such privileges, depriving those who are genuinely in need of low-cost housing.

Hence, in our efforts to build an inclusive and caring society, we need to put into practice what we preach, especially when it comes to respecting those whose social status are below ours or who are disadvantaged in some way.

In my work as an MP and as Chairperson of a Town Council, I have sometimes observed with angst how Singaporeans treat our cleaners and front-line officers. Few offer the words "sorry," "please," "thank you," or compliments when things go right.

CONCLUSION

In conclusion, we do not need to be policy-makers or regulators, or even be in politics, to make Singapore a more inclusive and caring society. Each of us can improve our society by thinking of and doing less for ourselves and our families, and more for others in our outer circles. Walk the extra mile. Arise from the seat of the armchair critic to really contribute. That way, Singapore can move one step close to a world in which everyone can potentially achieve the full measure of our humanity.

CHAPTER 10

The Singapore Spirit is not a Pontianak — What is it?

WOFFLES WU

Ambassador Ong Keng Yong, distinguished guests:

When I accepted the invitation to speak at this prestigious forum, I had no idea I would be so far out of my depth. I am neither a politician nor an academic. Travelling around the world to deliver lectures on plastic surgery is easy, as I know the topic well. But putting my thoughts together and wrapping my head around, a topic as intangible as the "Singapore Spirit," has been a challenge for me.

After reading *Singapore Perspectives* 2010, I realised that everything that needs to be said and discussed has already been covered by personalities more qualified than myself. Our Prime Minister, professors, political scientists, policy makers, and sociologists have succinctly and cogently spoken their minds on what Singapore is about, the direction it is headed in, and how this is to be achieved.

What can I possibly contribute to this forum? Have I been asked to speak because I am an artist, an actor, a failed restaurateur, a film-maker, a writer, or someone who is just passionate about the arts and heritage of Singapore? Is it because of my contributions as a doctor to the patients I serve and to the international world of plastic surgery? Or is it because being international in outlook, I get to observe Singapore from various angles?

I felt that the only way I could contribute meaningfully is to give my own perspective of why Singapore is my home and what it means to me, having grown up and made a career for myself here. I also wish to highlight the various people and talents whom I have been associated with and who I think have made Singapore the vibrant metropolis it is now. These individuals are living the Singapore Dream.

First, what is the "Singapore Spirit"? Is it like the Christmas Spirit, which celebrates family, fellowship, good cheer, the giving of presents, a time of worship, and a time to consider the less fortunate? Can we define it in similar terms?

To me the "Singapore Spirit" is about many things — some more immediately apparent than others. It is about the qualities and the drive that has enabled us to make a successful transformation from Third World to First World status in such a short span of time. This is founded on our "never say die, anything can be done" attitude and our belief that we can achieve anything.

It is this strong belief that we control our own destiny that has given us the confidence to go head to head with any country or body on a variety of issues. We have our political forefathers to thank for instilling in us this self-belief, and for providing us with the platform to springboard forward. But we also need to credit, as a people, our collective endurance, hard work, and our ability to change and adapt to new situations.

We also need to be mindful that the "Singapore Spirit" has a flip side and can manifest itself in negative ways. We must not be blinded by success and become cocky and arrogant, unfeeling, uncharitable, opportunistic, or eager to benefit from the misfortune of others.

We have to be less "kiasu" (Hokkien for "scared to lose") and curb our desire to win or benefit at all times. Queuing overnight to buy a condominium in order to resell it that very day or queuing for hours at a petrol station to get an additional 5% discount are laughable examples of this behaviour. But selfishly occupying public transport seats meant for the elderly and pregnant women or parking in handicap lots are a more disturbing manifestation of the "me first!" generation. Our society still needs to be guided and moulded in order to become more gracious and caring of others.

When I lecture or conduct surgeries overseas, I am often asked why I do not choose to live in London, New York, or Paris. Would I be not more successful in any of these great capitals of the world, have more patients, earn more, and have a better life? Would my star not burn brighter overseas?

The question is well-intended but it is based on a lack of knowledge of what Singapore has to offer and end up being condescending.

The answer is an emphatic NO. Why would I want to live in any of these places when I can live in Singapore?

In the 1950s and 60s, a young plastic surgeon named Ivo Pitanguy living in Rio de Janeiro in Brazil made a name for himself by pioneering several plastic surgery procedures. Soon patients, students, and fellows flocked from around the world to Brazil, bypassing the more traditional locations in the United States, and making Brazil a tourist destination and a plastic surgery hotspot. To this day, Pitanguy remains in Rio. He is proud that his achievements have contributed to the vitality and legend of Rio.

Our own Dr Arthur Lim has done the same thing for ophthalmology and put us on the international map.

My aspiration is to contribute in a similar way to plastic surgery, and to Singapore, as we become an international medical hub. I would like patients and students to come to me, and not me to them. I would like this to be my hub. I am in my comfort zone here.

This has required much groundwork over the past 15 years, during which I have travelled the world extensively, teaching, operating, establishing professional networks, and forging those invisible links with like-minded colleagues who believe in the highest standards of professionalism and results. International colleagues now have the confidence to send their patients to me here in Singapore. The hard work has paid off.

In my own way, like many others, I try to do the best for myself and my patients, my family, the community I belong to, and, if possible, my country. If I can contribute on an international level, it is a bonus and a privilege. Success means different things to each of us and some set their targets higher than others. No matter what level of success we attain, these are all positive contributions to the growth and prosperity of our country.

Some of us are cogs in the wheel, some are the wheels. But each component is indispensable, no matter how small it is.

I love Singapore. I do not love everything about it though. Certainly not the selfish behaviour — the *kiasu* behaviour I mentioned earlier — the terrible toilets, the rude, and dangerous drivers, the fact that we never greet our neighbours or say good morning in the lift.

I dislike some government policies, like scrapping cars that are more than ten years old, needing a Certificate of Entitlement (COE) in order to have a car, or paying Electronic Road Pricing surcharges at 10.30pm when Singaporeans tired from a day at work are rushing home to see their families or to rest. Clamping down on the official use of dialects when many citizens still speak dialect to communicate in a more intimate way is another pet peeve. I am aware why some of these policies are in effect, as they serve a greater good, but they often appear overly restrictive and punitive. Living in our version of Utopia has a price to pay but I still would not want to live anywhere else.

I have loved Singapore from the time it was a sleepy hollow. I still love it now, as it has transformed into an exciting, entertaining, and multifaceted cosmopolitan city, which offers everything from a safe business environment to excellent dining at all levels, superb education and an arts and cultural scene that rivals any Western country.

I travel every month. It is interesting to visit new countries, but after a few days away I cannot wait to board the Singapore Airlines plane that will take me back to Singapore, the land where almost everything works. Once I see the friendly smiles of the crew members, read my *The Straits Times* and order cup noodles, the stress of travel leaves me and I feel a tremendous sense of relief.

Singapore has transformed beyond recognition. Our physical environment, the cityscape, the clever town planning and the innovative architecture has allowed us to become one of the most beautiful cities in the world.

Just a few nights ago, as I sat in the gorgeously restored Collyer Quay (now the Fullerton Bay Hotel) gazing across the Marina at Marina Bay Sands, I was stunned by the scale, magnificence, and beauty of the vista before me. I felt I was in the middle of an illuminated jewel box that rivalled the splendour of anything in London, Paris, Barcelona, or New York. I told my foreign guests, who were here for Art Stage Singapore, that they were looking at Singapore at the peak of its development, the fruition of many years of planning and investment.

But it was not always like this.

When I was growing up in the 1960s and 70s, Singapore was still in its infancy as a nation. Chinatown was still a mass of people in dilapidated shop-houses, the Singapore River was a cauldron of debris and decay and bumboats lined up choc a bloc with stench to match. Traffic was sparse, a Mercedes Benz 280s cost $18,000 and bungalows were under $100,000.

Our biggest tourist attraction was the transvestites of Bugis Street and our most famous medical export was Professor Ratnam, who made Singapore the international hub of sex-change operations, long before Bangkok came into the picture. The bar at the Mitre Hotel was a crowd favourite with expats and locals on a shoestring budget and the Raffles Hotel was at its most decrepit state, all shabby and worn out.

Then things started to change rapidly. If we wanted to be plugged into the world's economy and become a First World country, we needed better infrastructure and operating systems in our quest to become a financial hub and the Switzerland of Asia. We needed a better city-scape, better tourist attractions and we needed to modernise. That we achieved this in a few short years is legendary and I will not dwell on these successes. The spirit of entrepreneurship and efficiency is a key component of the "Singapore Spirit" and we all know this.

But the success of a country does not rest only on its financial achievements or in the fact that we have provided a roof over everyone's heads. Once the basic necessities have been accounted for, a nation needs to develop a soul and to develop many layers of diversity to make life interesting and multi-faceted. This creates a place for people of different levels and backgrounds, different jobs, hobbies, lifestyle choices and allows us to meld and grow with one another. This is the spirit of tolerance and acceptance.

As teenagers, we all wanted to travel to Europe and the United States for further education or just to soak up the sights and sounds of countries with hundreds of years of culture and history. We were exposed to colourful lifestyles, different societies and were able to bring these influences back to Singapore to create our own versions of a modern Asian lifestyle.

I want to highlight the creative talents and the pioneers of the softscape who have enriched our social landscape and made Singapore a fun and exciting place to live in. This is not just about mainstream art and culture, but also about those who improve our lifestyle choices and add colour and diversity to our lives. These are the fashion designers, interior designers, creative directors, hairdressers, stylists, make-up artists, theatre practitioners, photographers, artists, gallery owners, film-makers, dancers, musicians, boutique owners, restaurateurs, disco and pub owners, furniture store owners, hobbyists, those involved in Chinese opera, Indian classical dance, Malay arts, ballet, and so many other different jobs and shops. They embody the spirit of creativity.

Even the old man in Arab Street selling beads and sequins, or the junk store owner Ah Keng who sells old, used furniture, are important parts of this aspect of our development, because they epitomize the spirit of creativity and fun and daring. Daring to live their lives in unconventional jobs or vocations, daring to show others that they can survive, that it can be done their way. They are our mavericks. They give us inspiration.

We owe a debt of gratitude to the pioneers who walked before us.

Before David Gan became a household name in hairdressing, there was Willie's of London at Tanglin Shopping Centre and the famous Roland Chow of Orchard Road. Before Takashimaya, we had Chotirmall, Melwani's, Khemco and C. K. Tang. Before X-tra, Space and other high-end furniture stores, there was Diethelm and Van Hin the local furniture maker.

Long before Stephanie Sun and J. J. Lin came onto the scene, there were the talented Anita Sarawak, Dick Lee, Chris Ho, and Jacintha Abisheganaden plugging away in the music industry. Tony, Terry and Spencer and Mathew and the Mandarins were just two of the music groups that originated in the 1970s and went on to attain international recognition. Long before drag queen Kumar became popular and acceptable, there was the irrepressible band Tania in the Hilton Hotel Lobby Bar, with their cross-dressing lead singer Alban.

Before there was Ashley Isham, we had Tan Yoong and Bobby Chng. Goh Poh Seng, a fellow doctor, started several arts-related food and beverage outlets that became hubs for creative types. First, there was *Bistro Toulouse Lautrec*, at the back of Tanglin Shopping Centre, where Tania subsequently moved to; and then the *Rainbow Lounge* in the same vicinity. Jacintha had her first solo concert there in 1982, singing songs from her debut album *Silence*. Many of her songs were produced by a young medical doctor, Dr Sydney Tan, who would later produce many songs and albums for local and international singers. He also wrote the musical score for the internationally released feature film *Singapore Dreaming*, which I co-produced in 2007.

I was lucky to be part of that creative group. In the 1970s, I used to play football with my neighbour and Jacintha's brother Peter Abisheganaden. I later took double bass and guitar lessons from their father Alex Abisheganaden, the guitar maestro. Dick Lee would often come to the house, as would other singers of the day, so it was an extremely creative environment to grow up in.

In 1977, Pat Chan, our swimming princess and multi-medalist at the SEA Games, turned her attention to producing a musical called "*Stardust*." This was a seminal and ground-breaking event because there had never been a musical of this scale featuring local performers before.

Held in the DBS Auditorium, the diverse cast hailed from all walks of life and this musical was to prove a springboard for many of them. Pat Chan, her brothers Mark and Roy (all National swimmers), Jacintha, Siva Choy, Wilson David, Moe Alkaff, Betty Khoo (the editor of *Female*), Terry Tan (who later became a celebrity chef in London), Winston Tan from the advertising industry, journalist Irene Hoe, Gerry Rezel, and Bob Fernandes (Singapore's James Ingram) were all part of this. At 17, I was the youngest singer and dancer in the group. New York-trained Gerald Chan choreographed our dance steps.

I remember in 1989 watching with pride the acclaimed play *M. Butterfly* at London's Drury Lane Theatre, where a young Glen Goei acted with the famed Sir Anthony Hopkins. Glen could have stayed on in London, but chose to return to Singapore to contribute to the diversity of local theatre. He has been responsible for numerous films and theatrical productions. Together with practitioners from TheatreWorks, The Necessary Stage and groups like the Dim Sum Dollies, we have developed our own brand of theatre and unique humour. Without these Singaporeans, who followed their passions and dared to live their lives differently, we would not have the vibrant city of today.

In fashion, daring individuals like Christina Ong, Farah Khan (then known as Kheng Lin) and Tina Tan paved the way, bringing in high-end fashion that made Singapore more interesting. Man and His Woman, the Link Boutique, Club 21, and other fashion stores offered variety beyond the safety of Robinson's, OG and Metro. In the early 1980s, Tina Tan opened the first Gianni Versace shop in the world outside of Italy. It was quite a coup to have beaten London, New York, Paris, Rome, and Tokyo for this honour. This in turn supported the modelling industry, which allowed agencies like Mannequin studios, Imp international and Carrie Models to grow from strength to strength. Carrie Models was started by Carrie Wong in a small office in the basement car park of the Hyatt Hotel in 1976. Brandon Barker, Dick Lee, and Linda Teo all contributed to its early success. Carrie Models is now international and has branches in Singapore, Malaysia, Hong Kong, and China. Even older than the Government Investment Corporation of Singapore (GIC), they will be celebrating their 35th anniversary this year.

In photography, before Chuando, David Tan, and John Clang, there were the likes of celebrity photographer Willie Tang and Russell Wong, who became famous after his glorious shot of Sebastian Coe was used for the cover of *Sports Illustrated*. When we were teenagers in the 1970s, I used to take photos with Russell and developed these photos in the bathtub of his Katong home.

In 1975, Jean Yip and Mervin Wee met. They were 16-year-old drop-outs who shared a love for hairstyling, and were armed only with ambition and guts. They went to London to train, honed their skills, brought these back to Singapore and started the Jean Yip chain of hair and beauty salons. They have never looked back. Today, with 66 branches in Singapore and Malaysia, they are living the Singapore Dream. They give back to the community by imparting their hair and business skills to young students and staff at their training centre, and by providing jobs to more than 1,000 people. It is amazing what hard work, determination, and talent can achieve.

This is just a small sampling of interesting individuals who have added colour and texture to our social fabric, and who have shown us their "Singapore Spirit." They paved the way for the success of today's entrepreneurs, with their beautiful boutiques, mega-salons, photography and film studios, which are able to live off the music, entertainment, beauty, and lifestyle industry.

We should remember that every time a Singaporean becomes successful internationally, be in the fields of commerce, business, sports, the arts, or sciences, it is not just a personal success but also a success for our country. It paves the way for others to follow. The "Singapore Spirit" is our collective spirit. It is the SPIRIT of SINGAPORE. Boomz!!

CHAPTER 11

Localism versus Globalism

JANADAS DEVAN

I visited a place called Little Gidding a couple of years ago, a tiny village in Cambridgeshire, England. It was difficult to find even with a Global Positioning System (GPS) device.

Nicholas Ferrar and his family had established a religious community there in 1626 and the poet T.S. Eliot had visited it 300 years later in 1936.

"If you come this way taking the route, you would be likely to take from the place you would be likely to come from...It would be the same," Eliot wrote in Little Gidding, the concluding poem in his magnum opus the *Four Quartets*.

"When you leave the rough road," "turn behind the pig-sty," walk round the hedges ("White again, in May, with voluptuary sweetness"), you would find, as always, "the dull facade and the tombstone."

I saw the tombstone — Ferrar's. I saw the dull facade — a small church that can seat no more than 30, built first in the 13th century, reconstructed in the 17th and repaired several times since. I saw the hedges. And I saw the pig-sty, now an all-purpose storehouse, with a motor-cycle in it.

Memory — personal, historical, and national — is always present in old countries like England; and even more so in ancient civilizations like China or India. Nostalgia in these lands, where the past lies thick on the ground, can readily find adequate objective correlatives for its yearnings.

Not so in Singapore.

Someone sent me a series of snapshots of "Old Singapore" about two years ago, around the time I visited Little Gidding. They were not of a particularly old Singapore, actually. The photos were of places and scenes and prospects that once existed within my lifetime, but are now no more: Queen Elizabeth Walk — not recognisable; National Theatre — demolished; Change Alley — changed beyond recognition.

My own personal memory is similarly bereft of stable external markers.

The houses I grew up in on Coronation Road — first an atap house and then a bungalow — have gone. The road I knew so well still wends its way along more or less the same path as it did 50 years ago, but past very different scenes. The Malay kampong folk, the Chinese shopkeepers, the Indian cowherds have made way for a string of semi- and detached bungalows, not all of them in good taste.

The school I attended, Anglo-Chinese School at Barker Road, does not look anything like it used to be; Safti has been transformed beyond recognition; the fields of the old Bukit Timah campus have been swallowed by the Botanic Gardens; Times House along Kim Seng Road has been obliterated.

About the only constructions in my personal memory that still look more or less the way they did when I first saw them are, strangely enough, Changi Prison — which I first saw as a child, visiting my father, when he was a political prisoner in the 1950s — and Conference Hall in Shenton Way, which used to be the headquarters of the National Trades Union Congress. I was very happy when they designated it a national monument the other day, and thus preserved it from obliteration.

If you came this way, taking the route you would be likely to take, from the place you would be likely to come from, it would almost invariably not be the same in Singapore.

It is difficult, almost impossible, to be nostalgic in this country, for its landscape is dotted with precious few *aides-memoires*. To love this country is to be attached, not to its past, but to its possibilities. Memory in Singapore is always oriented towards the future — projective, never retentive.

In part, this is due to our immigrant past and let us not forget, we are almost all, including a substantial number of Malay Singaporeans, descendents of immigrants. Our forefathers and mothers left things behind when they came here. Leaving things behind and setting out for the unknown is in our bones.

In part, it is due also to the circumstances of Singapore's birth as a sovereign state. Forty-five years ago, on 9 August 1965, nobody desired 9 August, for Singapore had not set out to be independent — not even Singapore's founding fathers, who had actually set out to find another country, not Singapore.

All of us came to wish for 9 August the day after on 10 August. It is difficult to see this straight, but that strange sequence, the way in which Singapore's desire for independence arose *ex post facto*, has shaped the way Singaporeans see themselves.

Because independence was not sought, we do not hark back to a founding moment. The founding moment, if it exists, exists not in the past, but rather, in that strangest tense of all, the future anterior — the tense that imagines the future as though it were already present: "You will have known what Singapore shall be when you see it." From the beginning, Singapore has always existed in the future-present.

This rare tense — common in the Romance languages — defines Singapore's self-conception. Unlike most other viable nation-states, Singapore never submits the present to the judgment of the past. Because it originated from the collapse of a prior promise — merger with Malaya — it has, from the beginning, submitted the present to the judgment of the future.

This memory of the future as the locus of hope characterises every aspect of life here. One cannot think of being Singaporean without projecting that identity into the future. The Singaporean is a being that can only exist as an ongoing, incomplete, forever half-finished project.

Similarly, one cannot see any corner of Singapore without imagining what it might look like in the future. The story of Singapore — economically and politically, materially, and spiritually — has always been oriented towards the future.

This condition is not without its costs. Ultimately, the benefits overwhelm the costs — but, still, there are costs.

The benefits: A society oriented towards the future has tremendous vitality. It tends to be open and supple, willing to absorb a wide variety of people and ideas. We remain barbarians, full of what Keynes called animal spirits. Forever a half-finished people, we are not decadent. We are primed to be members of S. Rajaratnam's "global city."

The costs: We tend to be a nation of *parvenus*. There is something of the *arriviste* in every Singaporean. A society where nostalgia is a near impossibility tends to lack refinement. We lack the stable identities that long-settled societies possess. We cannot be a nation after only 45 years, as Minister Mentor Lee Kuan Yew characteristically observed the other day. We are not Little Gidding, a comfortable and comforting village.

"If you came this way, taking the route you would be likely to take from the place you would be likely to come from..." — you will not find a familiar home.

Allow me at this point to advance two propositions that may help explain, among other things, the current controversy over the number of foreigners in our midst that Deputy Prime Minister Wong Kan Seng and others have addressed at this conference:

Proposition One: Socially meaningful life exists locally, in a particular time and place, or it does not exist at all.

Nobody can be directly acquainted with society in the mass. Someone living in Los Angeles, say, has no direct contact with something called American society. What that person has is a direct knowledge of his or her own family, circle of friends, colleagues in the workplace, and so on. This is not to deny that something called American society — or Chinese or Indian society, for that matter — has any reality. Far from it, Societies, nations, obviously act. Through the agency of the state, they go to war, make laws, administer justice, provide social safety nets and determine the socio-economic life of countless people.

But there are different levels of immediacy governing our existence as social beings. We tend to forget this when we read, say, a newspaper. By virtue of its ability to place events from different locations (Afghanistan, Shanghai, Washington, Jakarta, etc) on the uniform surface of a page, newspapers (like the rest of the media) foster the impression that all these geographically separated events can exist in a common mental space, as Ben Anderson observed once. That space does indeed exist, but the immediacy of its reality is in inverse proportion to its distance from the directly experienced facts of daily life, in particular local communities.

Proposition Two: The global economy is a fact completely at variance with the first proposition.

The global economy doubtless exists, but it has no location. It is a vast transactional system involving people who are far more unlikely to meet each other than are people who live in the same country, and are far less likely to understand each other when they do meet. If the first stage of industrialisation involved the reduction of all value to exchange value, the latest stage of capitalism involves the reduction of all communities to the status of symbols circulating in a space without location. The global economy, in other words, is everywhere and nowhere.

The problem here is how do we connect the first mode of social existence — here and now, in particular communities, in particular spaces — with that other, equally real mode, the global, which in essence has no location?

The solution obviously cannot involve shutting off the local from the global. That would be the route to economic suicide. But neither can the solution involve suppressing the local in favour of the global. There is no society that answers to a global "we"; there is no meaningful social life unless a group of people can say "we" — as in "we, the citizens of Singapore..."; and that is only possible in local communities.

Singapore and the United States are vastly different societies, but they wrestle with the same contradiction — that between the local and the global. It would be instructive to compare their experiences.

Take a look at the recent congressional elections in the US — or the 2008 presidential election, or 2004, or 2000. There is a "blue" America — Democratic — and there is a "red" America — Republican. The terms "blue" and "red" derive from the colours that CNN uses to designate Democratic and Republican states in the US presidential race. If you used those colours to designate Democratic and Republican areas down to the county level, you would see how geographically limited the Democrats are. California, for instance, a reliably Democratic state in national polls, is blue only along its densely populated coast. Apart from this sliver of land, the rest of the state is as red as the reddest of red states, like Alabama or Mississippi.

The same is true of New York and all the other states on the Eastern seaboard — blue only along their densely populated urban areas but Alabama otherwise. A US map showing how each county in each state voted would reveal a sea of red interrupted by only splashes of blue along the Pacific and Atlantic Oceans, the Gulf of Mexico, the Great Lakes, and the Mississippi and other rivers. As one commentator put it once, Democrats tend to be water people while Republicans tend to be land people.

Who are these watery people and what are the places they occupy like? The people are disproportionately young, secular, racially mixed; they are Davos people, people who would be comfortable in global milieus like the annual *World Economic Forum* in Davos. The cities — New York, San Francisco, Boston, Los Angeles — are cosmopolitan, globally connected service economies. The families with children, the churchgoers, have moved inland — the suburbs, exurbs, and rural towns of the interior. There are two Americas — one fluid, connected to global networks; and the other stolid, encased in insular communities — each marching (or not marching, as the case may be) to the beat of a different drummer.

The stolid, red America believes the fluid, blue America is rootless, feckless and un-American; and the blue America believes the red America is intolerant and anti-secular — in a word, redneck. Both views are certainly exaggerations. For example, people who distrust the cosmopolitan cultures of the coasts are not all hicks and bigots. What most of them are seeking is the shelter of stable communities, rooted in family and faith. But still the divisions continue and grow worse. Each America has a different culture, a different political party, even a different 24-hour cable news channel — Fox for the rednecks and CNN or MSNBC for the water-people.

The same thing cannot happen here? Well, the divisions here are not as pronounced yet. For one thing, it is not possible to be far from water anywhere in Singapore. Toa Payoh or Bishan are not Utah or Alabama. The cosmopolitans live in the heartland; and the heartlanders work in the cosmopolitan areas. We are so small, we cannot run away from one another. Even the most insular among us can neither avoid the world nor has any wish to do so. I doubt if there are many Sarah Palins in Singapore, with no passports. We can all swim then.

For another, politically and ideologically, we are more of a mixed bag. Consider the question of immigration — of foreign talent, etc. In America, the pro-immigrant party is the more liberal party, the Democratic Party. The iconic figure on immigration was that liberal lion, Ted Kennedy. In Singapore, the pro-immigration party is the more conservative party (at least on social and cultural issues), the People's Action Party. The iconic figure on immigration is Minister Mentor Lee Kuan Yew — a lion, but most assuredly, not a liberal. Strangely enough, it is the liberals in Singapore — at least as represented in the alternative media on the Internet and some of the speakers we have heard at this conference — who have adopted the anti-immigrant position. Such ideological confusion is sometimes productive: It helps prevent sharp divisions.

Still, it does not mean these divisions cannot arise. We have no alternative but to grapple with the contradiction at the heart of globalisation — the fact that socially meaningful life can only exist locally, here and now, but the global economy has no location and is therefore essentially rootless. We cannot solve this contradiction by abandoning one or the other side of the contradiction. We cannot shut ourselves from the world, for we would die; and we cannot abandon the local, for there is no country for rootless people.

What can we do? I think there is no alternative but to continue welcoming people from all corners of the world — and make them one of us. But we will have to better manage the process; these sudden spikes in immigrant numbers can obviously overwhelm the absorptive capacity of society. And finally, the elite in Singapore — and the Government — must continue to look out for the least among us. If the division between your globally-connected cosmopolitan elite and your locally-restricted grassroots comes to coincide dramatically with a sharp income and wealth gap, then Singapore is finished.

If you come this way, taking the route you would be likely to take from the place you would be likely to come from, then you must be able to find a more or less familiar community, a recognisable "we."

12

People's Association: Co-creating a Great Home and Caring Community

LIM BOON HENG

Thank you for inviting me to share with you the work of the People's Association (PA) and its GrasRroots Organisations (GROs) with regards to building social capital in Singapore.

The PA turned 50 last year. Its fundamental role of promoting racial harmony and fostering social cohesion in Singapore has not changed, although the mission statement — "To build and bridge communities to achieve One People, One Singapore" — was refreshed recently.

The Singapore of the past is very different from the Singapore of today. Attracting people to a community centre or club used to be very much easier. In the 1960s, all that was needed was setting up a black-and-white TV set, and the *kampong* folks would flock to the Community Centre (CC). As the two existing channels broadcast in English and Malay, and Chinese and Tamil respectively, Singaporeans watched most programmes in common, strengthening the message that we are a multi-racial society. No one has done a sociological study as far as I know, so we do not know how watching common programmes broke down racial barriers. As most people lived in the same neighbourhood for a long time, the opportunities for coming together at CCs helped to strengthen mutual trust and deepen bonds of friendship.

Thirty years ago, when I was first elected to Parliament, the Residents' Committees (RCs) were newly formed. Singaporeans were being uprooted from the *kampongs* and settled into Housing and Development Board (HDB) new towns. Old ties were disrupted. RCs were set up to build new communities. Block parties' organised by RCs were a novelty and attracted many residents. Children's parties, in particular, were a hit, and initially a sure way of bringing parents from different families together. Over time, however, the parents felt more secure about leaving their children with the RC members, and they stayed home to do housework instead! This challenged RC members to come up with new activities to attract residents.

As a rookie Member of Parliament (MP) in the 1980s, I was grateful for the advice that seasoned MPs gave. I remember what the late Mr Fong Sip Chee said to some of us: "You must remember what grassroots events are for. These events are not held for their own sake, but in order to bring people together, so that they can become friends and good neighbours. And at these functions, you should take the opportunity to address issues of the day, and explain policies."

The world has changed. The speakers before me spoke about the challenges of a global city, of an ageing population, of how rapid growth and developments such as the influx of foreign talent has brought about increasing disparities and created divides. They spoke about the need to strike a balance between globalisation and maintaining our local identity, about the need to nurture a caring society, and the need to build the Singapore spirit, with shared values and experiences, a commitment to the nation, and the common dreams and aspirations of citizens.

Indeed, the CCs and RCs have also evolved to meet the changing needs and aspirations of residents. CCs have evolved both in terms of offerings and in terms of infrastructure. Sports popular in the 1960s, such as boxing and weight-lifting, have been replaced by *tai chi, taekwondo* and yoga. Art classes for children, cooking, cake-making, Japanese language classes and flower arrangement were the most popular courses during the 1980s, and drew many residents to the CCs. Then, in the 1990s, the most popular courses became aerobics, international folk dance, choral singing, ballet and piano. Language and culinary classes have continued to be popular.

As the demand for and needs of CC courses changed, so has the infrastructure. In the 1990s, the CCs began to co-locate with major community agencies such as libraries, neighbourhood police posts, post offices, and polyclinics. In recent times, CCs co-locate with swimming pools and other sports facilities. These changes reflect the struggle of the grassroots organisations to bring people together, as more attention is given to multiple TV channels and the Internet in their own homes, or attractions elsewhere. It is a struggle against social drift, as described by Robert Putnam's book *Bowling Alone*.

Slowly, the attention of grassroots leaders turned to activities that would attract residents. The focus turned to the activities themselves, and GROs developed an over-reliance on lucky draws. While the numbers of attendees at grassroots activities stayed high, MPs observed that they tended to see the same familiar faces at these events.

When I was appointed PA Deputy Chairman in 2007, I looked at the performance, and, frankly, saw more output than outcome. Grassroots leaders and PA staff were all working extremely hard. But were we satisfied with the outcome? How well were we progressing in developing our common identity and sense of belonging, against the social forces at work? Should we attempt a review of PA and the work of GROs under its umbrella? We took the plunge, and went through a two-year exercise involving the PA Board, the Ministry of Community Development, Youth and Sports, advisors and grassroots representatives.

The result was the co-creation of one common vision for the community, that of "A Great Home and A Caring Community where we share our values, pursue our passions, fulfill our hopes, and treasure our memories." Our vision tagline is "Our Community, My Responsibility."

With this common vision, we asked grassroots leaders to envision what they wanted their community to be in five years' time, and to do their work-plans so that each year's efforts would contribute towards that community. In other words, all their efforts should lead to the accumulation of social capital. This they have done — their efforts have been compiled in the publication *Community 2015 Master Plan and Work Plan*.

The key components of social capital are: Trust and reciprocity between people, informal networks, and confidence in the government and public institutions. Robert Putnam's definition of social capital brought back to my mind the advice of the late Mr Fong Sip Chee. He defined the work of

MPs and their grassroots leaders in his own way that they add up to accumulating social capital!

In this light, the role of grassroots leaders is not that of event organisers, but that of community facilitators. High social capital must involve most, if not all residents, and not a minority. So how do grassroots leaders get more residents to participate, to take ownership? Getting thousands of residents to attend an event is not difficult, but when they come, do they participate and interact? There is more interaction and deeper engagement when people gather in small groups. When the group is large, many become passive attendees. When groups are small, everybody plays their part. Likewise, grassroots leaders observe a greater sense of ownership when residents organise pot-luck floor parties, compared to the block parties organised by the RCs.

Here, we can learn from what other organisations have done: Give everyone a role. When there is a sense of ownership, there is a sense of belonging. Both small- and large-scale events contribute to building social capital.. For example, large-scale events like the *National Day Parade* can allow people to participate in groups where they identify with one another. Large-scale events, like when Singapore wins a trophy in a sports competition, also give everyone a common high and a sense of common identity. But large-scale events must be complemented by many small-scale ones, such as interest groups.

How do we know when grassroots leaders have succeeded? When small interest groups are self-sustaining, and do not rely on the RCs or Community Club Management Committee (CCMC) to organise activities for them. When residents become good friends and look out for one another in what Dr Maliki calls "micro-communities," like when a nurse and a taxi-driver become community resources to help a diabetic neighbour improve his quality of life.

Local problems are solved by residents when they step forward and work with one another. For instance, when some people who make use of the HDB void deck become a nuisance, the block residents get together to regulate things and make sure they do not make noise at odd hours. These are scenarios that we will see, when our grassroots leaders, as Community Facilitators, put the resident — not the activity — at the centre of what they do.

There will be no end to this work. There will be changes in society, such as the influx of new immigrants, as we have witnessed in recent years, and each new decade will bring new issues and challenges. Some old trends, however, will continue too, such as the frequency with which Singaporeans change homes, at least in the immediate and medium-term future. And we must never take racial and religious harmony for granted.

There is a renewed sense of purpose among grassroots leaders today. They know what their role is: To harness their residents in a common effort to co-create "A Great Home and a Caring Community." There is also a new buzz and sense of excitement among the PA staff, as they now see their role clearly: To support grassroots leaders in bridging divides and communities, to forge a common identity and help us all become more rooted to this, our home.

CHAPTER *13*

Towards a More Equal, Self-Reliant Society

HO KWON PING

The bulk of public discussion about last year's general elections has been political governance and particularly, relations between the electorate and government. No doubt social media and a new, younger electorate have changed expectations and are redefining the relationship. But the divide is not just between the governed and the governing. Issues surfaced in the elections which indicate that other social fissures exist in Singapore society.

One such issue is widening income inequality. It is against this backdrop that other seemingly unrelated issues, such as ministerial salaries, or public disaffection against foreign workers, has to be viewed. In other words, what happens at the political superstructure is determined by the economic substructure.

Although the title of this panel is *Politics: A New Paradigm*, the talk about the "new normal", participatory politics, and other burning issues for young voters, must be seen within the context of a larger and longer-term plan to restructure Singapore society in a more fundamental way. We cannot construct a new vision or a social compact unless we also understand the source of income disparities and how they can be changed.

In my view, Singapore embarked on a major restructuring exercise in the mid-1980's but it remains unfinished. Our export-oriented manufacturing underwent a wage revolution some 25 years ago, but it was an incomplete revolution. It stopped short at the domestic service economy. We need to complete that revolution and bring Singapore completely into the ranks of a developed society, in terms of income relationships between our citizenry.   It is my contention that only when this is resolved can the political superstructure be harmonious.

If we achieve a complete economic restructuring, and there will certainly be transitional pain for affected industries, Singapore will be a more equal and self-reliant society even as we grow wealthier.

But if we continue as we have been, we will be an increasingly rich but unequal society with growing dependence on an underclass of low-wage, low-skill foreign workers.   And because of their wage dampening effect, young Singaporeans will always shun jobs in retail, hospitality or construction which young Australians and Scandinavians are willing to do in their own home countries.

The vision, put somewhat simplistically, is between say, a Denmark or a Dubai.

Has the vision of a Rugged Society become irrelevant in the nearly 50 years since MM Lee Kuan Yew tried to steel our population for the travails of independence, national service, and economic uncertainty?   Certainly, ruggedness as a value seems quaintly out of date and replaced by buzzwords such as creativity, personal self-realisation, or participatory politics.

But if ruggedness also means resilience, robustness, and self-reliance, then the values of our founding fathers remain relevant — and in danger of being lost in our thrust towards the holy grail of First World status and its accompanying accolade of having the most millionaires per capita in the world, more Ferraris and Lamborghinis per square mile of land, and so forth.

Before proceeding further, it may be interesting to look at comparative national data on wages.   The Institute of Policy Studies (IPS) was asked to provide specific examples of wage gaps between different occupational levels, recognising that they are not comprehensive but illustrative.

We chose doctors to represent the highest paid, professional class; nurses and self employed plumbers to represent the medium-skill occupations, and construction workers to represent the lowest-skilled class. IPS chose USA, UK, Germany, Australia, Japan, Hong Kong, Taiwan, and South Korea to be the comparative samples.

Here are the findings.

First, professionals like doctors and lawyers are paid slightly better in Singapore than the average of the IPS sample of developed countries.

Second, our lower income workers fare much worse than their counterparts in developed countries. A Singapore construction worker earns less than 10% of what a Singapore doctor earns, whilst that worker's counterpart in the other countries earn about a third of a doctor's salary in their own countries.

In fact, in Germany and Australia where immigration policies are more restrictive, construction workers earn about — believe it or not — half that of a doctor. This might seem hard to believe, but I guess this would include for doctors, young interns in government service, and for construction workers it would include older, highly skilled and self-employed home builders.

Lest one thinks that somehow European and American economies are not comparable to Singapore, let us compare with Hong Kong, which is not only closer to home, but is also a small city-state with abundant foreign labour from across the border.

Interestingly, doctors in Hong Kong and Singapore on average earn the same salary. You would, therefore, expect a similar wage ratio for other occupations.

But that is not the case. Construction workers in Singapore earn only 9% of what a doctor is paid compared to about 25% in Hong Kong. Self employed plumbers in Singapore, who are relatively skilled, earn about 12.5% of what a doctor earns compared to around 30% in Hong Kong. However, nurses in Singapore earn about 25% of a doctor's pay compared to about 33% in Hong Kong. So it appears that at the bottom of the occupational and income ladder, Singapore's disparities compared to other countries are very high, but narrow as the skill content increases.

Overall, the wage disparity between a Singaporean doctor and construction laborer or plumber, is three times higher in Singapore than elsewhere.

How can this be explained? Hong Kong has access to cheap and abundant labour from China, and yet construction workers earn a lot more. I do not have a definitive answer, but I can only surmise that this is because Singapore's construction industry uses a lot more low-cost, unskilled foreign workers, which depress wages for the few Singaporeans in the same jobs.

Singapore's building industry has argued that it cannot do without a large supply of foreign workers. That may well be the case, but Hong

Kong's building industry seems to be able to afford much better-paid workers amidst a thriving property industry.

The data is similar for other occupations such as in retail and hospitality but is less glaring. And so the question is: if in Hong Kong's laissez faire economy where one would expect higher wage disparity and also equally liberal access to foreign workers, and there is actually less disparity, why does Singapore have such high disparity?

How did these glaring disparities arise?

This presentation alluded earlier to a wage restructuring in the mid-1980's when Singapore's low-cost, low-skill industries were no longer competitive. The government induced a bold, even risky wage hike to force manufacturers to upgrade, move out, or close shop. In the meantime, the Economic Development Board (EDB) courted new, higher value added industries to come and our vocational schools and polytechnics produced more technically skilled school-leavers for these industries. Although painful for many companies, this effectively weeded out the labour-intensive and encouraged the skills-intensive export industries.

I recall those years vividly as I had just joined our family business, and witnessed the transition as many companies in Jurong — including some of ours — closed down or had to relocate to Malaysia or Thailand.

But the strategy worked. Today's life sciences, pharmaceuticals and other high-tech manufacturing industries testify to the correctness of that vision. It is no accident that the IPS wage data for the past ten years show that while wages actually declined in real terms for construction workers, plumbers, waiters, cleaners, etc — they rose substantially for technical workers in the life sciences and electronics industries.

But the wage revolution of the '80s stopped half-way. It did not extend to the domestic economy, and that is why the domestic services industries — construction, retail, hospitality, etc — were left untouched. There was frankly, no real need to restructure them. Though low skilled, their equally low costs also helped keep the cost of living down for Singaporeans. It also kept the business operation costs down for foreign investors.

So, we effectively ended up having a dual-income economy: an internationally competitive and well-paid economy, and a low-cost, low-skilled domestic economy. Nobody complained that the cost of hawker food was kept reasonable because of low-paid hawker assistants from China or Indonesia. Nobody complained that broadband charges or utility bills were kept reasonable because low-wage Bangladeshi workers were doing the digging and laying. On the backs of the South Asian construction worker, the Filipino nurse, the Chinese retail assistant, or the Filipino restaurant waiter, Singaporeans had a good life.

Furthermore, with virtually full employment, it was not as if foreigners were robbing Singaporeans of jobs. They were doing jobs that most locals shunned anyway. But there are two drawbacks. First, it dampened the wages of Singaporeans in low-income jobs. Second, there has been little incentive for the domestic services industries to invest in labour-saving technology. These drawbacks have existed for so long that it is no longer sustainable.

Politically, an under-class of Singaporeans and permanent residents stuck in low-skilled, low-paying jobs, and another under-class of low-income foreigners living at best in enclaves or at worst in *ghettoes*, can only lead to more social tensions which will inevitably flare up with ever-increasing population density.

Economically, growth due to low-cost labor but without real productivity increases, has diminishing returns. There will come a point when the economic cost of a large, low-skilled foreign worker population will become greater than their benefits.

Socially, the central ethos of our society, which is based on social mobility within an egalitarian culture, is being eroded. To have more millionaires per capita than anywhere else in the world — a questionable accolade awarded by several publications including Forbes — is one thing. It is another to have the highest income disparity in the developed world.

We need to complete the wage revolution started in the 1980's. We need to gradually but relentlessly increase wages in our domestic service industries, while reducing the influx of low cost foreign labour which keep these jobs low-skilled and low-paying. At the same time, we must incentivise businesses to invest in productivity-enhancing technology. Higher-skilled foreign workers working with labour-saving equipment should of course still be welcomed, because there will never be enough locals to fill our industries, regardless of wage levels.

The chairman of the Korean company which built Marina Bay Sands told me that his imported Korean workers are more expensive than those he could find locally, but their technical skills and productivity are so much higher. He also observed that Singapore construction sites employ about double the workers in developed countries and half that in developing countries, yet we are economically amongst the most developed countries. This is probably true not only in construction, but other domestic services like retail and restaurants. Somewhere on the way from Third to First World, our domestic service industries got stuck.

None of what I advocate is new. Every government agency involved agrees we should move in this direction. But the pace has been slow, and there is behind it, a sense that if we move too drastically, not only will we hurt our Small and Medium Economies (SMEs), but we will also lose the good life.

Hitherto, these issues were largely seen as economic policy problems for technocrats, employers and unions to deal with. But to not approach these issues with urgency and political sensitivity will mean allowing the divide to widen further. And in the next general elections, how will the disparity at the economic substructure be manifested at the political superstructure?

Most articulated visions of Singapore deal with things like education, the arts, or political governance. They usually do not deal with work relations, which actually are at the heart of a society's ethos and culture because work relations define how we treat each other. At the core of Japanese society is its unique values regarding self-reliance and respect towards work. Similar values, although manifested differently, also are at the core of Scandinavian or German culture.

In Singapore there is no such consensus. The supposed social compact between the government and its people must be underpinned by a consensus about the nature of Singapore society itself.

What is the benefit of more participatory politics if we have a society so hypocritical that citizens complain of poor service and how young Singaporeans are too soft to work in service industries, but in the same breath complain if costs rise because of higher wages? Or a society where a private housing estate raises a huge ruckus because a foreign workers' dormitory will be built in the same neighborhood, as if it were a leper colony?

Any attempt to become a more egalitarian and self-reliant society as in Japan and Scandinavia will require a paradigm shift. It is not something which our *nouveau riche* society, nor our young, have embedded in them as values.

Collective consensus is the ultimate goal of purposeful political dialogue. And in that exchange of views, informed debate will be necessary, or else xenophobia and other crude and emotionally charged issues will obscure rationality.

In conclusion, the presentation has tried to locate the presumably purely economic issue of wage disparity within the larger context of political and social change in Singapore. And unless we can collectively resolve the difficult trade-offs which inevitably accompany any movement towards a more equal and self-reliant society, any new paradigm will be empty and lacking in substance.

CHAPTER 14

Living with New Differences

SIM ANN

INTRODUCTION

I would like to begin by wishing those who are celebrating the Lunar New Year a happy Year of the Horse. The season of *loh-hei* is upon us.

This year, I began the Chinese New Year *loh-hei* season at the Sri Mariamman Temple. The oldest and probably most famous Hindu temple in Singapore, it is located in the heart of Chinatown.

For the past 11 years, the temple's management and volunteers have been organising Chinese New Year *loh-hei* for the less fortunate members of society, including residents from old folks' homes. To mark the occasion, representatives from partner organisations like Chinatown businesses and the mosque next door are also invited.

The meal was prepared by the temple's own kitchen and served by its volunteers. It featured vegetarian raw fish salad or *yu-sheng*, and the starters were a mix of spring rolls and pakoras. Halfway through the meal, the temple chairman and I went round distributing *ang pows*. I feel privileged to have been invited to such a special event.

I thought to myself, during and after the event, that there are not many places in the world where one can experience a meal like this. Examples like this reflect a commitment to racial and religious harmony that has taken many years to build. It also reflects the persistent effort of many community leaders who feel it is important to keep reaching out to each other. We have managed to make a big thing happen in a small place like Singapore.

DIVERSITY IS ALL AROUND US

One of the books by Japanese author Haruki Murakami, entitled *South of the Border, West of the Sun*, has a passage in it, which sticks in my mind. Written in the voice of the protagonist, Hajime, it describes growing up in suburban Japan:

> *The town I grew up in was your typical middle-class suburbia. The classmates I was friendly with all lived in neat little row houses; some might have been a bit larger than mine, but you could count on them all having similar entranceways, pine trees in the garden. The works. My friends' fathers were employed in companies or else were professionals of some sort. Hardly anyone's mother worked. And most everyone had a cat or a dog. No one I knew lived in an apartment or a condo. Later on I moved to another part of town, but it was pretty much identical. The upshot of this is that until I moved to Tokyo to go to college, I was convinced everyone in the whole world lived in a single-family home with a garden and a pet, and commuted to work decked out in a suit. I couldn't for the life of me imagine a different lifestyle.*

It sticks in my mind because this is more or less the complete opposite of my experience growing up — and probably those of many who grew up in Singapore. There are so many differentiators in our society that our childhood memories are probably a kaleidoscope of different lifestyles and habits.

OLD VS NEW DIFFERENCES — A HELPFUL DISTINCTION?

The topic of this panel is "living with new differences". That implies a distinction between "old differences" — which I take to be race, language and religion — and "new differences" — which, as the conference brief helpfully suggests, are borne of immigration, new media and globalisation.

I have three thoughts to share. The first thought is really a question. Is it useful to think of differences as being "old" and "new"?

To some extent, I can see how certain differences beyond race, language and religion might strike us as "new".

It is true that demographic changes, including those brought about by immigration, has introduced differences, some of which are quite visible.

Technology has also separated the world into digital natives and non-natives. It powerfully enables us to come into contact with people very different from ourselves, and yet also gives us an unprecedented ability to edit and control our own social circles. For example, if you have a Facebook account, you are more likely to be friends with people who share basic characteristics and the same outlook with you, and it is very easy to "unfriend" them if you find their views unpalatable. Scrolling through update feeds from the list of friends you have personally curated can feel like an echo chamber.

But it is less obvious that other kinds of differences are "new differences". Say, those between various age groups, or those of people with special needs, a topic that is close to my heart.

These are differences that we may talk about more often these days, or receive more public attention, as should be the case, but I do not think it necessarily makes sense to characterise them as "new".

Diversity is all around us, and this will continue to be the case. Even as some differences become less salient over time, others will emerge.

What matters is the philosophy underlying how we live with all kinds of differences. My take on this is that diversity well-managed is our strength. What does not pull us apart makes us stronger.

APPRECIATE DIFFERENCES

The second thought I have is that the basis for living well with diversity is the ability to appreciate differences.

I was reminded that the author Graham Greene once wrote, "hate was just a failure of imagination." Empathy is often identified as an essential ingredient for being able to appreciate and understand others. But what is empathy about?

It helps, of course, to have had personal experience that can be applied, so that we can tell someone "I know what it is like to feel a certain way" or "I know what it's like to have done something".

But how about the many times when we cannot say "I know what it is like"? How to instil and strengthen empathy, short of living another person's life?

My personal view is that reading, and the study of literature, are of great help here.

In the interest of full disclosure, I have to say that literature was my absolute favourite subject in school. It is more than a study in the beauty of thoughts expressed in words. It is a discipline for looking at the world with someone else's eyes, to seek to understand why a person might feel or do or say something, however unlikely it might be for us to feel, do or say those things. By requiring students to hunt for and interpret textual clues, literature builds sensitivity to nuances, and a habit of observation before judgement. It requires, and in turn enriches, the reader's understanding of history, psychology and many other fields.

I support the Ministry of Education's efforts in making literature as widely available to students as possible in schools, and the National Library Board's efforts to promote reading among the public at large.

PRESERVING THE COMMON SPACE

The third thought has to do with preserving the common space. I do not think anyone in this room doubts the importance of preserving shared experience and common space in a diverse society like Singapore. How else to hold us all together?

My thought in particular is that the preservation of the common space can be an untidy business characterised more by goodwill and give-and-take, than by the application of abstract rules of logic and consistency.

If we get the empathy part right, then it is not very hard to see why this is the case. Every life, every experience lived by individuals of different affiliations, identities and characteristics, is unique. To fully understand the perspective of someone different than you is to accept and embrace that uniqueness. To appreciate the accommodation that each group requires from society is also to recognise how important and singular it is to that group. It is difficult, if not impossible, to weigh one unique request against another. But if we agree that it is more important to stay together than to be apart, then it is possible to settle on *agar-agar* compromises. We can also let them evolve over time.

I was asked a question at a discussion yesterday about the government's role in preserving the common space. Is there really pushback from the other groups when one group asks for special accommodation?

The term "pushback" calls to mind the image of a thronging crowd, pushing and shoving against each other into a shrinking space, with government in the middle trying to persuade everyone to please stand back.

I do not think this image is one that many groups have of themselves.

I have a rather different picture in my mind. Imagine a village formed by a ring of houses of all shapes and sizes backing onto a village square. The square is not very regular to begin with. The backs of some houses jut out more into the square than others. But the square is a place that villagers enjoy using for gatherings or walks.

One day, a family starts to build an extension to the back of its house and claims a bit of the square. It is a very reasonable thing to do. The family is expanding, they need a bit more room, and in any case some houses already jut out into the square more than others and it was never regular to begin with. It is a small change that hurts none of its immediate neighbours. Not only is it a reasonable thing for the family to do, it is necessary. No one can find a basis to object to their action, in fact it would be churlish to do so.

Another family finds that they, too, need a small extension onto the square, and builds it. A third family voices its support for the first two and quickly adds its own extension. This carries on for a while, and the village decides to regularise the practice for fairness. After vigorous and exhausting debate, the village comes up with a complex set of rules on how much of the square each family is entitled to. Eventually there is no square left.

A few things are true about this picture. Every family who wishes to make an extension has an eminently reasonable request. Applying a set of abstract rules, too, was a very logical thing to do. But it is also true that, at the end of the day, the village lost something.

That is the mental picture I have of the challenges of preserving the common space. Losing the village square, either bit by bit, or even altogether, is not necessarily the end of the world. But it does mean changing what the village looks like, and the experience of living in it. If we are that village, then we have to decide whether this is the approach we want.

CONCLUSION

Allow me now to recap my three main points.

First, diversity is all around us. Whether it is living with "old" or "new" differences, we need a shared understanding that what doesn't pull us apart makes us stronger.

Second, it is important to enable appreciation of differences. Literature helps.

Third, we need to preserve the common space. It is not a neat approach of rules and logic, more an untidy business of give-and-take, but it is our best bet.

Thank you.

CHAPTER **15**

Approaches to Emergent Group Differences

DAVID CHAN

INTRODUCTION

Our traditional narratives on Singapore's vulnerability and strengths relating to multi-culturalism, social harmony and national identity are primarily based on the official groupings of race and religion. With the rapid changes in Singapore's economic, social and political environment, particularly those associated with the significant increase in Singapore's population due to the inflow of foreigners, we need to go beyond these traditional and official groupings to examine "new" ways of grouping people in various contexts and for various purposes to address emergent differences. A segmented approach to policymaking is effective only if we know what the relevant groupings are or how to segment the population relating to the issues in question.

Issues of emergent differences across "new" groupings of people in Singapore are much more complex than simply including additional group membership variables such as age, education or nationality. To unpack the complexity, we need to examine how people think, feel and act in various situations and contexts, including individual, social, organisational and cultural settings. These variations in human cognitions, emotions and behaviours may account for or be accounted by emergent group differences.

To examine issues in emergent group differences, I will begin by providing an overview of the macro contexts and evolving concepts, particularly those related to the population challenges facing Singapore. Next, I will explain the need to go beyond the conventional approach that relies on the traditional narratives associated with the major race and religion groupings in Singapore. I will propose that we adopt a strategic focus and principled approach, be it in the contexts of science, policy and practice.

MACRO CONTEXTS AND EVOLVING CONCEPTS

Singaporeans are classified into distinct racial groupings of Chinese, Malay, Indian and other races (i.e., CMIO). This CMIO model is used for many official purposes. For example, the CMIO model is used to determine which language constitutes the mother tongue of a student in school. It is used to set racial quota for residency in public housing to prevent formation of racial enclaves and promote integration. The model is also used to specify a necessary criterion that at least one individual in the group of potential candidates contesting an election in a Group Representation Constituency (GRC) must be of Malay, Indian or another non-Chinese race, which enshrines racial minority representation in Parliament.

The CMIO model is much more than a convenient convention used to guide policies and socio-political actions. It is a national narrative that, through the power of a collective tradition, has guided how people think, feel and act in interpersonal and intergroup contexts. The CMIO model is therefore a cognitive, affective and behavioural framework that both creates and constrains our thoughts, feelings and behaviours in relation to an individual or group of individuals. Similarly, the official classification of people according to religious beliefs into various major religion groups has influenced the way we construe and converse about religious harmony and the separation of the secular state and the freedom of religion in Singapore.

Both the social sciences underlying public discourse and the evidence-based approach to policymaking have relied much on the official race and religion groupings. This is evident in the way survey findings on social attitudes are analysed and presented. Respondents are classified into distinct and mutually exclusive race or religion groups and the survey results are then compared across groups, typically in terms of between-group differences in mean score or proportional agreement on the relevant survey item.

In short, the official CMIO classification of race and religion has underlined and guided public discourse and policy decisions across our life domains or what I call the research-policy-practice (i.e., RPP) context.

The CMIO model has ascribed and constrained the meanings of various traditional terms and concepts used in the RPP context whenever we refer to group differences and inter-group relations in Singapore. For example, in practically all national surveys in Singapore, the CMIO model is used to determine the response options in the demographic item on respondent's race or ethnicity. More subtly, the traditional race and religion groupings are assumed whenever there are survey items on substantive issues about race and religion in Singapore. For example, in attitudinal items on perceptions of inter-racial or inter-religious group relations (e.g., "I am satisfied with the race relations in Singapore" or "I am optimistic about the relations between religious group in Singapore"), the assumption held by the researcher, and likely also the respondents and the readers of the reports on the survey results, is that the CMIO groups or the major religion groups are the referents in the items.

Similarly, the CMIO and major religion groupings are salient but assumed when we speak about Singapore's national interests vis-à-vis the race or religion group sectorial interests, and when national education efforts and politicians' policy speeches describe and emphasise the concepts of multiculturalism and social harmony and describe the value of social cohesion, national values, and national identity.

While these traditional terms and concepts continue to feature in school textbooks and policy speeches, several important new terms and concepts on groupings and group differences have emerged in the past few years. Many of these concepts entered into public discourse and policy decisions because of the relatively recent changes in Singapore's population profile and the associated societal challenges. Examples of these group-centric or intergroup-related terms and concepts include social identities, social divides, social integration, social capital and social resilience. These emerging terms and concepts are likely to continue to dominate national discussions and they need to be seriously and systematically taken into account in the RPP context so that we can better understand and address the critical issues in emergent group differences in Singapore.

ISSUES IN EMERGENT GROUP DIFFERENCES

The discussion on issues in emergent group differences is likely to be more fruitful when there is general agreement on the kind of society that we want to be as a country. One way to construe this common aspiration is to explicate the major societal end goals on which we are likely to collectively agree. I have previously suggested five such goals (Chan, 2013).[1] First, citizen's well-being and quality of life should be central as the desired outcomes of policy and public actions. Second, there must be real and good opportunities for all Singaporeans, regardless of background. Third, we want a compassionate and inclusive society. Fourth, we want people to be rooted and committed to Singapore, not only for citizens but also permanent residents (PRs) and even foreigners, probably in different but important ways. Finally, Singapore needs to be an adaptive and resilient society in order to cope with the novel demands that are brought about by rapid changes and uncertain situations, which may be either global or local conditions.

The details of these five goals are complex and we may not get clear consensus on the specifics because of the diverse contexts of their manifestations and interpretations. Nevertheless, it may be useful to think of these five major goals in general terms and remind ourselves that they can serve as societal end goals, so that we have a framework to help facilitate the evaluation of policy intent and content as well as public collective actions related to emergent group differences.

In a recent report on social capital and development, my colleagues and I discussed several issues concerning emergent group differences which we considered critical in the context of Singapore population challenges. We also made several recommendations on how to tackle them (Chan et al., 2014).[2] Our analyses highlighted the fact that issues in emergent group differences are much more complex than merely including another demographic variable such as age or marital status in our national surveys or reporting a more detailed cross-tabulation breakdown analysis of the results. To illustrate, consider the example of how new group differences may emerge when changing population demographics create new dynamics for the family unit.

---

[1] Chan, D. (2013), "Population matters: Contributions from behavioural sciences", Behavioural Sciences Institute Conference 2013, Singapore.
[2] Chan, D., Elliott, J., Koh, G., Kong, L., Nair, S., Wee, A., and Yeoh, B. (2014), "Social capital and development", in *Population Outcomes: 2050*, Institute of Policy Studies Exchange Series, Number 1, 2014.

Public policy and public discourse regarding the family in Singapore have largely been centred on the concept of a nuclear family consisting of two generations, with both parents present, or an extended family comprising three generations living under one roof. In order to understand the emergent group differences associated with changes in the family institution, it is necessary to go beyond this narrow conception of family (i.e., nuclear or extended family) and to take into account several trends in population changes that are likely to persist into the future. These include rising singlehood, low total fertility rate (TFR), ageing and longer life expectancy, and increased immigration and influx of foreigners. Specifically, these trends are likely to lead to a diversity of family forms that are qualitatively different from the traditional concept of a nuclear or extended family, some of which are either already evident today or likely to become pervasive in the near future. Examples include double-income married couples with no children; double-income married couples with children brought up by foreign domestic workers; single-parent households; multi-generational families comprising more than three generations; and trans-national marriages. These heterogeneous family forms, which are currently not explicitly accounted for in policymaking, will need to be examined in detail and taken into consideration in the efforts on family development and relating family to emergent group differences.

The combined trends of rising singlehood, declining TFR and increasing lifespan in Singapore imply that there will be an increase in the proportion of elderly living alone. Hence, it is critical to correctly identify and adequately address the relevant and emerging issues of health and community care. For example, elderly who are living alone do not have the type of financial, physical and social support that a family can provide for their healthcare needs. This has implications for early health promotion, relevance of various initiatives to enhance active ageing, and infrastructure planning including the type and accessibility of facilities.

Rising singlehood itself is a trend with social capital ramifications for Singapore. As more Singaporeans do not get married, either by choice or constraint of circumstances, they will form an increasingly large and significant segment of the population. Public policies, especially those formulated with the intent to promote family formation and procreation, will need to recognise the needs of Singaporean singles and their contributions and rights (both actual and perceived) as citizens. This is particularly relevant in the area of housing policies, given that current policies explicitly provide family support (e.g., financial incentives for family support). Failing to do so will lead to a sense of alienation and perception of unfairness and discrimination among Singaporean singles. Singles constitute a large and significant segment of the population that can contribute either positively or negatively to emergent marital status and family-related group differences in Singapore.

In short, when examining an issue of emergent group differences, it is important to locate it in the specific inter-group relation setting and policy contexts, as opposed to discussing group differences in abstract. In addition, each issue is likely to be embedded in the ongoing social-political context, and so we cannot remove the politics from it. By politics, I mean linking the issue to nation building — not in the sense of a national propaganda but in terms of the end goals that we want to achieve as a society. Such an approach is more likely to produce a constructive debate.

STRATEGIC FOCUS AND PRINCIPLED APPROACH

I propose that we adopt a strategic focus and principled approach in examining and addressing emergent group differences. There are five aspects in this approach.

First, we need to think about strategic social futures by specifying the new group differences that could emerge and possible social divides that could occur. We can learn much from the strategic futures thinking that the Government has adopted for the country's water supply. In the case of water, we thought about various scenarios and made plans well ahead into the future. This has led to very positive outcomes for Singapore's current and future state of affairs with regard to water supply. The scenario and strategic futures thinking involve both prevention and promotion approaches, where we thought about and planned for various negative consequences that could occur and also positive outcomes to aspire to. The complexity and inter-dependency of social issues make it all the more important for us to adopt a strategic social futures thinking on how various population profiles and dynamics could impact group differences and social cohesion in Singapore in different ways.

A second aspect of strategic focus is to move beyond thinking of an individual as a member of a single group (e.g., race) and to think in terms of the individual's multiple social identities in a dynamic way. This requires some elaboration.

Social identity is the part of an individual's self-concept derived from perceived membership in a social group (Tajfel and Turner, 1986).[3] People possess multiple social identities corresponding to their social group memberships (e.g., nationality, ethnicity and religion), and these identities may vary in strength. Different identities can be activated in different situations. Individuals from different groups may differ in the weights and priority to which they assign to their different social identities. Since social identities influence the way an individual thinks, feels and acts, they are primary drivers of behavioural manifestations of group differences. Social identities can be potentially unifying or divisive forces through their direct impact on cognition and emotion, which in turn influence individual and intergroup behaviours.

Research has shown that different social identities in an individual can be activated in different situations. Therefore, it is important to think about the co-existence of multiple social identities in an individual (e.g., race, religion and nationality) in terms of activation-in-context rather than in terms of competition between different identities leading to dilution in each identity. In managing inter-group relations and designing policy interventions, it is useful to examine how different social identities can be activated by various contexts to prevent inter-group conflict and enhance inter-group under-standing and cooperation through commonalities or complementarity of social identities. This dynamic way of construing multiple identities is more productive than the traditional static way of categorising individuals according to fixed group membership.

According to our population statistics, out of every 10 individuals living or working in Singapore, there are six Singapore citizens, one permanent resident and three non-resident foreigners on various work or dependency passes. A strategic focus and principled approach to emergent group

---

[3] Tajfel, H. and Turner, J. C. (1986), "The social identity theory of inter-group behaviour", in S. Worchel and L. W. Austin (Eds.), *Psychology of Intergroup Relations*. Chicago: Nelson-Hall.

differences associated with local-foreigner issues will need to explicitly consider concepts that can be applied to these three major groupings.

This leads to the third aspect of my proposed strategic approach. I propose that we use the concept of what I call "home-in-community" as a building block of Singapore society. This concept will facilitate discussions on commitment, social cohesion and local–foreigner relations. It could also help integrate Singapore's goal to be a global city and the goal to maintain and enhance national cohesion, so that Singapore remains vibrant and cohesive as a "city-in-a-country" (Chan, 2014a).[4]

The concept of "home-in-community" applies to all people in Singapore. For example, a whole-of-society approach involving not just the Government, but also the people and private sectors, should be used to enhance integration and community development through social interaction, mutual help and volunteerism. In this way, Singaporeans can feel a strong sense of belonging, national identity and rootedness to the country. Permanent residents can see the community as their current second home, with the potential and prospect of making Singapore their first home by becoming citizens. Non-resident foreigners can see the community as a good transient home away from home — one that is attractive to work and play in but also worthy enough for them to contribute to.

The fourth point in my proposed approach to addressing emergent group differences is the need to be rooted in shared values and core principles that we can all agree to adopt as a country and society (Chan, 2014b).[5] Values are convictions of what is important and beliefs of what ought to be. For example, if we agree on the core values of integrity, fairness and social harmony, we will have a common basis and guiding goals for discussing issues, negotiating differences and resolving conflicts between groups. To translate these abstract values into concrete policy and public actions, we will need to agree on core guiding principles such as rule of law, accountability and "people-centricity".

---

[4] Chan, D. (2014a), "Strike the right balance to make Singapore a "city in a country"", *The Straits Times*, April 5, 2014.

[5] Chan, D. (2014b). "From emotions to shared values", *The Straits Times*, December 28, 2013.

Finally, a strategic and principled approach must be evidence-based. This requires us to be more scientifically defensible and well-informed when conducting research and interpreting results reported from empirical studies. I will illustrate with two examples of simplistic treatment of group differences — one on the use of singular grouping of individuals and the other on the use of group mean scores.

As mentioned above, the CMIO model is used to group individuals based on ethnicity for many social-political purposes. However, the CMIO model does not adequately reflect the complex realities of how people perceive themselves and one another, especially with regard to local-foreigner perceptions. For example, based on the CMIO model, PRC Chinese foreigners and new Singapore citizens who were PRC Chinese nationals are classified in the same Chinese ethnic category as Chinese Singaporeans who have grown up in Singapore or lived here for many years. While belonging to the same ethnic category according to CMIO classification, Chinese Singaporeans are clearly distinguishable from PRC Chinese foreigners and naturalised citizens in terms of some cultural beliefs, values, attitudes, norms, habits and perceptions. Moreover, PRC Chinese themselves are not a homogeneous group given the immense cultural diversity across different regions of origin in China. Such "within-PRC Chinese" differences create new layers of complexity.

The cultural differences among the various groups within the same ethnic classification are likely to result in important group differences in how they behave and react to the same situation. When not adequately managed, these practical group differences could lead to violations of expectations, misunderstanding and conflicts, which in turn threaten inter-group relations and social cohesion. Using the same ethnic category (e.g., Chinese) as a basis for policies (e.g., ethnic-based self-help groups) and predictions of behaviour is unlikely to achieve the desired goal. Instead, it is likely to lead to negative unintended consequences because important actual group differences are masked when individuals from these different groups are classified together into the same ethnic category.

Challenges similar to the issues on ethnicity also apply to the classification of individuals into religious groups. Religious customs and practices differ among distinct communities which could occur even within the same religion. These differences can sometimes alienate people or lead to conflicts between people who possess differing beliefs or between locals and foreigners who are unfamiliar with the religious landscape in Singapore. As with the CMIO model, the current classification of the major religions in Singapore does not capture the complexities and heterogeneity within the same religion. Failing to adequately manage differences that are rooted in religions group identities will threaten inter-group relations and social cohesion.

Policy deliberations and public discourse on survey findings have focused almost exclusively on the comparison of mean scores between groups. Two groups can have an identical mean score but differ greatly in their patterns of within-group dispersion of scores. It is the pattern of dispersion (or within-group variance) that provides information on the dynamics of within-group differences such as whether there is high agreement, high disagreement or polarisation of attitudes within the group. It is possible for three groups to differ substantively, with each uniquely exhibiting one of these three within-group patterns and yet all three groups having an identical group mean score. The exclusive focus on mean scores and failure to consider between-group differences in within-group variances will miss important group differences and result in misleading inferences from the data (Chan, 1998).[6]

In conclusion, there is much more to group differences in Singapore than the CMIO model can describe and explain. There are many emergent group differences that we need to understand and address. Given the rapid changes associated with our population challenges and the criticality of the consequences of policy and public actions, we need to adopt a strategic focus and principled approach for examining emergent group differences in research, policy and practice contexts.

---

[6] Chan, D. (1998), "Functional relations among constructs in the same content domain at different levels of analysis: A typology of composition models", *Journal of Applied Psychology*, 83, 234–246.

CHAPTER 16

Beyond the "Global City" Paradigm

LINDA LIM

THE ECONOMY AT INDEPENDENCE

At independence in 1965, Singapore's economy remained heavily dependent on its colonial-era role as a regional entrepôt, or import-export hub, linking South-east Asia to world markets through the provision of port, transport, commercial and financial services as well as British military services, which constituted nearly a third of the gross domestic product (GDP). Though Singapore's per capita income was already Asia's second highest, after Japan, unemployment was 12% of the labour force.

A decade earlier, a World Bank mission to Malaya (including Singapore) had recommended that the two British colonial territories embark on import-substituting industrialisation for what became known after the merger in 1963 as a "Malaysian Common Market" (International Bank for Reconstruction and Development, 1955).[1] Political separation in 1965, and the circumstances under which it occurred, made this an unlikely, or at least difficult, prospect. At the same time, there was occasional social unrest at home and political turbulence abroad, including Indonesia's *Konfrontasi* against Malaysia, the war in Vietnam and the Cultural Revolution in China.

---

[1] International Bank for Reconstruction and Development. (1955). *The Economic Development of Malaya*. Baltimore, Maryland: Johns Hopkins Press.

THE POST-INDEPENDENCE DEVELOPMENT STRATEGY

Fortunately for Singapore, another promising development strategy had already emerged elsewhere in the developing world — that of labour-intensive manufacturing for export to world markets. Puerto Rico's "Operation Bootstrap" began as early as 1948, soon to be followed by the export of garments manufactured by Chinese industrialists who fled to Hong Kong after the communist takeover of China in 1949. In 1965, Mexico established its Border Industrialization Program, or *Maquiladora*, and in 1966 the Kaohsiung Export Processing Zone (EPZ) was inaugurated in Taiwan, followed by the Masan zone in South Korea in 1970 and multiple EPZs in Malaysia and the Philippines in the 1970s.

This development strategy fit with the theory of comparative advantage, which argues that countries should specialise in the production and export of items that intensively use their relatively abundant factors of production. High unemployment suggested that Singapore too might be competitive in relatively labour-intensive industries. But the strategy was driven not just by comparative advantage, or supply-side factors. Technological and public policy changes in developed countries also contributed to favourable demand-side conditions for labour-intensive manufactured exports from developing countries.

Most notable in trade policy was the institution of Items 806.30 (in 1956) and 807.00 (in 1963) of the US Tariff Schedules, which exempted US-origin value-added from import duty (U.S. Tariff Commission, 1970).[2] In the contrary case of textiles and garments, low-wage developing countries were so successful in displacing production in developed countries that the General Agreement on Tariffs and Trade (GATT, precursor of the World Trade Organization) imposed Multifibre Arrangement (MFA) quotas limiting exports from individual countries from 1974 to 2004. Fortunately, as a relatively early exporter, Singapore, like Hong Kong, retained textile quotas much larger than those awarded to lower-wage later entrants like Bangladesh, giving it a measure of protection that preserved competitiveness in this labour-intensive sector longer than market forces would allow. From 1975, Singapore

---

[2] U.S. Tariff Commission. (1970, September). *Economic Factors Affecting the Use of Items 807.00 and 806.30 of the Tariff Schedules of the United States.* Tariff Commission Publication 339, Washington, DC.

also benefited from the GATT/WTO's Generalised System of Preferences (GSP) for developing countries until, together with the other Asian newly industrialised countries (NICs) of Hong Kong, Taiwan and South Korea, it was "graduated" (ruled ineligible by income level) by the US, (1989), European Union (1997) and Japan (2000) (Ow-Taylor & Ow, 1991).[3]

Technological developments in the semiconductor and consumer electronics industries also enabled and encouraged subdivision and offshore sourcing of labour-intensive parts and components of the electronics value-chain by multinationals like Fairchild Semiconductor, Texas Instruments and Hitachi, a subject I examined in 1975–76 through field research in Singapore and Malaysia for my PhD dissertation (Lim, 1978).[4] The other industry that Singapore bet big and successfully on was the then-also-labour-intensive shipbuilding and repair, transforming the abandoned British naval base facilities into commercial shipyards run by new government-linked companies (GLCs) like Keppel and Sembawang.

Resource-based comparative advantage was not the sole reason why these labour-intensive export industries developed. Also key to Singapore's success here was the parallel development of complementary competitive advantages through strategic industrial and social policy that built on the country's already established economic assets of good geographical location, deep-water harbour, free trade and capital flows, and commercial and physical infrastructure.

---

[3] Ow-Taylor, C. H., & Ow, C. H. (1991). Graduation from U.S. GSP: The Case of Singapore. *Journal of Asian Economics*, 2(2), 285–299.

[4] Lim, L. Y. C. (1978). Multinational Firms and Manufacturing for Export in Less-Developed Countries: The Case of the Electronics Industry in Malaysia and Singapore (PhD dissertation in Economics). University of Michigan, Ann Arbor. See also Leontiades, J. (1971). International Sourcing in the Less-Developed Countries. *Columbia Journal of World Business*, 6(6), 19–26, Moxon, R. W. (July 1974). Offshore Production in Less-Developed Countries: A Case Study of Multinationality in the Electronics Industry. Bulletin, Nos. 98–99. New York University Graduate School of Business Administration, Institute of Finance and Reynis, L. A. (1976). The Proliferation of U.S. Firm Third World Sourcing in the Mid-to-Late 1960s: An Historical and Empirical Study of the Factors Which Occasioned the Location of Production for the U.S. Market Abroad (PhD dissertation in Economics). University of Michigan, Ann Arbor.

Industrial policy measures undertaken by new state institutions (primarily the Economic Development Board, or EDB, founded in 1961) consisted mainly of a streamlined bureaucracy (then called a "one-stop shop" for investors), the provision of infrastructure such as subsidised industrial estates (e.g., Jurong Town Corporation, or JTC) and industrial financing (Development Bank of Singapore, or DBS), and various tax incentives, including one to explicitly encourage manufacturing for export, that were introduced in 1967.[5] Taiwan and Korea had similar policies but Singapore's were distinctive in two ways.

First, they focused largely on promoting inward foreign direct investment whereas policies in the other NICs privileged domestic private enterprises, which soon came to dominate their export manufacturing sectors. Second, Singapore integrated social policies into industrial development to a much greater extent than in other locations. Its signature social policy — "public" housing (Housing Development Board or HDB flats) that residents paid for through their own "forced savings" (in the Central Provident Fund, or CPF) — co-located labour-intensive factories, including the then iconic "flatted factories", with HDB residential high-rises. This facilitated employers' access to workers, especially young females who made up the vast majority of workers in textiles and electronics factories and typically worked around the clock (requiring rotating shifts). It also helped maintain low labour costs by reducing workers' costs of housing (due to a combination of scale economies and state subsidies) and transportation. At the same time, large state investments in healthcare and education raised labour productivity, and in education also provided vocational and technical training for specific manufacturing industries (Lim, 1989).[6]

---

[5] Singapore's industrial policies during the first two decades of independence have been extensively discussed in many studies, including Pang, E. F., & Lim, L. (1986). *Trade, Employment and Industrialisation in Singapore*. Geneva: International Labour Office and Chia, S. Y. (1989). The Character and Progress of Industrialization. In K. S. Sandhu and P. Wheatley (Eds.), *Management of Success: The Moulding of Modern Singapore* (pp. 250–279). Singapore: Institute of Southeast Asian Studies.

[6] Lim, L. Y. C. (1989). Social Welfare. In K. S. Sandhu and P. Wheatley (Eds.), *Management of Success: The Moulding of Modern Singapore* (pp. 171–197). Singapore: Institute of Southeast Asian Studies.

Political stability and labour peace were necessary to encourage investment because they ensured that export manufacturing for distant global markets, especially in short product life cycle industries like fashion garments and electronics, would not be disrupted by political upheaval or labour unrest. Notably, among the other NICs, Taiwan and Korea were under military rule with strict labour controls until democratisation in the late 1980s while Hong Kong was a British colony, all throughout the period of labour-intensive export manufacturing. Unlike these NICs, Singapore was nominally a parliamentary democracy, albeit one that had seen the left-wing political opposition eviscerated in the early 1960s, resulting in a one- or dominant-party government by the People's Action Party (PAP) that helped ensure political stability (Chan, 1989).[7] On the labour front, the PAP's control of the labour movement (National Trades Union Congress, or NTUC) and legislation restricting labour organisation and action (particularly the 1968 Employment Act) ensured that there were virtually no incidents of significant labour unrest over the next four decades (Raj, 1989).[8]

Thus both market forces (comparative advantage) and domestic government policies (creating competitive advantage) made Singapore's new export manufacturing industries competitive in a fortunately favourable global market context. At the same time, the focus on foreign investment linked its economy closely to the developed home markets of multinational employers. Between 1965 and 1973, just before Singapore suffered its first globally-induced recession as an independent nation, manufacturing value-added grew by 23.2% per year at current factor cost and 18.1% at 1968 constant prices while its share of GDP rose from 15% to 23% and the share of manufacturing output exported rose from 27% to 54%, and to 63% by 1985 (Chia, 1989, pp. 253–256).[9] By then, less than a decade after independence, the combination of very rapid labour-intensive growth and Singapore's small

---

[7] Chan, H. C. (1989). The PAP and the Structuring of the Political System. In K. S. Sandhu and P. Wheatley (Eds.), *Management of Success: The Moulding of Modern Singapore* (pp. 70–89). Singapore: Institute of Southeast Asian Studies.

[8] Raj, V. (1989). Trade Unions. In K. S. Sandhu and P. Wheatley (Eds.), *Management of Success: The Moulding of Modern Singapore* (pp. 144–197). Singapore: Institute of Southeast Asian Studies.

[9] Chia, 1989, op. cit.

labour force meant that "surplus labour" had been absorbed, full employment had been reached and labour shortages appeared, indicating a shift in comparative advantage.

Yet the initial policy response was to seek to maintain GDP growth and preserve the eroding competitiveness of labour-intensive activities by holding down wages through the institution of a tripartite National Wages Council (NWC) in 1972 and importing low-wage foreign labour. It was not until 1979 that a "second industrial revolution" was launched, with the goal of moving into higher-value industries, increasing productivity and wages, and reducing reliance on low-skilled and foreign labour. It was recognised that:

> *The economic success of the 1970s was, in retrospect, achieved not so much because of improvements in labour productivity but as a result of the influx of foreign labour and the increased numbers of women joining the labour force...*
>
> *... the availability of cheap low-skilled workers allowed many employers to continue with inefficient operations, thus threatening to defeat the national plan to move up the technological ladder.*
>
> *In line with the wage-correction policy introduced in 1979 to help employers automate their operations, the government decided to phase out all foreign workers and have a wholly Singaporean work-force by 1991... A foreign worker levy ... was introduced in 1982... in order to deter employers from becoming overly dependent on them.*[10] (Pang et al., 1989, p. 134)

THE "SECOND INDUSTRIAL REVOLUTION" AND AFTER

One of the downsides of being a "global city" hitched to the wagon of multinationals based in distant foreign markets is vulnerability to economic shocks in those markets. The externally driven recession that Singapore suffered in 1974–75 was partly responsible for the delay of policymakers to

---

[10] Pang, E. F., Tan, C. H., & Cheng, S. M. (1989). The Management of People. In K. S. Sandhu and P. Wheatley (Eds.), *Management of Success: The Moulding of Modern Singapore* (pp. 128–143). Singapore: Institute of Southeast Asian Studies. See also Pang, E. F., & Lim, L. (1982, Fall). Foreign Labour and Economic Development in Singapore. *International Migration Review, 16*(4), 548–576.

adjust to the loss of comparative advantage in labour-intensive manufacturing. Another severe recession in 1984–85 led to hesitation in following through the "Second Industrial Revolution", as its high-wage policy was blamed for the severity, though it was not the cause, of the recession.

> In the 1970s, a low-wage policy encouraged labour-intensive activities, thus negating attempts to achieve high productivity. In the 1980s, wage increases were to be tied to productivity, but instead the high increases recommended across the board did not reflect inter-industry differences in productivity growth. In most cases, wage increases exceeded productivity and pushed labour costs beyond internationally competitive levels.[11] (Pang et al., 1989, as cited in Pang & Lim, 1989, p. 136)

Dependence on foreign manufacturing investment for which there was growing international competition arguably also reduced the degrees of freedom that Singapore's policymakers had in adjusting to declining competitiveness. In retrospect, they appear to have responded in two ways: first, by seeking to change the factor endowments that underlie comparative advantage, specifically by relaxing immigration rules for highly educated or skilled professionals (Pang et al., 1989, p. 134)[12]; second, by continuing to add location-specific competitive advantages that would particularly appeal to capital- and skill-intensive industries, primarily infrastructure and investment incentives targeted to specific industrial "clusters". These policies reflect the

---

[11] See also Pang, E. F., & Lim, L. (1989). Wage Policy in Singapore. In *Government Wage Policy Formulation in Less-Developed Countries: Seven Country Studies* (pp. 75–101). Geneva: International Labour Office. Other relevant studies include Rodan, G. (1985). *Singapore's Second Industrial Revolution: State Intervention and Foreign Investment*. ASEAN-Australia Joint Research Project, Rodan, G. (1987). The Rise and Fall of Singapore's 'Second Industrial Revolution'. In R. Robison, K. Hewison and Richard Higgot (Eds.), *Southeast Asia in the 1980s: the Politics of Economic Crisis* (pp. 149–176). Sydney, Australia: Allen and Unwin and Leggett, C. (1994). Labour and Singapore's Second Industrial Revolution. In S. Jackson (Ed.). *Contemporary Development in Asian Industrial Relations* (pp. 77–97). Sydney, Australia: University of New South Wales Studies in Human Resource Management and Industrial Relations in Asia.

[12] Pang & Lim et al. (1989), op. cit., p. 134.

view of Professor Michael Porter (1990)[13] who states that a nation can escape the limitations of its factor endowments like land, natural resources, labour and the size of the local population by creating "new advanced factor endowments", such as skilled labour, a strong technology and knowledge base, government support and culture.

The policies were successful in maintaining and even growing manufacturing's share of GDP, which went from 22% in 1985 to 26% in 1990, where it remained through 2005 (Choy, 2010, p. 129).[14] This was in striking contrast to the sharp (roughly 50%) share drop in all other developed economies, except Korea, and the virtual disappearance of manufacturing in Hong Kong (Perry, 2012)[15], as predicted by the Fisher-Clark hypothesis that demand for, and employment in, services rises with income over time. The share of high-value-added (capital-intensive) sectors also increased, as reflected in the decline in manufacturing's share of employment from 26% in 1990 to 17% in 2005, and the "steady migration of industrial production over the last twenty years into technologically advanced and skill-intensive clusters, in particular electronics, petrochemicals, specialty chemicals and pharmaceuticals" (Choy, 2010, p. 131).[16]

However, this policy-induced move up the manufacturing value-added ladder was accompanied by a more concentrated industrial structure, heavily reliant on an electronics and, more recently, pharmaceutical cluster, both of which transmitted their highly volatile business cycles to Singapore's own GDP growth (Choy, 2010, p. 131).[17] In addition, studies have shown that in all stages of Singapore's industrial development — from the labour-intensive

---

[13] Porter, M. E. (1990). *The Competitive Advantage of Nations*. New York, NY: The Free Press.

[14] Choy, K. M. (2010). Singapore's Changing Economic Model. In T. Chong (Ed.), *Management of Success: Singapore Revisited* (pp. 124–138). Singapore: Institute of Southeast Asian Studies.

[15] Perry, M. J. (2012, March 22). Manufacturing's Declining Share of GDP is a Global Phenomenon, and It's Something to Celebrate. US Chamber of Commerce Foundation. Retrieved from http://www.uschamberfoundation.org/blog/post/manufacturing-s-declining-share-gdp-global-phenomenon-and-it-s-something-celebrate/34261.

[16] Choy, op. cit.

[17] Ibid.

1970s to the capital- and skill-intensive 2000s — productivity growth has been weak to non-existent.[18] This most likely reflects the input-intensive nature of Singapore's growth, which has been achieved by adding mostly foreign capital, skills and labour to production rather than by increasing the productivity of domestic factors of production. As an example, a recent international innovation index ranked Singapore No. 1 in "Overall Innovation Input" each year from 2011 to 2014, but only No. 17 in "Overall Innovation Output" in 2011, declining to No. 25 in 2014, and No. 94 in "Innovation Efficiency" in 2011, declining to No. 110 in 2014 (INSEAD 2015).[19] Other studies have attributed Singapore's high inequality, stagnant median wages, low wage-to-income and low consumption-to-GDP ratios and comparatively weak performance on "well-being" indices to this input-intensive growth model

---

[18] See, for example, Lee, T. Y. (1985). Growth without productivity: Singapore manufacturing in the 1970s. *Journal of Development Economics, 19*, pp. 25–38; Young, A. (1992). A Tale of Two Cities: Factor Accumulation and Technical Change in Hong Kong and Singapore. In O.J. Blanchard and S. Fischer (Eds.), *NBER Macroeconomics Annual 1992.* MIT Press; Young, A. (1995). The Tyranny of Numbers: Confronting the Statistical Realities of the East Asian Growth Experience. *Quarterly Journal of Economics, 110,* 641–80; Krugman, P. (1994). The Myth of Asia's Miracle. *Foreign Affairs* 73/6, 62–79; Chuang, P. M. (2009, March 23). S'pore scores low in labour productivity. *The Business Times,* citing a comparative study of 17 developed economies by the U.S. Department of Labor; and Nomura, K., & Amano, T. (2012, September). Labor Productivity and Quality Change in Singapore: Achievements in 1974–2011 and Prospects for the Next Two Decades, KEO Discussion Paper No. 129, Keio Economic Observatory, Keio University. The most detailed and excellent analysis of Singapore's productivity policies and performance since independence can be found in a three-part case from the Lee Kuan Yew School of Public Policy, *Singapore's Productivity Challenge,* Parts I, II and III, prepared by Hawyee Auyong under the supervision of Donald Low. Auyong, H. (2014). Singapore's Productivity Challenge, Parts I–III. Case Study Unit. Singapore: Lee Kuan Yew School of Public Policy. Auyong's analysis shows that economic planners expressed concerns about excessive dependence on foreign capital and labour, the limits of the export manufacturing model and their depressing impact on productivity growth from very soon after independence, and continuing to the present day.

[19] INSEAD (2015), *INSEAD Global Innovation Index.* Retrieved from: https://www.globalinnovationindex.org/content.aspx?page=past-reports.

(Lim, 2014).[20] Professor Tan Kong Yam's contribution to this volume explicitly links social discontent to the fact that "the bottom 30% and some of the aspiring members of the middle class" have lost out from globalisation while the government, local and global elites, and owners of capital have benefited.[21]

SINGAPORE'S ECONOMIC MODEL AT 50: A LOOK BACK

Becoming a "global city", and specifically a "node" in the evolving global supply chains of multinationals, was the best and probably only path to economic development that Singapore could have followed fifty years ago. It succeeded because external global forces, including multilateral trade liberalisation and the information and communications technology revolution, and internal domestic policies and outcomes were conducive. Comparative and competitive advantage together created the international competitiveness that enabled Singapore to develop a successful export manufacturing sector within a few years of independence. But comparative and competitive advantages are dynamic, and Singapore's small size and high growth meant that shifts in international competitiveness happened very rapidly, with comparative advantage in labour-intensive activities yielding quickly to skill- and capital-intensity.

Singapore's policymakers recognised all of the limitations and weaknesses of its economic model as they emerged. The Ministry of Trade and Industry reviewed the model and recommended new policies in 1986 (after the 1984–85 recession), 1991 (after a 1990 downturn), 1998 (after the 1997–98 Asian financial crisis), 2003 (after the tech bubble burst, the September 2011 terrorist attacks in New York and the SARS crisis) and 2010 (after the 2008 global financial crisis) (MTI 1986; 1991; 1998; 2003; 2010).[22] All the reports

---

[20] Lim, L. Y. C. (2014). After the Miracle: Singapore's Success. In R. E. Looney (Ed.), *Handbook of Emerging Economies* (pp. 202–226). London: Routledge.

[21] Please see the chapter by Professor Tan Kong Yam in this volume.

[22] Ministry of Trade and Industry, Singapore (MTI). (1986). *The Singapore Economy: New Directions*, Report of the Economic Committee; MTI. (1991). *Strategic Economic Plan: Toward a Developed Nation;* MTI. (1998) *Committee on Singapore's Competitiveness Report*; MTI. (2003) *Economic Review Committee*; MTI. (2010). *Economic Strategies Committee.*

emphasised the need to increase productivity[23] and move into higher value-added activities, though the actual sectors prioritised changed over time (to eventually include a cumulatively broad slate of industries and services). All assumed a continued global role for Singapore in multinational networks, and a leading role for government in the "restructuring" or "transformation" of the economy. Until the 2010 committee report, all featured a continued major role for manufacturing, referred to in 2003, as in 1986, as one of "the twin engines of manufacturing and services". And despite the earlier (1979) stated intention to reduce dependence on foreign labour, all reports emphasised the need for continued, if reduced, imports of foreign labour and, especially, foreign talent. To varying degrees, they also mentioned the need to develop domestic private entrepreneurship, recognised as a deficiency of the Singapore model compared with those of Hong Kong, Taiwan and South Korea.

Interestingly, relatively early on, as well as recently, Singaporean economists, myself included, voiced scepticism about high-tech manufacturing as a durable and desirable development strategy for Singapore in the long term, as these representative remarks show:

> *The question may be raised as to whether the government should be creating an artificial comparative advantage for Singapore in high-technology manufacturing, and indeed, whether it can succeed in doing so. The new strategy requires, apart from the foreign capital, technology and markets that Singapore's labor-intensive export manufacturing sector is already dependent on, increasing dependence on foreign skilled labor and expertise.[24]* (Lim, June 1983, p. 758)[25]

> *It is not apparent that Singapore has a comparative advantage in high-tech industry, at least in the short term. The prerequisites for success in high-tech industries are an abundance of scientific skills, large expenditure on R&D, and the availability of venture capital*

---

[23] For details, see Auyong (2014) op. cit.

[24] This paper refers to alternative development strategies discussed in Pang, E. F., & Lim, L. (1982). Political economy of a city-state. In *Singapore Business Yearbook*, 7–33. Research Collection Lee Kong Chian School of Business.

[25] Lim, L. Y. C. (June 1983). Singapore's Success: The Myth of the Free Market Economy. *Asian Survey, 26*(6), 752–764

and dynamic entrepreneurship…. Although much has been spent on technical, scientific, and engineering education and training in the past decade so that the talent pool is growing, it lacks experience and critical mass, and is expensive in comparison with that available in the other NICs, and even in some advanced countries…. Singapore does not have a ready availability of venture capital, in spite of its very high savings rate and its well-developed financial markets. (Chia, 1989, p. 274)[26]

In manufacturing, though, the planners are banking heavily on the biomedical industry… to spearhead industrial upgrading. Unfortunately … biomedical output tends to be as volatile as electronics exports, being constantly subject to unpredictable demand fluctuations and changes in product mixes. Furthermore, the government is taking a calculated gamble in picking this industry as a putative winner. It is well known that the huge R&D investments in biotechnology have long gestation periods before basic research can be applied to the commercial production of new drugs and medical technologies, not to mention stiff competition in this area from other countries such as Korea, which arguably has a comparative advantage over Singapore. (Choy, 2010, p. 136)[27]

Reservations were also voiced about the continued dependence on both foreign and state enterprises

Secondly, the dominance of foreign enterprises and the public sector have to some extent crowded out domestic private enterprise. Foreign-owned enterprises and state-owned enterprises compete with domestic private enterprises in both the product and factor markets….

The crowding-out effect is likely to be more serious in the labour market, as foreign investors and the public sector compete for scarce skills, and cream off the best talents by offering attractive salaries and career perks, thus inducing an upward pressure on salaries. The ready availability of remunerative jobs in government and MNCs, continuing full employment, and rising wages tend to discourage entrepreneurial risk-taking among the younger generation.

---

[26] Chia, (1989), op. cit.
[27] Choy, (2010), op. cit.

The crowding-out effect also operates with regard to access to capital. The high contribution rates for employees set by the Central Provident Fund (CPF) have reduced personal disposable incomes and voluntary savings, and thus contributed to a scarcity of personal and household venture and risk capital....

Thirdly, the rising cost of doing business also penalizes domestic entrepreneurs in SMEs. Large-scale urban redevelopment, for instance, has led to serious dislocations of many small businesses ... as relocated businesses often face higher rentals in their new premises. Rising labour and utility costs, compliance with ... business regulations, have also impinged harder on the SMEs.

Fourthly, the tax system is biased against local entrepreneurs in manufacturing activities. The high tax rate on corporate profits and the absence of taxes on capital gains and windfall incomes have distorted entrepreneurial returns, thereby diverting entrepreneurial energies away from industrial production, which is characterized by long gestation periods, towards speculative activities in real estate and the stock market. And while the government offers wide-ranging tax incentives to promote industrial investments, local SMEs tend to benefit less than foreign MNCs because of the selection criteria.

Finally, social attitudes have bred risk aversion rather than the entrepreneurial spirit. This is the result of a paternalistic government, a strong regulatory environment, an emphasis on social conformity, an educational system emphasizing scholarship rather than creativity and innovativeness, and a growing intolerance of failure. (Chia, 1989, pp. 265–266[28])

and about the dependence on foreign workers:

The question we must answer sooner or later is this, 'When do we stop growing?'... at what point do we stop importing foreign workers and cease to encourage foreign entrepreneurs and capital in Singapore? Because of our limited land area, industrial expansion, together with the concomitant population expansion,

---

[28] Chia, (1989), op. cit.

will produce overcrowding to increasingly uncomfortable limits.
(Goh Keng Swee, as cited in Teh, 2014)[29]

[Given official projections of annual economic and productivity growth rates] ... the population of foreign workers, temporary and permanent, will rise in Singapore in the 1980s. The benefits of such workers to the local economy are well known, but the potential social and economic costs they pose have yet to be closely examined. These include the costs of providing housing, public transportation, social services and recreational facilities.

... These costs will spill over to the local population, who will have to compete with the foreigners for scarce and increasingly costly housing, and for services such as transportation, recreation and public health facilities. Costs will escalate rapidly and Singaporeans may have to subsidize the increased services to accommodate the foreigners. Their dissatisfaction with the declining quality of life may lead to hostility against foreigners.

... These social problems will intensify as the composition of the foreign labor force becomes increasingly weighted toward workers from countries other than Malaysia.... As the nontraditional sources of labor increase, so will ethnic, cultural and linguistic differences, which may limit productivity as well as intensify problems of social cohesion and integration.

... The short-term flexibility foreign workers offer must be weighed against the need for a restructuring of the economy.
(Pang & Lim, 1981)[30]

To avoid an overdependence on imported labour, however, the government ought to review its policy on the intake of low-skilled foreign workers. By augmenting the size of the labour force, these migrant workers have held down economy-wide wage increase. But the same workers depress earnings at the lower end of the nominal wage scale because of their low productivity, thus

---

[29] Teh, K. P. (2014). Globalisation and Singapore's Discontent, talk given at the Asia Pacific Real Estate Association (APREA) Chairman/CEO Series, September 5.
[30] Pang, E. F., & Lim, L. (1981, August 4). Singapore's Foreign Workers: Are They Worth the Costs? *Asian Wall Street Journal.*

impacting on income distribution adversely. Worse, relying on them indefinitely implies that Singapore's economic progress would still be achieved primarily by increases in labour inputs rather than productivity improvements. Since there are upper limits to immigration and the population size, sustainable growth in the long run can only come from the latter. Hence, a slower pace of economic growth might not be a bad thing if it is achieved through productivity gains and is accompanied by less macroeconomic volatility. (Choy, 2010, p. 135)[31]

These consistent analyses reflect traditional economics, which is the "science" of the allocation of scarce resources among competing alternative uses. As I have explained elsewhere:

Comparative and competitive advantage both allow for government policy to influence a location's competitiveness in particular sectors, through selective investments that shape resource endowments, and tax incentives and subsidies to target resource allocation toward particular sectors.

However, these policies can be imitated with relative ease, leading to "beggar-my-neighbour" outcomes and excess capacity....

As a national economy moves up the technology ladder, the capital and opportunity cost of further state-directed shifts in comparative or competitive advantage escalates, given diminishing returns. Further, competition created by government policy rather than market forces introduces a large element of political risk into business decisions, encourages inefficiency in the allocation of resources, and reduces world welfare.

... These time-tested economic maxims boil down to one prognosis for Singapore's economic model—you can't have everything, even without size and resource constraints. Trying to achieve comparative advantages in too many sectors at once will only push up resource costs, aggravate negative externalities such as inflation and environmental degradation, and result in reduced competitiveness overall. Competitive advantage based on economies of scale, first-

---

[31] Choy, (2010), op. cit.

*comer and agglomeration or cluster advantages derived from
government policy rather than geographical advantages, are probably
unsustainable.* (Lim, 2009)

Singapore itself likely suffered recently from a "beggar-my-neighbour" event
when Broadcom, a large US fabless semiconductor firm, announced that it was
moving some of its operations out of Singapore to Ireland, leading to
speculation that this could be due to the expiry of tax incentives.

*Tax incentives reduced Broadcom's Singapore taxes by US$423
million (S$528 million) last year, and by US$399 million in
2012 — significant sums given that its net earnings were US$424
million last year and US$719 million in 2012...*

*[The company's annual report] said tax incentives such as those it
enjoyed in Singapore "often require us to meet specified employment
and investment criteria" in the relevant jurisdictions.*

*It added: "In a period of tight manufacturing capacity, our ability to
meet Singapore content requirements in our products may be more
limited, which may have adverse tax consequences".*

*Broadcom's decision to use its Irish trading company for some foreign
operations was expected to "result in a similar foreign tax provision
as our current Singapore tax incentive", it said.* ("Clarity needed
on whether chip dip a cause for worry", 2014)[32]

SINGAPORE'S ECONOMIC PROSPECTS: THE NEXT 50 YEARS

Singapore's "global city" economic model, successful in terms of delivering
rising incomes and living standards for its citizens through high GDP growth
in the first decades of independence, has recently come up against domestic
resource and social constraints:

*Singapore's continued policy of importing foreign capital, foreign
labour, and foreign technology, and privileging foreign/global
companies, to serve foreign markets, poses obvious local political,
social, and cultural challenges for the nation and the state....*

---

[32] Chia, Y. M. (2014, September 2). Clarity needed on whether chip dip a cause for
worry. *The Straits Times.* Retrieved from http://www.straitstimes.com/st/print/2792236.

These policies, together with changes in the global economic environment and the globalization processes of multinational companies, have resulted in much more ambiguous impacts on the local population. GDP growth, hinged to globalization in specific ways dictated by the state, has in the past decade suffered multiple setbacks that reflect continued if not increased vulnerability to the vicissitudes of volatile regional and global economies.... The growth which has occurred has seen low shares in GDP for labour incomes (relative to capital returns), and consumption (relative to investments and government expenditures), increased income inequality, and a decline in the relative incomes of local Singaporeans relative to foreigners. The specific forms and requirements of GDP growth have also contributed to the undermining of national identity and social cohesion which previously held together the people of this "hub economy" and sustained their support for their government. (Lim & Lee, 2010, pp. 153–4)[33]

A great deal of policy and public interest has been devoted to these issues since the general election of 2011, in which opposition political parties made unprecedented gains in popular votes and parliamentary seats (Low & Vadaketh, 2014).[34] This suggests that the industrial and social policies so critical to past success have been found wanting in the current stage of development.

The PAP government has responded by working to improve housing affordability, reduce inflation and transport congestion, expand healthcare and social safety net provisions for the elderly and the lowest-income. It is also slowing (but not stopping) the inflow of foreign workers, subsidising wage increases, putting in place (relatively minor) affirmative action provisions for Singaporeans in the job market and trying (yet again) to increase productivity,

---

[33] Lim, L. Y. C., & Lee, S. A. (2010). Globalizing State, Disappearing Nation: The Impact of Foreign Participation in the Singapore Economy. In T. Chong (Ed.), *Management of Success: Singapore Revisited* (pp. 139–158). Singapore: Institute of Southeast Asian Studies.

[34] Low, D., & Vadaketh, S. (2014). *Hard Choices: Challenging the Singapore Choices*. Singapore: NUS Press.

so far without success.[35] As noted on the Ministry of Manpower's website (MOM, n.d.)[36]:

> Over the past decade, Singapore's economy grew by an average of 5% per annum. Singapore's productivity growth over the same period averaged about 1% per annum, a rate on par with that of other developed countries. The broad majority of Singaporeans also enjoyed real wage growth and a rise in living standards.
>
> Nonetheless, productivity gains have declined in recent years due to heavier reliance on labour inputs to generate economic growth, especially inputs of foreign manpower.
>
> Productivity is the only sustainable way to increase our value-add and grow our incomes and it must be the key driver of our economic growth. The Government will focus on helping businesses and workers improve their productivity and continue to provide support through many programmes and schemes.

Significantly, the government has also announced a lowering of the target rate of GDP growth to 2% to 3% per year, similar to that in other developed countries, rather than the 3% to 5% (with 2% to 3% annual productivity growth) recommended by the Economic Strategies Committee in 2010 ("PM Lee redefines 'economy faring well'", 2015).[37] Clearly, it now accepts the limitations on growth imposed by domestic resource — and political — constraints, and maturity as a developed economy, which also undermine the continued viability of the "global city" model itself.[38] As I noted in a 2009 interview:

---

[35] Productivity dropped dramatically in 2014. See http://www.tradingeconomics.com/singapore/productivity.

[36] Ministry of Manpower (MOM). (n.d.). Skills, Training and Development. Ministry of Manpower. http://www.mom.gov.sg/employment-practices/skills-training-and-development.

[37] Lee, U.-W. (2014, January 17). PM Lee redefines 'economy faring well'. *The Business Times*. Retrieved from http://www.businesstimes.com.sg/government-economy/pm-lee-redefines-economy-faring-well.

[38] See *The Economist*. (2014, March 7). The world's most expensive city: Sing on a shoestring. Retrieved from http://www.economist.com/blogs/banyan/2014/03/world-s-most-expensive-city and Milman, O. (2015, January 5). The price of life in

Certainly, to generate growth, just by adding more input, you can get more output. But what is the opportunity cost? How much did we pay to attract such investment and what else might have been done with the money, tax revenue foregone and other local resources? Because we are a small economy, big, lumpy, capital-intensive investments that we do not control also increase our risk and our vulnerability to downturns, rather than protect us from them.

Ultimately, economic growth… should seek to increase the "income, welfare, stability and security of all Singaporeans". It should be "growth for people", not "people for growth".

In the long run, a lower rate of growth which delivers a higher ratio of benefits to Singaporeans may be more desirable than a higher rate of growth which is more unstable and inequitable. (Long, 2009a, p. 10)[39]

The global economic environment, so favourable in the first few decades after independence, is also very different today, presenting both challenges and opportunities for the future.

First, there will be a slowdown, if not a reversal, in the pace of globalisation in the next fifty years; world trade growth has fallen to, or below, world GDP growth, which it dramatically outpaced in previous decades (*The Economist*,

---

Singapore, city of rules: 'It's a Faustian deal'. *The Guardian*. Retrieved from http://www.theguardian.com/cities/2015/jan/05/the-price-of-life-in-singapore-city-of-rules-its-a-faustian-deal. While Singapore has been promoting urban density as a positive attribute of its "liveability" as a city, this does not mesh with studies that show a strong preference of rising middle classes in Asia, particularly China and India, major source countries for immigrants to Singapore, for more physical space, as reflected in growing suburban sprawl. See *The Economist*. (2014, December 6). A planet of suburbs: Places apart. All dense cities also have very low fertility rates, which I, and others have commented on in the Singapore context. Ever-increasing density, including through large-scale immigration, could thus compound Singapore's extreme demographic dilemma; see Lim, L. Y. C. (2014), How land and people fit together in Singapore's economy, in Low & Vadaketh, op. cit., pp. 31–47.

[39] Long, S. (2009a, March 11). Why it can't be more of the same. *The Straits Times*.

2014, December 13).[40] The reasons for what some have called "deglobalisation" include, on the supply side:

- Acceleration in shifts of comparative advantage, with automation in situ taking over from offshoring to more labour-intensive locations as manufacturing wages rise, whether in the US, where "reshoring" is picking up (*The Economist*, 2013, January 19)[41] or China, where electronics contract manufacturer Foxconn is planning to replace its one million workers with robots (*The Economist*, 2011, August 6)[42];

- Revolutionary technologies like 3-D printing enabling mass customisation and small-batch production at or close to where the final consumer resides (*The Economist*, 2013, September 7)[43];

- Continued shrinkage of the already fractional share of manufacturing in the value-chain of physical products like the Apple iPhone, most of whose value is embedded in services like design, marketing, software, retail and return to capital (of the roughly US$500 iPhone retail price in 2011, less than US$10 went to manufacturing in China) (Schuman, 2011)[44];

- Producing: where you sell to save on transport and inventory costs and turnaround time, and to reduce currency exposure and risk;

- Lower marginal benefits from further trade and investment liberalisation when most countries have already liberalised, with further liberalisation and standardisation more likely to occur on a regional than global level;

---

[40] *The Economist*. (2014, December 13). International Trade — A troubling trajectory. Retrieved from http://www.economist.com/news/finance-and-economics/21636089-fears-are-growing-trades-share-worlds-gdp-has-peaked-far.

[41] *The Economist*. (2013, January 19). Reshoring Manufacturing: Coming home. Retrieved from http://www.economist.com/news/special-report/21569570-growing-number-american-companies-are-moving-their-manufacturing-back-united.

[42] *The Economist*. (2011, August 6). Foxconn: Robots don't complain. Retrieved from http://www.economist.com/node/21525432.

[43] *The Economist*. (2013, September 7). 3-D printing scales up. Retrieved from http://www.economist.com/news/technology-quarterly/21584447-digital-manufacturing-there-lot-hype-around-3d-printing-it-fast.

[44] Schuman, M. (2011, May 16). Adding up the iPhone. *Time*. Retrieved from http://content.time.com/time/magazine/article/0,9171,2069042,00.html.

- Environmental and social policy pressures to reduce carbon footprints and thus streamline and shrink currently far-flung global supply chains;
- Narrowing of competitive advantage differences between geographies based on relative productivity levels, infrastructure and government incentives increasingly constrained by international agreements and protocols to "level the playing field", as economic development proceeds around the world.

On the demand side, we see:

- A slowdown in global macroeconomic growth as the rich world ages and stagnates and booming emerging markets become more mature;
- Manufacturing's shrinking and services' expanding share of value-added in global value-chains as world incomes rise, populations age and the heavily services-oriented "app economy" takes hold;
- Social innovations like the spread of the "sharing economy" (Lever, 2015)[45], the "on-demand economy" (*The Economist*, 2015, January 3)[46], conservation culture, buy-local norms and a values shift from material to experiential "goods" (like social media communications);
- A much lower rate of employment creation by large companies: for example, Facebook has annual revenues of US$12 billion and a market capitalisation exceeding US$200 billion but serves 1.5 billion customers with only 8,500 employees worldwide, most of whom are its home country.

All these add up to slower growth in output, a lower ratio of goods to services in output, a lower ratio of manufacturing to services value-added in goods, a greater localisation of goods and services production, and a much lower employment to output ratio, occurring at much lower levels of per capita income than in the present-day developed world. This is the post-industrial society on a global scale.

---

[45] Lever, R. (2015, February 3). 'Sharing economy' shapes markets as complaints rise. Agence France-Presse.

[46] *The Economist*. (2015, January 3). The Future of Work: There's an app for that. Retrieved from http://www.economist.com/news/briefing/21637355-freelance-workers-available-moments-notice-will-reshape-nature-companies-and.

For Singapore, these global trends indicate a need for transformation beyond the "global city" paradigm of the past fifty years. Today, there are also many more "global cities" competing for this role — Hong Kong, Shanghai, Sydney, Seoul — and more will emerge in the next fifty years. The gap in every dimension (physical infrastructure, income levels, social amenities, shopping, cultural activities) between the first-tier global cities of Shanghai and New York has dramatically narrowed while Shanghai's share of world GDP has increased as New York's has shrunk.[47] The same will eventually be true of the gap between Bangkok and Manila with that of Singapore.

Domestically, Singapore's comparative advantage long ago shifted decisively away from labour- to capital- and skills-intensity, despite decades of this market adjustment being slowed by compensating policy-created competitive advantages such as a liberal foreign-labour-and-talent policy. Such policy advantages will be increasingly difficult to sustain given heightened competition and spreading global norms like the reduced acceptability of tax-avoidance incentives for multinationals, a major feature of Singapore's attractiveness to foreign investors, many of whom would not locate here without them.[48]

However, is the real risk to Singapore that the age of the hub in MNC business models is coming under pressure and potentially to an end? A number of Beps proposals could make having a hub in somewhere like Singapore less palatable, if it means higher taxes on a global basis. For example, MNCs could end up paying more

---

[47] In 2000, China's share of world GDP was 3.6% while the U.S. share was 31%. By 2012, China's share had increased to 11% while the U.S. share had fallen to 22%. During this period, China's per capita income rose from 2.6% to 12.2% of the U.S.'s per capita income. See World Development Indicators at www.data.worldbank.org.

[48] I have heard this from many multinational subsidiaries in Singapore that I interviewed for my research. For the declining global acceptability of "tax arbitrage", see e.g., "EU to accuse Apple of taking illegal tax aid from Ireland", *The Guardian*, September 28, 2014; "More than 50 Countries Sign Tax Deal", *Wall Street Journal*, October 29, 2014; "UK Targets Tech Firms with 'Google Tax'", *Wall Street Journal*, December 3, 2014; "New Leak Shows Scope of Luxembourg Corporate-Tax Deals", *Wall Street Journal*, December 10, 2014; "EU to Widen Sweetheart Tax Deal Probe", *Wall Street Journal*, December 17, 2014.

in taxes when paying dividends from profitable subsidiaries with a hub in Singapore than if they had just paid to the headquarters directly. In that case, would this negate the operational benefits of having the hub in Singapore?

In a more extreme scenario, MNCs could choose to just invest into territories directly rather than through a hub location such as Singapore. This could be bad news for Singapore.[49] (Pickford, 2015)[50]

Changing US financial regulations such as those removing expatriate tax benefits, enforcing taxation of offshore bank accounts (under the Foreign Account Taxation Compliance Act, or FATCA) and imposing more restrictive credit rating standards on sovereign wealth funds like Temasek and GIC also impact Singapore's financial services sector ("Singapore isn't Greece, Singapore tells S&P in 29 pages", 2015).[51]

LOOKING TO SERVICES AND THE REGION

While Singapore's chosen development strategy of becoming a "global city" was the right one for its time and circumstances fifty years ago, the challenges of remaining internationally competitive in this role emerged rather quickly. It was only sixteen years after independence that Pang Eng Fong and I (1981)[52] wrote:

Ultimately, Singapore will have to face up to a fundamental strain in its domestic economy: the competition for labor between the services and the manufacturing sectors.

---

[49] Beps stands for the Base Erosion and Profit Shifting project that is being carried out by the Organisation for Economic Co-operation and Development (OECD). The current move towards corporate tax reform in the U.S., if effected, would also reduce the need for MNCs to shelter overseas income in offshore tax havens like Hong Kong, Singapore, Luxembourg, Ireland, Bermuda and the Cayman Islands.

[50] Pickford, B. (2015, January 27). Responsible taxation — the impact on Singapore's hub status. *The Business Times.* Retrieved from http://www.businesstimes.com.sg/opinion/responsible-taxation-the-impact-on-singapores-hub-status.

[51] *The Straits Times.* (2015, February 6). Singapore isn't Greece, Temasek tells S&P in 29 pages.

[52] Pang, E. F. & Lim, L. (1981, August 4) op. cit.

... Because of its labor-intensive base, and the rigidities imposed by fixed capital investments, restructuring in the manufacturing sector must be slow, and its success in the competitive international arena is by no means assured. The projected demands for high-skilled and experienced technical personnel are great and can't be met from the domestic labour pool. It's possible that they can't even be met internationally, given the shortages in skilled labour in most competing countries, including the advanced industrial nations.

... Singapore has a much stronger international competitive advantage in the export of services — banking, finance, commercial services, transportation, telecommunications — based on its long experience and large human and capital investment in these sectors. Another asset is its location in a rapidly growing regional economy of which it is the service hub. The service sector is intrinsically labor-intensive, and will become more skill-intensive as it upgrades into high-value services.

At the same time, even in export manufacturing industries, Singapore's competitiveness is shifting toward service-oriented activities such as regional warehousing, purchasing, servicing and research and development. Both commercial and industrial services have a demand for skilled professionals that can't be supplied adequately from domestic sources. And, as the Singapore population grows more affluent, it will consume more labor-intensive social and personal services than goods, further increasing the domestic demand for labor.

One solution to the long-range problem of labor shortage is to concentrate Singapore's limited domestic resources in the one area in which it has the greatest competitive advantage — the supply of services, including industrial-based services. This would mean the phasing out of production-oriented manufacturing, in which Singapore's potential advantage on a global basis is problematic.

Unskilled labor would be released for the nontraded services sector, and skilled labor would be available for professional jobs in the highly competitive traded services sector. Reliance on both unskilled and skilled foreign labor would be reduced, and Singapore's historic complementary role to countries in the region would be enhanced.

A few years later, the Report of the Economic Committee (1986) made similar recommendations:

[Singapore should] move beyond our being a production base, to being an international total business centre. We cannot depend only on companies coming to Singapore solely to make or assemble products designed elsewhere. We need to attract companies to Singapore to establish operational headquarters, which are responsible for subsidiaries throughout the region. In Singapore such headquarters should do product development work, manage their treasury activities, and provide administrative, technical and management services to their subsidiaries ...

Services account for an increasing share of our GDP, and our service exports have been growing as quickly as world trade in services. Scope for growth is still huge. We need to promote not just Singapore-based activities like tourism or banking, but also offshore-based activities, like construction firms building hotels in China, and salvage firms operating in the Middle East ... we have expertise in hotel management, air and sea port management, town and city planning. These skills should be systematically marketed ...

Our greatest potential for growth lies in this area: banking and finance, transport and communications, and international services. It has been growing rapidly.... The government must promote services actively, the same way it successfully promoted manufacturing.... Suitable incentives, including taxation of income from international services at a lower rate, will speed the shift toward a service economy. (As cited in Lee, 1989, p. 293)[53].

---

[53] Lee, S. A. (1989). Expansion of the Services Sector. In K. S. Sandhu and P. Wheatley (Eds.), *Management of Success: The Moulding of Modern Singapore* (pp. 280–299). Singapore: Institute of Southeast Asian Studies.

However, the committee did not recommend any reduction in the promotion of manufacturing:

> *As manufacturing is to be treated equally with services, there appears to be a continuity of the old pattern of concentrating on the overall growth rate as the target of economic policy and of emphasizing the visibility of manufacturing, despite the possibilities and the strength of the services sector.* (Lee, 1989, p. 297)[54]

Furthermore, the Economic Review Committee (2003) continued to emphasise manufacturing as one of the "twin engines" of GDP growth. Services continued to expand, growing from 60% of the GDP in 1985 and 1990 to 63% in 2005; its share of employment rose from 67% in 1990 to 77% in 2005 (Choy, 2010, p. 129)[55], enabled by the liberal foreign labour and talent policy as competition continued with the heavily-subsidised manufacturing sector for scarce resources. As the theory of *comparative* advantage tells us, a comparative advantage in one sector means a comparative *dis*advantage in another, and even large economies like the US and China cannot be equally competitive in every sector.

Choy (2010)[56] argues thus for a change in Singapore's economic model[57] away from manufacturing to services:

> *the service sector is less risky. Due to its very nature, service industries are less dependent on foreign capital and tend to be influenced to a smaller extent by business cycles. As Singapore establishes itself as a reputable exporter of final services such as financial wealth management, the media business, marketing and design services, tertiary education, and medical treatment — moving away from the current reliance on activities that are cyclically tied to manufacturing production such as intermediate trading, transportation, and banking services — the economy's vulnerability to external shocks will be reduced accordingly. The*

---

[54] Ibid.
[55] Choy, (2010) op. cit.
[56] Ibid.
[57] The definitive quantitative longitudinal study of the Singapore economy and its institutions is in Abeysinghe, T., & Choy, K. M. (2002).

construction of two world-class integrated resorts to attract high-spending visitors to Singapore can be construed as a step in this direction, though it must be acknowledged that international tourist traffic will remain sensitive to global economic conditions and geopolitical events.

More to the point, the development of a heterogeneous and diversified service sector offers the prospect that monetary policy will be a potent tool for mitigating economic fluctuations, as a result of the greater sensitivity of tradable services to exchange rate movements. Since exportable services have much higher domestic value-added and lower import content compared with manufactured goods, theory predicts and empirical evidence confirms that a currency depreciation stimulates the foreign demand for services much more than it does commodity exports.

For all this to come to pass, however, government bureaucrats need to intensify greatly their efforts to promote the service sector in general, and expand regional markets for tradable services in particular. Servicing the needs of the burgeoning middle classes in China and India could easily add a percentage point or two to Singapore's potential growth rate. One should also not neglect to mention the untapped potential of domestically-oriented service industries catering to a richer and ever-growing local population. Economic planners in Singapore must, therefore, shed their long-held bias in favour of manufacturing, stemming perhaps from the perception that service jobs are less glamorous and that the average level and growth rate of productivity in the service sector are lower compared with the goods industries. However, service industries have the virtue of being relatively labour-intensive, thus generating more employment and helping to keep both structural and cyclical unemployment at bay. The same cannot be said for high-technology manufacturing. For example, the biomedical sciences cluster currently accounts for only a small proportion of the workforce, its forward linkages with the health care industry notwithstanding. Moreover, if Singapore is going to be compared to the leading cities of the world such as New York and London, having a vibrant and progressive service sector will be essential for success....

... the manufacturing-based export growth engine which Singapore and other Asian economies have relied on so heavily for economic success has run out of steam and left them without domestic demand stabilizers. Therefore, it is time for the government to change Singapore's economic model to meet the new economic circumstances and challenges. (pp. 136–137)[58]

The next question one might ask is services for whom? The Strategic Economic Plan (1991) recommended the launch of what was called a "second wing" for the Singapore economy, encouraging local enterprises to venture out and invest in booming neighbouring countries, with the assistance of government fiscal incentives, tax concessions, equity financing and infrastructure provision to support overseas ventures.

By 1997, S$75.8 billion in cumulative outward direct investments had been committed by local firms, though the lion's share was, not surprisingly, attributed to government-linked companies (GLCs).

Sadly, though, the Asian financial crisis erupted in July 1997 with the devaluation of the Thai baht and brought to a dramatic end the golden era of strong regional and domestic economic growth that had lasted for nearly a decade. (Choy, 2010, p. 126)[59]

Despite this slowdown, both large and small Singapore companies have continued to invest abroad, with Asia their top source of overseas revenue, and ASEAN particularly important for SMEs.[60] Recently, Dr Teh Kok Peng

---

[58] Choy, (2010), op. cit.

[59] Ibid.

[60] See "Asia remains biggest source of overseas revenue for Singapore companies", *The Straits Times*, January 29, 2015, citing the Singapore International 100 ranking by the DP Group.

(2014)[61] has called for "creating a second Singapore outside Singapore" (as cited in Teh, 2014):[62]

> *while the particular globalization strategy that Singapore embarked on soon after independence was the right one ... we may have overstayed in applying this strategy as the dominant one. As a result, our shortage of land, labour and other capabilities is becoming more obvious and severe. I believe it is time to have a second strategic pillar, which I would describe in short as "creating a second Singapore outside Singapore." ... the economic space of Singapore and Singapore companies should be much bigger than the geographical space of Singapore....*
>
> *Singapore's land and labour constraints are immutable. Since independence in 1965, our planners have done a remarkable job in land reclamation and urban planning such that we have been able to increase our population and the intensity of our land use without the residents feeling unduly overcrowded or congested until recent years.... Nevertheless, in the long term, there is clearly a limit as to how much more we can do in land use intensification, given how much we have already done.*
>
> *With regard to labour, Singapore had actually run up against domestic labour constrains early on, and had begun importing foreign workers, mainly Malaysians, by the early 1970s.... Since then, our dependence rate of foreign workers as a proportion to our total work force has risen sharply, to possibly the highest in the world, with the exception of the Gulf States.... It is this surge in our resident population ... that has given rise to ... discontent.*
>
> *... It may well be that Singapore can support a population of 6.9 million without being congested or over-crowded, with clever planning and after the current massive construction of MRTs, highways, hospitals, schools, HDBs etc. all reach completion. But*

---

[61] Teh, op. cit.

[62] Dr Teh, an economist, was President of the Government of Singapore Investment Corporation (GIC) Special Investments division from 1999–2011, and is currently a non-executive director of several large Singapore companies.

it may also be the case that one man's buzz is another man's claustrophobia.

The question also arises as to the marginal benefit of such further large capital investments in a limited space and … with the limited supply of labour. In economic theory, when one factor of production — land — is largely fixed, and another factor — labour — can only grow slowly, adding more and more capital leads to diminishing returns. About twenty years ago, Paul Krugman argued that Singapore's growth … was largely driven by inputs of labour and capital rather than productivity. If this is true, are we in the process of doing more of the same, even if the declared intent is to develop a more innovation-based, productivity-driven economy? (pp. 100–101)

Dr Teh goes on to note that more mature developed economies are all large importers *and* exporters of foreign direct investment, which yields higher returns than the portfolio investments in which Singapore currently concentrates its massive foreign reserves (resulting from high savings and large cumulative budget and current account surpluses, managed mainly by MAS and GIC). Given this large stock of accumulated capital and other capabilities, and a per capita income that is one of the world's highest, a "second Singapore" is clearly feasible as well as desirable. Income from foreign investments would also help counter the long-term balance-of-payments outflow of investment income from the huge stock of inward foreign direct investment in Singapore itself. In Dr Teh's opinion, "it seems to me that we are at a stage of development where the greater risk by far is not venturing out".[63]

Such outward direct investment has the following benefits: easing the pressure on Singapore's own land and labour market, as foreign labour is employed in their home countries instead; enabling SMEs to achieve scale more easily and deploy their developed technologies and capabilities more profitably in lower-cost locations; avoiding potential exclusion from promising markets, and acquiring new knowledge and capabilities abroad that could be transferred to enhance parent firms' competitive advantages; and higher returns

---

[63] Comment made at IPS Singapore Perspectives 2015.

on investments enabling the payment of higher taxes to help fund the domestic transfer payments put into place to serve growing social needs.

Fortunately, in addition to the physical, financial and human capital built up over the past fifty years, Singapore benefits from an excellent geographical location in the centre of South-east Asia. This is the next large emerging regional market to which global multinationals are already turning their investment attention, as are Singapore and national companies in our neighbouring countries.[64] The tapering off (*note:* not total disappearance) of the 20th-century development model of manufacturing for export through multinational networks to rapidly-ageing, slowly-growing, distant rich markets will be replaced by domestic consumption-led growth in faster-growing nearby middle-income markets like China (as it "rebalances" its economy away from the current investment-driven export-led manufacturing model towards increased domestic consumption of services)[65] and the more youthful India and Indonesia. Singapore's well-developed industrial services referred to above can also integrate with developing manufacturing capabilities in neighbouring countries, for both regional and global markets

Singapore can build on our natural differentiating advantages versus other "global cities" by playing a role in regional value-chains catering to the hundreds of millions who are already entering the middle class all around us. Based on comparative (capital, skills) and competitive advantage (infrastructure, first-comer advantage, location, culture), our edge is likely to be in value-added services — finance, education, health-and-wellness, recreation — that we already provide to the world's and region's wealthy, and which market research studies already show strong demand growth for in these

---

[64] See, for example, "Indonesia sees surge in foreign investment", *Wall Street Journal*, January 20, 2012; "Foxconn moves into Indonesia, worrying labor groups", *Christian Science Monitor*, September 5, 2012; "Indonesia to Big Chains: Share the wealth", *Wall Street Journal*, May 12, 2013; "Facebook.ers in Indonesia Rise to 69 million", *Wall Street Journal*, June 27, 2014; "Japan Inc. goes deeper into Southeast Asia" (*Wall Street Journal*, September 28, 2014; "Japanese Investment in Southeast Asia: Outward bound", *Economist*, November 1, 2014.

[65] This is the same economic model that Singapore should also rebalance away from. See Lim, L. Y. C. (2010). Rebalancing in East Asia. In S. Claessens, S. Evenett and B. Hoekman (Eds.), *Rebalancing the Global Economy: A Primer for Policymaking* (pp. 32–35). London: Centre for Economic Policy-Making.

markets.[66] What we need to do is cater more explicitly to the much larger numbers just slightly further down the regional income distribution, who are likely to consume similar services and at similar price-points to the bottom 80% of our local citizens by income level, who can provide and benefit from such services themselves as skill capabilities and scale economies develop.

Put simply, we will move from manufacturing physical goods for customers richer than we are to providing services to customers poorer than we are. The good news is that services for our regional neighbourhood are more location-specific and scalable, and less capital- and energy-intensive, than manufacturing for distant markets, less reliant on rare specific technical skills unlikely to be found in adequate scale among our small population and more open to small entrepreneurs with different levels of formal education, providing a channel for employment creation, upward mobility and reduced inequality (through SME ownership and the capital returns from operating in regional markets). As I have written elsewhere:

> In both high-tech manufacturing and financial services, Singapore lacks not just market scale and supply-chain depth and diversity, but also a sizeable globally-competitive labour and talent pool. So far it has succeeded by importing the narrowly specific skill sets that these sectors require — like electronics engineers from China and financial and IT experts from India — but this has already bumped up against ... constraints. In the next 50 years it will also become more difficult to attract top talent from other Asian countries as their economies develop, giving their talented citizens better career opportunities and lifestyles at home.
>
> Fortunately, Singapore's scale also confers certain advantages, in that it only needs to excel (on the supply side) in relatively few, smaller but higher-value, product niches in order to compete globally and provide sufficient employment opportunities for its

---

[66] Some examples include McKinsey (March 2012), "Meet the Chinese Consumer of 2020"; Accenture (February 2013), "Meet the New Chinese Consumer"; Boston Consulting Group (March 2013), "Indonesia's Rising Middle Class and Affluent Consumers".

resident population, with the help (on the demand side) of expanded domestic consumption by the local population, and demand from increasingly affluent regional neighbours. Looking forward 50 years, two major intrinsic assets that the country possesses are its geographical location in the centre of what will be the world's largest fast-growing middle-income regional market (the currently 600-plus million in Southeast Asia, together with the 1.5 billion-plus in South Asia), and its own population's cultural affinity with the populations in that market, which will be particularly important in various professional, personal and social services.

In financial services, for example, the principle of portfolio diversification alone will dictate that some segment of the burgeoning mass middle classes of Southeast Asia will place some portion of their savings in or with Singapore-based financial institutions and finance professionals, just as high-net-worth individuals from the region and the world already do. In tourism, there is already a large and vibrant regional market, which will only grow as more families are able to afford short holidays in neighbouring countries. Health and educational services are already well-developed and have further room to grow, especially for average-income customers. (Lim, 2015, p. 101)[67]

Note that Indonesia is already the largest source of international visitors to Singapore, followed (at some distance) by China, while elder services (that Singapore's rapidly-expanding ranks of elderly could also benefit from at home) are already beginning to take off in China ("China's aging boomers are lucrative market", 2015).[68] From a trade policy perspective, for all its likely disappointments, the ASEAN Economic Community, which is due to be

---

[67] Lim, L. Y. C. (2015). Singapore in the International Economy. In E. Quah (Ed.), *Singapore 2065: Leading Insights on the Economy and Environment from 50 Singapore Icons and Beyond.* Singapore: World Scientific (pp. 98–102).

[68] Burkitt, L. (2015, January 20). China's aging boomers are lucrative market. *Wall Street Journal.*

launched by the end of 2015 (ASEAN Secretariat, 2014)[69], will enhance the prospects for regional services integration, given its vision of a "single market" for services, regulatory standardisation, infrastructural connectivity (e.g. in telecommunications, to facilitate e-commerce) and promotion of SMEs and SME collaboration.

What of the role of state industrial and social policy, which I argued above was critical to the success of the post-independence "global city" economic model? This transition from being one of many global cities to becoming a one-of-a-kind regional city requires shifts in Singaporean mindsets, educational choices, labour market behaviours and government policies that directly or indirectly influence and incentivise them.

> Focusing on employment and income creation for the average native Singaporean as opposed to income maximisation for footloose foreign corporations ... requires a shift in economic policy and individual thinking from, among others, the global to regional, manufacturing to services, capital to labour and skills, high-end to middle, foreign to local, state to market, large to small, profits to wages, corporate to entrepreneurial, and so on. (Lim, 2015, p. 101)

Given the strong underlying market advantages, I do not see a role for state industrial policy to micro-manage this shift. Rather, I would propose a downsizing, if not dismantling, of the whole bureaucratic infrastructure that has for decades strived — with some, if incomplete and declining, success — to "manage" Singapore's international competitiveness as a "global city", particularly in manufacturing. Not only is such state management of competitiveness no longer effective or even possible in the changed global environment that is already with us today, but it also distorts resource allocation at home and abroad, discouraging entrepreneurial investments. A reduction in the role of state intervention in the forces of dynamic comparative and competitive advantage would, among other things, release scarce resources of capital and local talent to find their way into the most market-advantageous economic activities which I, and others, have argued are likely to be in services

---

[69] ASEAN Secretariat. (May 2014). *Thinking Globally, Prospering Regionally— ASEAN Economic Community 2015*. Jakarta: ASEAN.

for the domestic and regional market, a process which is already taking place. As noted in my 2009 interview:

> *The way forward for Singapore… is to allow the market to 'diversify on its own', with resource allocation done by market forces and entrepreneurs, instead of the state and bureaucrats.*

> *Do we devote our carefully husbanded national savings, accumulated over generations, to letting the state make big bets on a few major, capital-intensive, risky and expensive projects?*

> *Or do we privatize the economy, releasing capital and talent to local entrepreneurs to create value in smaller but nimbler enterprises? At least, if they fail, it will take only small parts, rather than big chunks, of the economy down with them.*

> *It's much better to send out 100 motorboats, rather than one huge aircraft carrier, into the unknown. I would bet on at least some of the motorboats making it, instead of the aircraft carrier, a sitting duck, which could get blown up.* (Long, 2009b, p. 10)[70]

I have been visiting Myanmar for thirty years. About eight years ago, I interviewed some Singaporean businesses there and found to my surprise and delight that there were already about 350 of them, mostly SMEs in services like trading, schools, hair salons, small hotels, shops and restaurants. This was well before Myanmar started opening out to foreign investment in 2011, after which Singapore GLCs, banks and government agencies like International Enterprise Singapore (IE) and SingBridge, as well as MNCs from many countries, moved in in a big way. Our SMEs had ventured into a very difficult business environment ahead of most of the "big boys", and they were doing well.

Since the 1991 "second wing" initiative, many of our GLCs have also ventured into the region. Mr Chow Yew Yuen, CEO of Keppel Offshore and Marine, shared his company's experience:

---

[70] Long, S. (2009b, March 11). New growth model beyond Jack-of-all-hubs needed. *The Straits Times.*

As offshore and marine, we operate in 15 countries and we have 20 yards worldwide. Most of our operations we manage with a few Singaporeans. We find that Singaporeans are actually, because of our background, able to operate in those countries quite well if you compare with people of maybe more homogeneous societies like the Japanese or the Koreans.... In our case, we are moving a lot of our less skill intensive types of operation overseas. For example, we have moved to the Philippines, Indonesia and some of the other regional places. But to protect the mothership, we are consciously making decisions on where we keep our R&D development, our project management development and our supply chain management (in Singapore).[71]

Individual Singaporean entrepreneurs have also ventured into our South-east Asian neighbours.

One example is Kwok Kian Tow, a Singaporean economist-by-training whose company runs granite quarries and processing facilities in Singapore, Malaysia and China, branching out into construction materials in Vietnam and Myanmar, and into property development in Malaysia and China. His company also manufactures die-cast aluminium parts in Malaysia. To quote Kwok:

The British East India Company sent ordinary Englishmen to the 'Far East' and many became leading businessmen thousands of miles away from home. Each of us who went away from Singapore shores to do business in Southeast Asian countries and beyond had an EIC "eureka moment" — that these lands held opportunities equal to or better than home. As for the drive and the flow to do business in unfamiliar settings, most of us had no EIC to give us a start, a leg up. Each had his own story.[72]

Some younger Singaporeans are also doing the same thing, and for the same reason, namely, they see the Singapore market as "saturated".

---

[71] Comment made at the post-panel discussion at IPS Singapore Perspectives 2015 on 26 January 2015.
[72] Kwok Kian Tow, personal communication with author in February 2015.

And Sharifah Yuhaniz, a Singaporean MBA entrepreneur in Malaysia, says:

> *In my business, the opportunities are in South East Asia. With lower oil prices, many downstream projects like in situ small-scale power generation projects are becoming viable and are taking off. Especially in an archipelago of small land masses like South East Asia, producing power near demand makes a lot more sense than dealing with expensive transmission.*[73]

Social policy could also have a role to play in enabling or encouraging more Singaporeans to become entrepreneurs, develop service enterprises and venture into Southeast Asia. For example, if Singaporeans did not have to devote so much of their savings to CPF and housing, they would have more disposable income and time to spend on consuming domestic services,[74] creating jobs at home and accumulating start-up capital and developing capabilities that could be invested both at home and abroad. They might even be able to marry at a younger age, have more children and be able to support themselves in their post-retirement years ("Top concerns for Singaporeans", 2015)[75]. A universal social safety net for poverty and pension relief might reduce the risk aversion that discourages entrepreneurial activity. And educational options could be increased at all age levels to provide experiences (e.g. active learning projects in neighbouring countries) and skills (e.g. studying South-east Asian languages, non-university accounting, finance and marketing courses) that would

---

[73] Sharifah Yuhaniz, personal communication with author on 23 February 2015.

[74] Tilak Abeysinghe and Choy Keen Meng, "The aggregate consumption puzzle in Singapore", *Journal of Asian Economics* 15 (2004), pp. 563–578; Tilak Abeysinghe and Jiaying Gu, "Lifetime income and housing affordability in Singapore", *Urban Studies* 48 (2011), pp. 1875–1901; Linda Lim and James Cheng, "Why Singapore is not Iceland", *The Business Times*, Singapore, January 24, 2014; "'Meaningful correction still unachieved': Tharman", *The Business Times*, October 29, 2014; "Not kicking the habit", *Economist*, February 7, 2015, all refer to the high level of household debt in Singapore. In contrast, in the U.S., entrepreneurs often resort to home mortgages for start-up capital.

[75] Channel NewsAsia. (2015, February 16). Top concerns for Singaporeans: Retirement adequacy, healthcare and cost of living. *Channel News Asia*, Retrieved from http://www.channelnewsasia.com/news/singapore/top-concerns-for/1663084. html.

encourage and enable entrepreneurship.[76] Given vested (and competing) interests, including entrenched bureaucratic interests, and the multiple other needs that social policy must fulfil, bold policy changes are unlikely here.

CONCLUSION

The "global city" model served Singapore's economic development well in the early decades of independence when it comported well with the country's mostly market-based comparative and competitive advantages. As these changed, strategic government industrial and social policy interventions managed to preserve international competitiveness, mostly by importing foreign capital, talent, labour and technology to serve global markets. However, this was at the cost of ever-increasing subsidies for foreign investors ("corporate welfare"), distortions and rigidities in the allocation of resources, disappointing productivity growth, increased volatility, inequality and negative externalities, and the "crowding out" of local entrepreneurs and non-favoured sectors, calling into question the model's continued economic, social and political sustainability.

Looking forward to the next fifty years, dramatic and rapid changes in the global economy further undermine the viability of the "global city" model. However, a fortunate geography, and valuable national assets accumulated over the past half-century, provides Singapore with a new opportunity to prosper as a regional city serving the growing service consumption needs of the increasingly wealthy middle classes of South-east and South Asia, and connecting them with the wider world as necessary. This transition requires an entrepreneurial spirit that will enable us to create our own jobs rather than slot ourselves into the declining number of jobs that will emanate from large foreign companies. In addition, a mindset shift in geographical orientation is required:

> *For the last 40 years, Singapore has viewed itself as 'an outpost of Western empire, catering to those scared of the jungle and needing an intermediary'...*

---

[76] For a more extended discussion of what Singapore and Singaporeans can do to prepare for the employment challenges of the present and future, see Lim, L. Y. C. (2014), What's wrong with Singaporeans? In Low & Vadaketh, op. cit. pp. 79–96.

... Instead of trying to be a 'secondary global node', Singapore should focus on being a 'primary regional one' and leverage its 'unique location-specific advantages'. (Long, 2009a, p. 10)[77]

From the 1910s to the 1930s, my great-grandfather Kung Tian Siong, the first of now six generations of my family to study in Anglo-Chinese School (and, beginning with my great-grandmother, Methodist Girls' School), frequently travelled to and readily conducted business in cities as diverse as Batavia (now Jakarta), Surabaya, Pontianak and Shanghai on the one hand, and Los Angeles, Chicago, New York, London and Frankfurt on the other, while his younger brother Kung Tian Cheng lived and worked for some years in Bangalore and Mysore as well as Penang, Shanghai and Beijing. Their widowed mother was an illiterate seamstress who spoke only dialect, yet both men became fluent and literate in English, Malay, Mandarin and several Chinese dialects, and were clearly comfortable in many different cultural milieus.[78] There have always been Singaporeans like them, and there should be many more in our next fifty years, as we increase the regional, while retaining the global, content and context of our city, and of our nation's economy. Conserving our multicultural national identity will then go hand in hand with economic progress and social well-being.

For more, please refer to:

Lim, L. Y. C. (May 2009). Singapore's Economic Growth Model: Too Much or Too Little?" *Ethos, 6*, 32–38.

Pang, E. F., & Lim, L. (1989). High Tech and Labour in the Asian NICs. *Labour and* Society, *14*, 43–57.

---

[77] Long, (2009a) op. cit.

[78] For more details on their lives and careers, see Lim, L. Y. C. (2014). *Four Chinese Families in British Colonial Malaya: Confucius, Christianity and Revolution* (3rd Ed.). Retrieved from www.blurb.com. Also available at the National, NUS and ISEAS libraries in Singapore.

17

Economic Dynamism Amidst Demographic Change

RAVI MENON

I will focus my presentation on the economic implications of demographic change: what it means for economic growth and economic dynamism. The two are different. My presentation will centre around two broad themes. First, I will describe our demographic trilemma — the constraints and the choices we need to make. Second, I would like to argue that demographics is not destiny — why economic dynamism is not a numbers game and how we can remain dynamic amidst this demographic challenge.

Decline in fertility has dragged down resident population growth

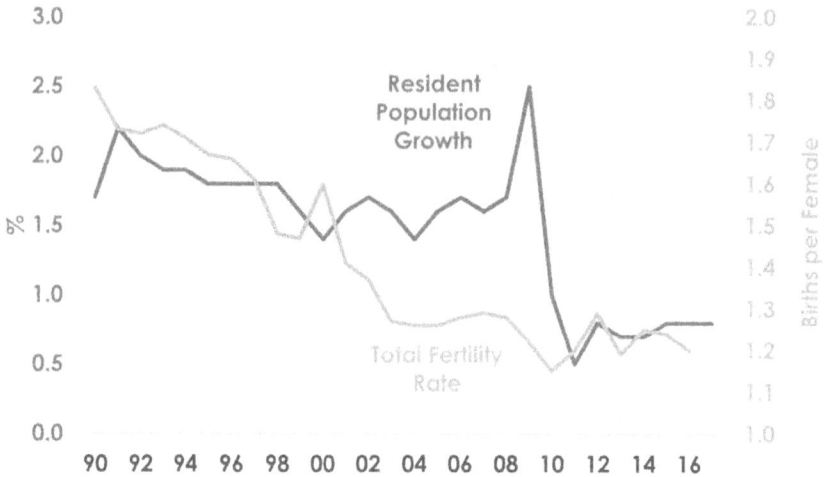

Source: Department of Statistics

Let's start with the total fertility rate, or TFR. By the way, we must be one of the few countries in the world where most people know what TFR stands for! It is indeed an existential issue for us. The TFR is the starting point of all demographic analysis. Singapore has had a sustained decline in its TFR. Our TFR fell from around 1.8 in the 1980s (which is already below the replacement level of 2.1) to about 1.3 in the early 2000s. This has weighed heavily on resident population growth as seen from the relatively close correlation with the TFR. There appears to be three distinct phases in the last 30 years. In the 1990s, both the TFR and resident population growth declined in tandem. In the 2000s, the TFR continued to decline but resident population growth recovered. This reflected net positive immigration as the number of new citizens and permanent residents grew. In this decade, the TFR appears to have stabilised at around 1.2–1.3 while resident population growth fell sharply reflecting the tightening of immigration flows.

Assuming zero net migration, working-age population will start to shrink soon

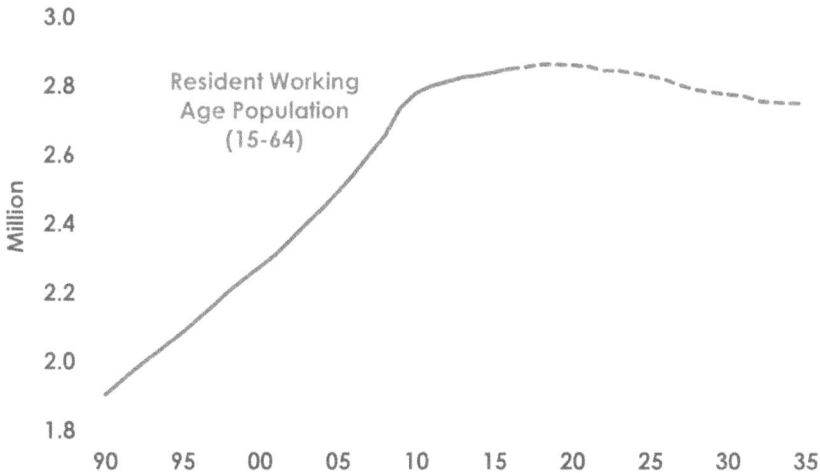

Source: Estimates from Department of Statistics Singapore and Monetary Authority of Singapore

The next two slides are a thought experiment. They are not a forecast or prediction but aim to illustrate the implications of having very low resident population growth. First, let us assume that we have zero net immigration starting from this year. The resident working-age population — this is defined as citizens and permanent residents between the ages of 15 to 64 — will begin to shrink from around 2020. The exact year is not key. What is important to note is that it is not far off. By 2035, the working-age resident population will possibly decline by a cumulative 3.5 per cent.

Assuming zero increase in foreign workers, labour force will similarly decline

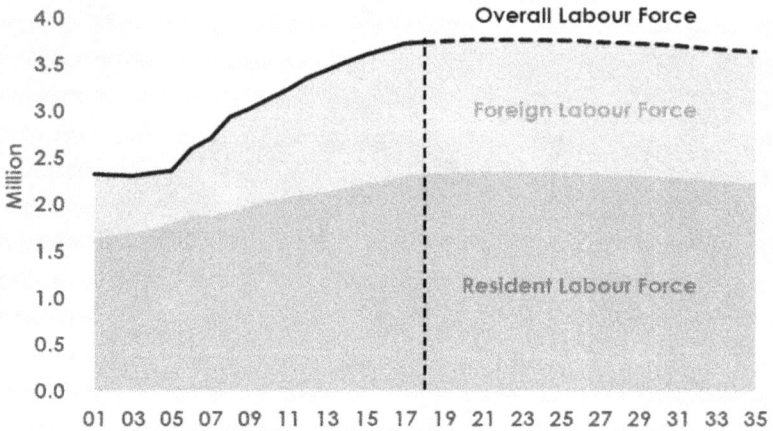

Source: Estimates from Ministry of Manpower and Monetary Authority of Singapore

Second, let us assume zero net increase in foreign workers from now on. The overall labour force will decline gradually from around 2022, driven fundamentally by the shrinking resident labour force.

If labour force declines*, GDP growth will also decline

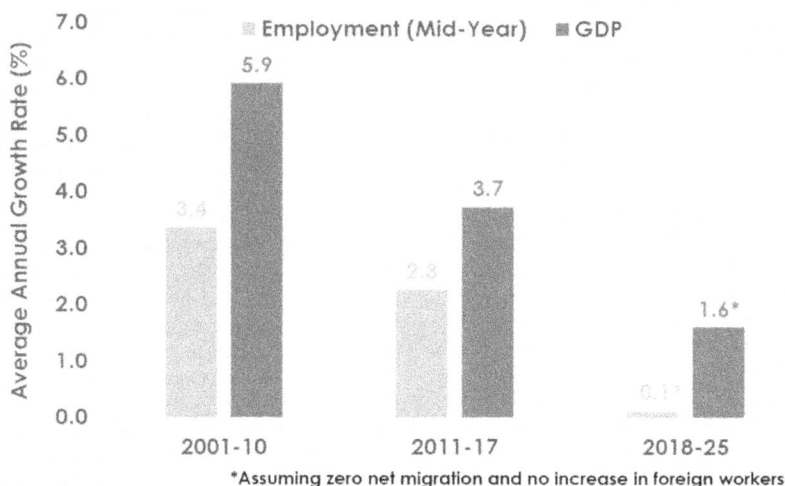

*Assuming zero net migration and no increase in foreign workers

Source: Estimates from the Department of Statistics, Ministry of Manpower and Monetary Authority of Singapore

These two assumptions taken together — zero net migration (i.e., no additional new citizens or permanent residents on a net basis) and no additional foreign workers — will have important implications for economic growth. From the perspective of the supply-side capacity or potential of the economy, GDP growth can be seen as the sum of productivity growth and labour force growth. This means, holding productivity growth constant, a decline in labour force growth will have a direct impact on economic growth. This correlation appears to be borne out in the past empirically. If labour force growth falls to near zero, then the only source of GDP growth is productivity growth. If productivity growth stays at about 1.5 per cent, which is what we have likely averaged over the last seven years (based on mid-year employment), then GDP growth will approach that level.

The demographic trilemma

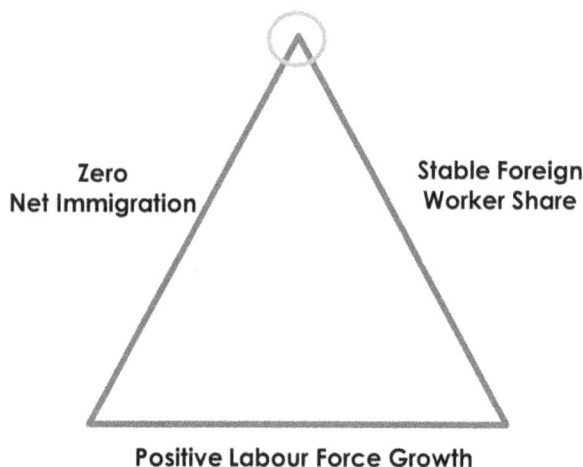

**Zero
Net Immigration**

**Stable Foreign
Worker Share**

Positive Labour Force Growth

This then is the demographic trilemma. We have three possible objectives that various people in Singapore have advocated in the past. The reality is, at any one time, we can achieve only two out of the three objectives.

The three possible objectives are:

- Positive labour force expansion
- Zero net immigration, that some would prefer
- No increase in share of foreign workers in total workforce

So, what are the trade-offs? If you look at the corners of the triangle, that's where the trade-offs are: If we want labour force to grow and have zero net immigration, then we have to allow the share of foreign workers in the workforce to rise. That's the bottom left of the triangle. If we want the overall labour force to grow and the share of foreign workers to be stable, then we have to allow net immigration. That's the bottom right of the triangle. If we want zero net immigration and the foreign worker share to be stable, then we have to accept zero labour force growth. That's the top of the triangle.

The trilemma represents the constraints. I've put them in rather stark terms, to reflect vividly the trade-offs we face. Collectively, as a society, we have to decide which corner of the trilemma we want to be at, or which corner we want to be close to. I'll argue later on that we may be able to soften these constraints and reach more balanced outcomes. But the fundamental constraints and choices implied by the trilemma are real.

A recovery in fertility is the best solution but will help only in the long run

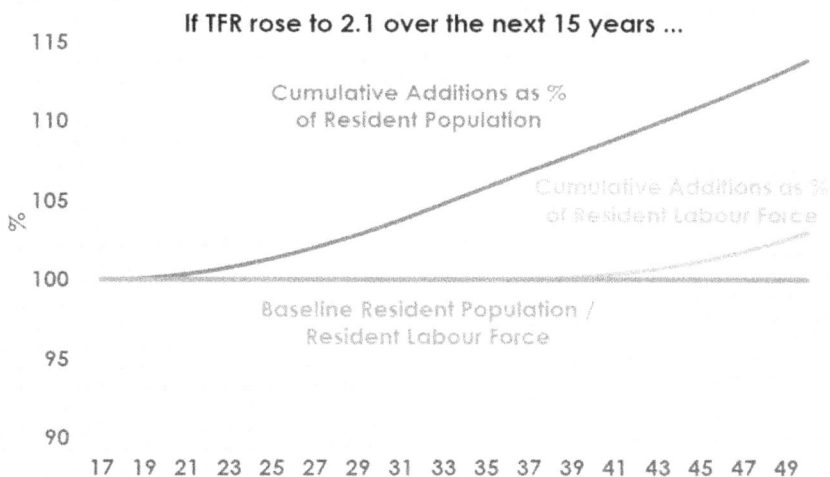

If TFR rose to 2.1 over the next 15 years ...

Cumulative Additions as %
of Resident Population

Cumulative Additions as %
of Resident Labour Force

Baseline Resident Population /
Resident Labour Force

Source: Estimates from the Monetary Authority of Singapore

Are there ways to escape the trilemma? Or at least soften its hard constraints? There are two solutions that have often been mentioned. First, an increase in fertility. Second, an increase in resident labour force participation rate. A recovery in Singapore's TFR is the best and most lasting solution that we can have, but its positive effects on labour force will only occur in the very long run.

So here's another thought experiment: Assume our TFR rises steadily from the current level of 1.2 to 2.1 (replacement rate) over next 15 years. Obviously, it will have an immediate impact on resident population and its effect will cumulate over time. That is shown by the blue line which is

189

shooting up quite nicely. But crucially a recovery in the TFR will not have any perceptible impact on labour force and GDP growth until nearly 2040. This is shown by the yellow line. It will take time for the extra babies born in the next 15 years to start entering the labour force. So while it's the most lasting solution to our challenges, TFR effects will only impact the economy in the long run.

Improvements in labour force participation will help in the near term but not by much

If gender gap in LFPR narrowed to German levels by 2035 ...

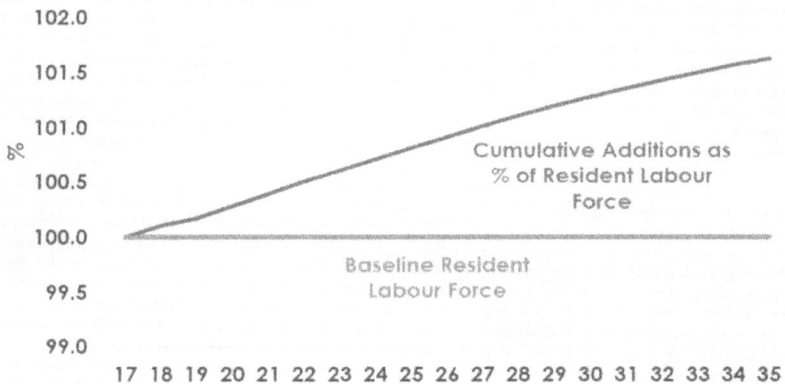

Source: Estimates from the Monetary Authority of Singapore

The second way to soften the trilemma is to increase our resident Labour Force Participation Rate (LFPR). This will have more immediate payoffs. But even at plausible stretch targets, its effects on resident labour force growth will be quite limited. Singapore's LFPR — defined as share of the resident population aged 15–64 who are in the labour force — is currently 76.1. It is not bad by OECD standards but there is scope to improve it. Japan is at 76.8; Germany is at 77.9; the Netherlands is at 79.9; Sweden is at 82.1.

Our LFPR for older workers is not bad; it is female LFPR where we are lagging behind. There is currently still a fairly large gender LFPR gap between male and females in their 40s and 50s. This gap in Singapore is higher than that in leading OECD countries. In many advanced economies, women tend to return to the work force after their prime child-bearing years. In Singapore, this is much less prevalent. If we can make it easier for our women to return to the workforce after they have had their children, we can narrow the gender gap vis-à-vis the advanced economies.

This slide demonstrates another thought experiment. Assume we narrow our gender gap from the current 15 percentage points to 11 percentage points by 2035 — approximately the level seen in Germany and Netherlands. This will only translate into a cumulative labour force increase of about 2 per cent in 2035.

How can we soften the hard constraints of the demographic trilemma?

1   **Make it easier to set up a family; make it easier for women to return to workforce**

2   **Seek balanced solutions – some net immigration, some increase in labour force, some flexibility in foreign worker share**

3   **Focus on size and type of foreign workforce that will maximise job and wage opportunities for Singaporeans**

The demographic trilemma presents the constraints and choices facing us. We can soften it by raising the TFR and LFPR. Of course, having babies or returning to work are deeply personal choices. No one makes these choices in order to boost labour force growth or GDP growth, and we should not suggest doing so. The government tries to facilitate fertility and labour force participation because that is what many people desire for their own fulfilment. Many women would like to return to work, but they face a number of constraints. We must make it easier for them to do so. The government has made significant efforts in recent years to invest in childcare and facilitate more flexible working arrangements. We must continue to push on this front and collectively as a society enable more who want to work enter the workforce.

Likewise, many married couples want to have children — not for GDP but because children are a source of joy and fulfilment of love. Government policies on marriage and parenthood are guided by this higher purpose. And of course, a growing labour force is a happy, economic by-product.

We must make balanced choices in addressing the trilemma. We must accept a slower rate of labour force growth. The underlying demographic slowdown is so severe that it is neither feasible nor desirable to try to completely offset it through immigration or foreign workers. But we must also allow a certain rate of net immigration to augment our resident population. This is not just about numbers but about rejuvenation and expanding our talent base. And while we cannot keep increasing our share of foreign workforce indefinitely, we must be flexible in allowing fluctuations in the ratio according to economic cycles, changing circumstances, and opportunities.

Finally, we must reframe our question on foreign workers. It is not about how many foreign workers industry wants or society can afford to have, but what number and kind of foreign workers we need to maximise the job and wage opportunities for Singaporeans. Foreign workers must be a complement to the local workforce.

Let me move on to the second broad theme — that demographics is not destiny. We can sustain our economic dynamism in the face of demographic change.

We cannot grow as fast as before ...

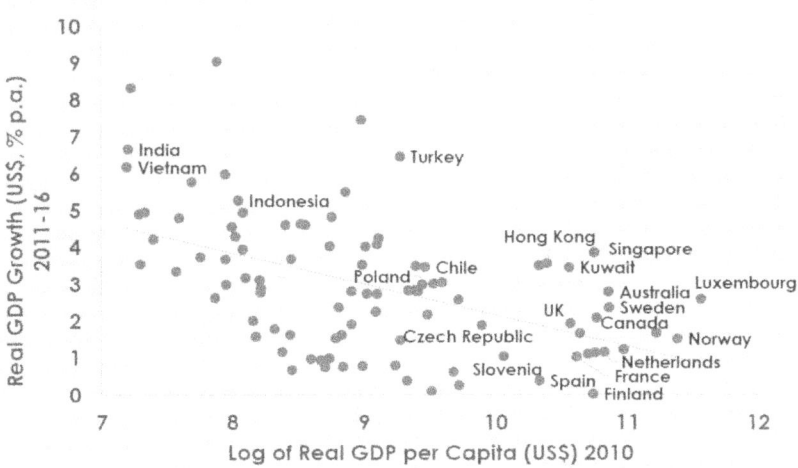

Source: World Bank, World Development Indicators

First, we should not grow despondent over our slowing rate of economic growth. The empirical experience of countries over time shows a negative relationship between level of income and the growth of income. It is not a perfect negative relationship as you can see from the scatter but it suggests that countries with low levels of GDP per capita tend to have higher rates of GDP growth. This is called "catch-up" in the literature.

Meanwhile, countries with higher levels of GDP per capita tend to grow at slower rates as they are more mature. Singapore is a mature economy as you can see; it has one of the highest levels of per capita income in the world. We will not be able to sustain the 6–7 per cent rates of growth that were seen a decade ago. And there's nothing to be unhappy about this. In fact, our position above the downward sloping line in the slide shows that we have managed to grow faster in recent years than countries with similar levels of per capita income.

... but as a city we cannot afford to grow too slowly either

Real GDP Growth Per Annum (2010-2016)

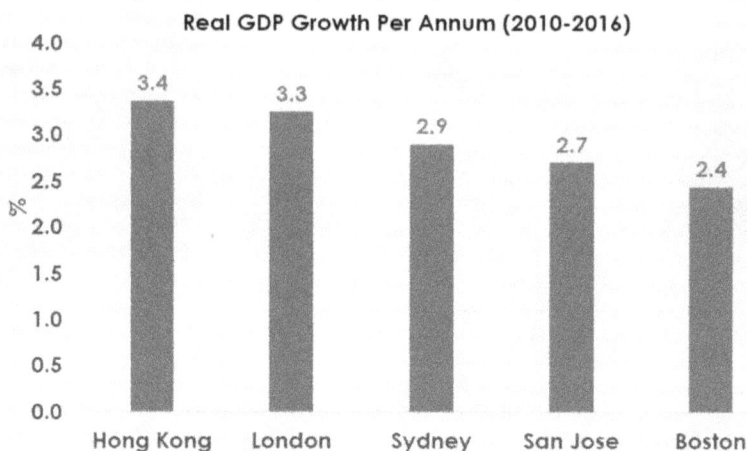

Source: U.S. Bureau of Economic Analysis, Office for National Statistics (U.K.), Haver Analytics, SGS Economic & Planning, Monetary Authority of Singapore

But while we must accept a lower rate of growth than before, as a global city, we cannot afford to grow too slowly either. It seems many leading global cities grow at rates between 2.5–3.5 per cent, faster than the national average of the countries they are a part of. London has averaged 3.3 per cent annual growth since the financial crisis while Sydney has averaged around 2.9 per cent. San Jose (which encompasses Silicon Valley) has averaged 2.7 per cent per annum.

It is hard to imagine a dynamic city growing at less than 2 per cent or worse still, 1.5 per cent. It will be unattractive to investors and talent, including the city's own investors and talented people. A reasonably good rate of growth helps to create opportunities and preserve a sense of progress and hope, particularly among the young. It will also facilitate upward social mobility.

In leading cities, productivity is the key source of economic growth and dynamism

Sources of GDP Growth (2010-16)

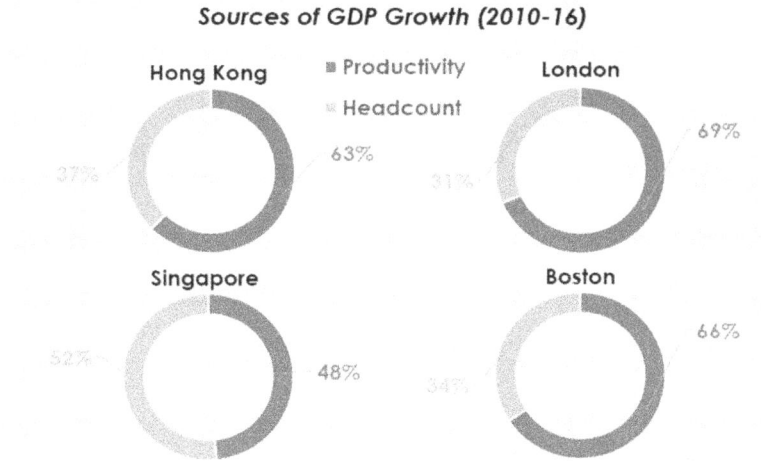

Hong Kong ■ Productivity ■ Headcount

63% 37% 31%

London 69%

Singapore 48% 52%

Boston 66% 34%

Source: U.S. Bureau of Economic Analysis, Office for National Statistics (U.K.), CEIC, Monetary Authority of Singapore

The experience of other leading cities suggests that demographics is not destiny. Yes, vibrant cities do attract people — and their additions to the labour force add to growth. But the main source of their growth and dynamism is not headcount but productivity.

This is not an in-depth study but it appears that about two-thirds of overall GDP growth in the cities shown is due to productivity improvements. In comparison, productivity has accounted for about half of Singapore's GDP growth. There is clearly scope for us to do better and thereby sustain our dynamism.

Scope to reap human capital dividends

Highest Qualification Attained by Residents 25 Years & Over

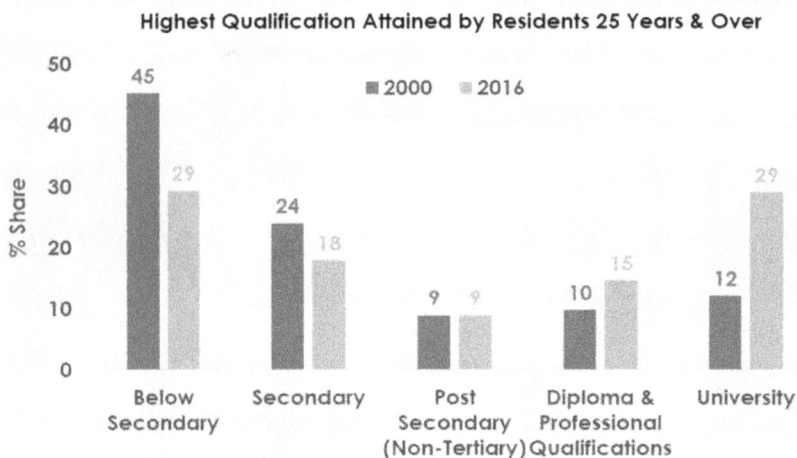

Source: Department of Statistics Singapore

How can we do this?

First, Singapore has scope to reap the human capital dividends that are arising from the continuous investments we have made in education and training in past decades. As recently as 2000, 45 per cent of the resident workforce had below secondary school education, and only 12 per cent had university education. In just one-and-a-half decades, those ratios have converged, reflecting the cumulation of efforts made over preceding decades. The proportion with less than secondary education has dipped below 30 per cent; while the proportion of the university-educated has more than doubled to nearly 30 per cent.

The effects of this transformation in human capital will continue to be felt in the productive capacity of the workforce. With higher levels of education, the ability of the workforce to take on more complex tasks and to leverage on technology is substantially stronger. There is more to come. The share of the university-educated may not continue to as rise sharply but there is still plenty of scope to increase the share of those with secondary, post-secondary and diploma & professional qualifications. They will be better placed to transform the nature of many jobs, raising standards and quality, thus enabling productivity and wages in these occupations to rise.

Scope to improve quality of foreign workforce

Source: Ministry of Manpower

Second, there is scope to improve the quality of the foreign workforce. We should increasingly be concerned about the skills of the foreign workers that we take in, rather than just the numbers. In fact, more skilled foreign workers will mean that we will need less of them. The trend of improving quality in our foreign workforce has already begun. The proportion of work permit holders has declined by about 10 percentage points over last 10 years, while the proportion of S Pass and employment pass holders has increased by around 10 percentage points. This trend must continue as we restructure our economy towards higher value-added activities, seek deeper skills, and undertake more pervasive digitalisation.

Scope to raise productivity in domestic services jobs

Wage as % of Country's Median Wage

■ Plasterer　　Childcare Worker　　■ Baker　　■ Security Guard

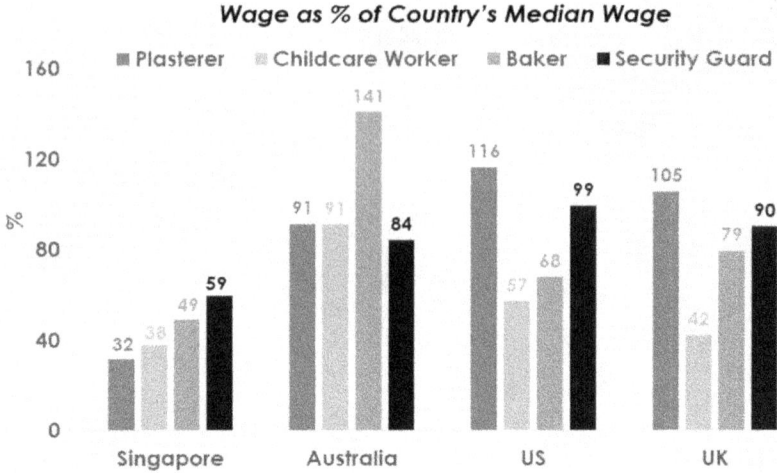

Source: Australian Bureau of Statistics, U.S. Bureau of Labour Statistics, U.K. Office for National Statistics, Ministry of Manpower, Monetary Authority of Singapore

Third, there is scope to increase productivity and efficiency in many domestic services jobs. Consider wages in four occupations (Plasterer, Childcare Worker, Baker, and Security Guard) across four countries (Singapore, Australia, the US, and the UK). The slide shows the median wage in these occupations relative to the overall median wage in that country. In Singapore, the typical pay in these occupations range from 30–60 per cent of the local median wage. In Australia, these occupations have wages much closer to the median wage. Wages in these occupations are also higher in the US and the UK, though the pattern is slightly different across countries. There is scope to further professionalise these jobs in Singapore. In particular, to increase the skills content, leverage on technology, improve business processes, and raise the quality of output. This will enhance productivity and help to support higher wages in these occupations.

Professionalising rank-and-file jobs will broaden and strengthen middle class

Wage as % of Country's Median Wage

■ Bank Teller ■ Vehicle Mechanic ■ Hairdresser ■ Bus Driver

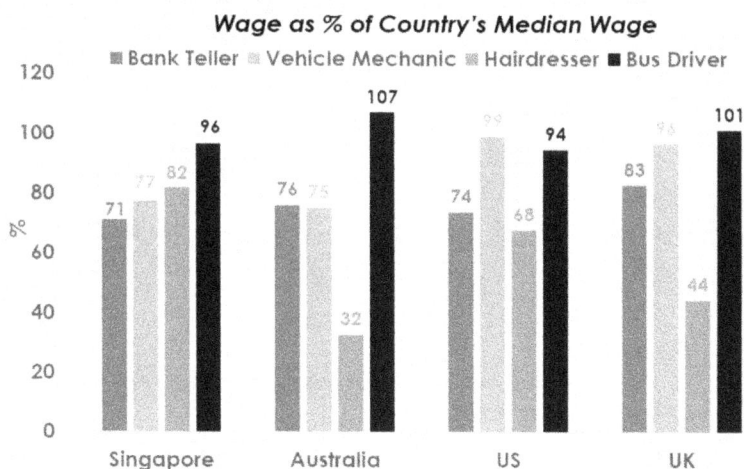

Source: Australian Bureau of Statistics, U.S. Bureau of Labour Statistics, U.K. Office for National Statistics, Ministry of Manpower, Monetary Authority of Singapore

In fact, the professionalisation of more of such so-called "rank-and-file" jobs in Singapore will help to strengthen and broaden the middle class, and make for a more equitable society. And Singapore can do this. We have good examples of jobs that have historically been perceived to be less skilled that have now been successfully upgraded. These jobs now command much relatively good wages, close to that seen in Australia, the US and the UK, controlling for median incomes. This slide shows that our bank tellers, vehicle mechanics, hairdressers, and bus drivers earn a good (median) wage that is quite close to the median. In fact, our bus drivers appear to be paid just below the median in Singapore, comparable to their counterparts in Australia, the US and the UK. And hairdressers in Singapore are doing amazingly well. They earn much closer to the median wage compared to their counterparts in Australia, the US and the UK.

The story of our bus drivers is interesting. Since the introduction of the Bus Contracting Model by the Ministry of Transport and the entrance of foreign bus operators, there has been greater competition in the bus industry, raising the game. Bus driving became more professional. The focus is on driving well, increasing fuel efficiency, and meeting the targets set by the Ministry of Transport on frequency and timeliness. More women have also been drawn into the industry with the introduction of flexible working arrangements and maternity leave. The result is that the dependency on foreign workers has been reduced, and productivity and wages have increased. Now our bus drivers are making close to the median wage in Singapore.

Dynamism is not about numbers but quality

1 Economic dynamism is about efficiency, entrepreneurship, innovation, and talent

2 Internationally competitive advanced manufacturing and modern services complemented by high-quality domestic services

3 An open, resilient, innovative, and inclusive society

In sum, demographics is not destiny and economic dynamism is not about numbers. Dynamism is about quality — the quality of our workforce, the quality of our enterprises, and the quality of our institutions. It is about high levels of efficiency and productivity. It is about growing the Singaporean talent base as well as being a magnet for the world's talents. It is about a vibrant entrepreneurial and innovation base, characterised by a lot of start-ups, a lot of experimentation, and a lot of R&D.

A key aspect of dynamism is also high rates of churn in the labour and capital resources in our firms. There needs to be continuous flux and reallocation of resources in response to changing economic and market conditions. Both capital and labour need to be nimble and highly adaptive. The structure of the Singapore economy is well suited for sustaining our dynamism. Singapore's strong advanced manufacturing and related trade and logistics activities are internationally competitive. In modern services, comprising financial, professional services, and info-communications technology, we enjoy an international hub status. Together, these sectors make up some 40 per cent of our economy. If our domestic services can be further professionalised — job by job, each worker possessing deep skills and delivering a high quality of service, we will be a dynamic economy.

Finally, dynamism must be about our people. We must remain an open society. Not just in being open to foreign trade, investment, and talent, but being deeply connected to the rest of the world. Not just attracting foreign talent to Singapore but Singaporeans venturing abroad as our companies and industries internationalise. Most of all, being open in spirit and mindset, staying open to diversity, being comfortable working in multi-cultural settings, thriving in a globalised world.

We must also remain a resilient society. Able to ride the ups and downs of business cycles and structural changes. Able to adapt, learn new skills, continually improve. We must become a more innovative society to be dynamic. Willing to experiment and accepting failure as a halfway house to success. Investing in R&D, leveraging on technology. Most of all, having an enterprising spirit — always seeking new and better ways to do things.

In the end, we must be an inclusive society. It is probably not a coincidence that IPS has chosen to make the theme of this conference "Together". The two forces that offer the most promise for sustained economic dynamism are globalisation and technology. But how far we can reap the benefits of globalisation and technology will depend on how well we bring all our people together. The path of dynamism is also the path of continuous disruption, even dislocation. To sustain the momentum and consensus in favour of globalisation and technology, we must help those adversely affected by them and equip Singaporeans to succeed. And to maintain cohesion in the face of population ageing and growing healthcare burdens, those who have benefitted from our growth and dynamism must contribute to the larger society — through taxation, philanthropy, community service.

We then become not just a dynamic people but also a compassionate one. Now that is a combination worth having, and I think the only one worth having.

CHAPTER 18

The Future Politics of Ageing

CHAN HENG CHEE

The ageing population is undeniably one of the major issues of our time. It is inevitable and will happen in all societies globally. Demographic trends have the quality of certainty, short of dramatic change due to war or a catastrophic disaster. No one has denied population ageing. The other issue of our time is climate change but there are some who deny it. A common concern for most countries is that as the population grows older, there may be emerging conflicts in society between the population who are growing older and the working age population which is not growing commensurately. We frequently highlight the uncomfortable truth that the old age dependency ratio will rise. There will be far more dependent people then there are working people. The *IPS Background Paper* has projected this. Christopher Gee has pointed out that the dependency ratio will be 24 older people per 100 persons of working age in 2020 and 54 older people per 100 persons of working age in 2040. Now, contrast this with 8 older aged persons per 100 working age persons in 1980 and 11 to a 100 in 2000. The burden is great, but is it just about who pays the taxes, who pays the bills and who gets what space?

Sociologists and gerontologists write about generational wars or age wars and age conflicts. Generational conflict sounds familiar but generational war and age war seem overstated. The only age war I can think of — if it is one — is the conflict in the United States over the Vietnam War on the rights and wrongs of the war between young men — many college students who were drafted to fight and die in a country far away — and middle-aged older politicians and generals who were making decisions about the war. As some of you remember, protests spread across the campuses and industries. The Vietnam War triggered the counter-culture revolution in America in the 1960s and a major "value disruption" with it. By the time they realised that it was about "values-change", all ages were pulled in. Young people did start the process but it became intergenerational. One can also think of young Chinese students in Tiananmen protesting against the economic and political issues of the day against the central authorities. It had nothing to do with age conflict; it was a protest against the Communist Party and government on issues of inflation, unemployment and corruption. The Arab Spring, which has been associated with young people did not only involve young people, it involved older people too. In the end, the protests included everyone and they were not about age-related issues.

Now, if generational wars and age wars sound far-fetched, generational conflict and tensions do exist in Asia as well as in the West. Lester Thurow, the late political economist and Dean of the Massachusetts Institute of Technology (MIT), Sloan School, went so far as to say in 1996, that in the years ahead, class warfare is apt to be redefined as the young against the old rather than the rich against the poor because of the explosion of public pension costs and healthcare. His prediction has not come true — in the 20 years since he made the statement — in the United States, in Europe or elsewhere. In Asia, culture, tradition and context will play a role in shaping the acceptance of burdens and the allocation of resources.

So, what will happen to our politics in the coming decades, given the growing senior vote? How will Singaporeans react to the claims of an ageing society? What will happen to the politics of integration as it pertains to allocation and redistribution? Integration in ageing societies inevitably raises the question of immigration.

Let me talk about allocation and redistribution first. I have commented before that we do not have the same resistance to the allocation of budget monies to subsidies for the old, the disabled, the poor and single mothers with children that you will find in some industrialised societies. There, it is an ideological issue because Republicans in the United States and the Conservative Party in the United Kingdom may not support welfare subsidies for those who cannot support themselves. There is usually a huge debate. In Singapore, it is different. If anything, Singaporeans applaud moves to increase welfare payments to the needy and say that the government should give more. But of course, the government has not really raised taxes yet to pay for the subsidies though they talk about it. Our attitude can partly be explained by the exposure to the many years of early PAP's democratic socialism. We have been socialised into a sense of egalitarianism and a sense of the larger good.

I read a post recently by Dave Chew of Singapore. It was in Quora[1]. I quote him because he reflects the public sentiment. He was answering the question, "Do Singaporeans still favour the PAP?" and this is what Dave Chew wrote and I quote, "The Singapore electorate is probably conservative financially, centrist in politics, pragmatic and not so idealistic. We are altruistic and believe in equality but pragmatism is more important to us. We have little interest in the highfalutin ideals of freedom of speech, of human rights in the Western sense. We prefer to gauge our lawmakers by real changes they make to our lives. We are not stuck-up by the Left or Right battles, and what we are keen on is to see our fellow citizens having a better life. If it means more subsidies, we're cool. If it means more taxes, which happened in GE2015, it normally goes without so much as a whimper. Fundamentally, it is about what works and not about what should. Dave Chew went on to discuss "Yes, we support the PAP but...!" So, he is not a flag waver. It is interesting that he makes this comment. I ask, "Will Singapore's tolerance for tax increases remain?"

Healthcare costs are indeed rising rapidly. The topmost line is the United States in purple. The thick orange line represents Singapore and only South Korea is rising less than Singapore. So, while compared to other OECD countries, our healthcare costs are not as high. There is no doubt they are going northwards.

---

[1] Quora is a question-and-answer website where questions are asked, answered, edited and organised by its community of users.

Healthcare Expenditure Per Capita, $US

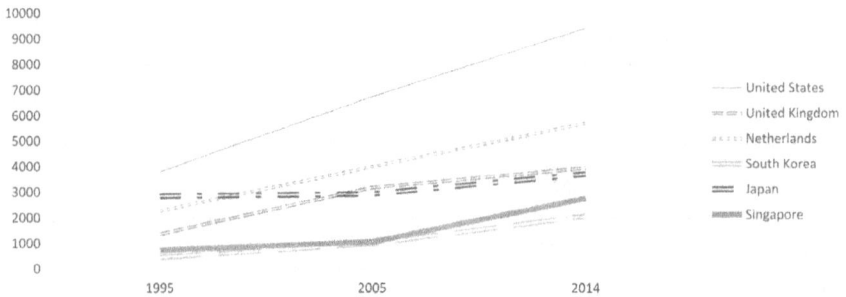

Total Healthcare Expenditure, % of GDP	Country	1995	2005	2014
	United States	13.09%	15.15%	17.14%
	United Kingdom	6.69%	8.24%	9.12%
	Netherlands	7.44%	9.60%	10.90%
	South Korea	3.67%	5.33%	7.37%
	Japan	6.62%	8.18%	10.23%
	Singapore	2.94%	3.74%	4.92%

Source: World Bank

We can have smart policies to try to moderate costs, but in the end, with the projected figure of 900,000 seniors aged 65 and above in 2030 — which is only 12 years away — and the numbers will increase as we live longer and have better health — health costs will be hefty.

I believe if taxes continue to increase, there will be unhappiness as per what the IPS survey shows, although there is a large group of neutrals at this point. Will this result in younger Singaporeans demanding a reduction in older citizens' benefits? I am sure there is a tipping point but we are not there yet, judging by the political debate. There is the matter of public policy choices about what proportion of the budget should be allocated to the expenditure for the young and for the older citizens before there is a contestation. I do not think we have that argument yet. Today, we have simple conflicts of interests between bicyclists and users of personal mobility devices (PMD) — usually younger people — using the walkways reserved for the senior citizens in the housing estates. It is a contestation over space.

Now, some have argued that what may temper opposition to these allocations is the reality that everyone will age, and the expectation of the below 65 that one day, they too will benefit from the same subsidies. This casts a different light on things. When the Pioneer Generation Package

(PGP) was offered, not only were the Pioneers made a happy lot, their children were happy too because the healthcare costs for the family were lightened. But will there be pressure from those who just missed the package?

As Singaporeans live longer, it is not only healthcare costs that will be a political issue, there could be conflict or tensions over jobs and power positions. Today, we find that older persons do not do well in finding the appropriate kind of work. 25.8 per cent of elderly residents are in the labour force. Where are senior Singaporeans working? Which areas? Cleaners, labourers and related workers form the largest group. The number of older services and sales workers, legislators, senior officials and managers is declining but the professionals are keeping up. The number of older clerical support workers is also growing.

Percentage of Elderly in various occupations (1990-2015)

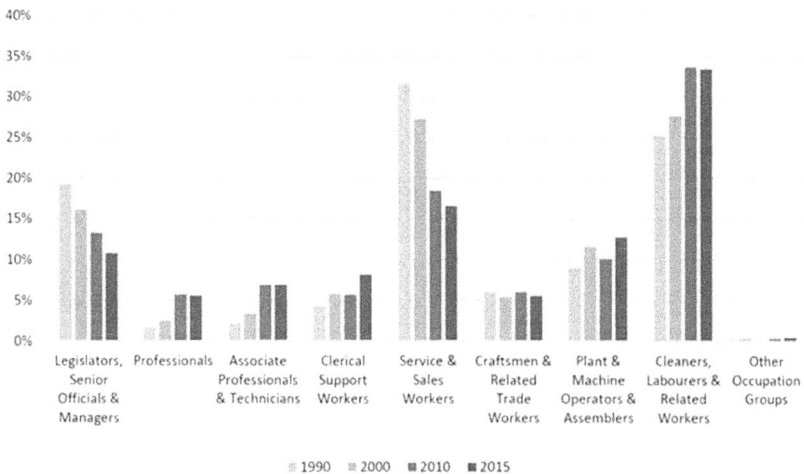

Source: Department of Statistics

The senior citizens that are growing older are better educated, even as they age, and they may want to hold on to their last jobs or aspire to a better job. Some countries such as the United Kingdom do not have a retirement age at all.

I was told by a young colleague at my Centre that she would resent it if she were told she should give up her job simply because she reached a determined number like 65 or 67 if she were still mentally or physically capable to hold the job. That would be "ageism" — bear in mind that there is the enabling technology to help the older workers. At the same time, I think we have to be aware that increased automation will do away with many jobs. The problem for us in Singapore, as in most societies, is to find the sweet spot — the jobs for seniors that have to be created now that some jobs are taken away. Where do they fit?

Next question: the next generation will be impatient, waiting to take over positions at the top or near the top. How does society deal with these pressures? I believe there will be tensions. In Singapore, we have a tradition of circulation at the highest echelons of the Civil Service. No Permanent Secretary gets more than ten years as "Perm Sec". In politics, we are also pushing the circulation of leaders. We have the fourth generation now, and I read that the Workers Party will be changing leaders too. Will we see a group of "grey panthers" emerging, fighting to hold their place in society and the economy? Will they demand more job opportunities and the right kind of jobs? Do they have to fight against "ageism"? I saw many American corporate leaders keeping very fit. They made sure they went to the gym, looked fit and good so that their younger colleagues would not be able to push them aside. So, please keep fit. Look good!

Looking ahead, the "grey vote" will be a substantial constituency. In 2030, it is projected that 900,000 persons will be 65 and above. In 2030, the population of Singapore citizens, if you hold that there will be no immigration at all from 2013 — I am taking this from the White Paper (A Sustainable Population for a Dynamic Singapore: Population White Paper) — will be 3.4 million. With 900,000 aged 65 and above, in a population of 3.4 million, that makes your vote about 24 to 26 per cent. So, it is a substantial vote. For the PAP, it has been something of a vote bank. In recent years though, because of job disruption, some in their mid-50s and mid-60s may be more disgruntled. Inflation and the inability of pensioners or retirees to make ends meet is an effective slogan to rally votes in any country. It is also true that among the high-income groups in many countries, Singapore included, older citizens form a substantial proportion. Amongst the rich, there are also the old — you'll get there too. The aged do not form a monolithic vote. In Singapore, ethnicity and religion will further impact on voting behaviour, depending on the issues of the day, and it need not be just age-related.

There are two other issues concerning age integration that I would like to highlight. I speak of age harassment. While there may not be public conflict or protests against the ageing population, age harassment takes place. Not the "hashtag me-too" (#MeToo) harassment but the abuse of the elderly in the homes by family members unable to cope with an ageing relative who is bedridden and hard to care for. There could also be poor treatment in ill-run institutions. Government and society need to find ways to alleviate stress in the family and monitor institutions for the aged. Laurence Lien will tell you about that. Now, I mentioned "ageism" earlier. What is "ageism"? It is prejudice and discrimination on the grounds of a person's age — most frequently seen in employment. This is an issue everywhere, and in Singapore, though there are some exceptions made to the possession of special skills. You can say that those who are older can be innovative as well. I will say, "Yes they are very innovative." In a situation of declining population, this ought to be less of an issue but change in the mindset does not happen automatically.

A tight labour force can help too. The re-employment age in Singapore has been raised in 2017 from 65 to 67 for eligible employees. This is a good step but there must be job growth for this to work well. You just cannot say "hire the older people". There must be job growth and there needs to be genuine rethinking on the concept of ageing and viewing the elderly people as an asset rather than liability.

Now, let me talk about immigration, regeneration and renewal. How can ageing societies cope with renewal or regeneration? Anti-immigration is a global sentiment. Singapore is not like every society and every country; we are a city and we are a city-state. This debate will be continuing and the future debate could be contentious, but as a city-state, our working population cannot be replenished by internal migration. In other countries like Indonesia and China, people from the rural areas come to the city to work. Inevitably, immigration therefore comes up as a partial solution to augmenting population numbers and the workforce. Pro-birth policies are the other measure but there are limits to their success. If Singapore turns off the immigration tap altogether and does not take in any new foreign non-residents, the Singapore population is expected to start shrinking in 2025 — seven years away.

Japan, it has been discussed, which has a population of a 127 million today, will shrink to 50 million by 2100 if they do nothing. The Japanese government has been slowly but surely turning to immigration to deal with a population decline, though they are a long way off. Foreigners constituted only 1.8 per cent of their population in 2016. Some say Japan has robots, they produce robots to step up productivity. But what is a population of robots? There is no soul to the nation. Immigration is deeply unpopular in Japan, and Japan is homogeneous and generally closed society.

Like it or not, the issue of immigration must be addressed in Singapore. The conversation, I think, has shifted a little. Singaporeans generally accept that some immigration is necessary. They realise that older citizens and young children need caregivers, which the working family cannot provide adequately. But they would like sustainable immigration and would like to be assured that their core identity will not be eroded. Singaporeans are most concerned about job security. It is an issue then of moderated immigration. The issue is not immigration or no immigration. We have gone past that! The question is how many and what types of immigration? We need the creative and the innovators, as well as caregivers and unskilled workers. As I said, there has to be job growth. Philip Yeo, in his interview with Sumiko Tan, said, "We don't want so many masseurs, we want people who can come in and also create jobs, the innovators."

Now, when the numbers shrink drastically and the economy and society is affected, I think Singaporeans will be pragmatic. The critical issue is how we will integrate new citizens and how we can integrate them better.

Fortunately, we are not the first ageing society in the world. We can learn from the example of others.

CHAPTER 19

Creating a Golden Age for Ageing: Opportunities We are Missing

LAURENCE LIEN

Looking 30 years forward, my children will be around my age now. Their children would be young. I do not want to be a burden to them. I want to be independent, so I need to look at what life will be like if I want to be independent. In terms of the end of life, there are four main scenarios: sudden death, terminal illness, frailty and organ failure. Organ failure is usually associated with losing functionality and chronic illness. Experiencing frailty is also a slow decline towards death. With a terminal illness, it is a relatively quick but painful decline, while sudden death is immediate.

Proposed Trajectories of Dying

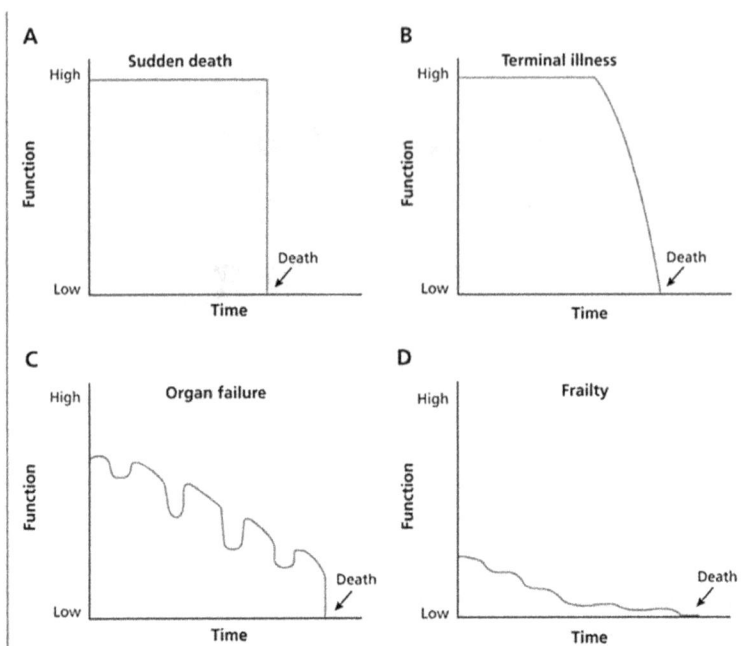

Source: Lunney, J. R., Lynn, J., & Hogan, C. (2002). Profiles of older Medicare decedents. *Journal of American Geriatric Society*, 50: 1109.

When faced with terminal illness, it is important to reduce futile end-of-life (EoL) treatments, of which there is too much. In fighting chronic disease, we should focus on preventative care. In my view, there are too many people in Singapore who are chronically sick and frail, and there is too much organ failure. Thankfully, the kidney disease numbers have improved for the first time in decades. A chief executive officer of an Australian nursing home operator came to visit our nursing homes. I asked him about his first impression of nursing homes in Singapore and to highlight differences from those in Australia. He said, "Too many wheelchairs! Why are there so many wheelchairs in your nursing homes? We don't see so many in ours. People are more independent and the age profile is a lot older." We are not keeping people well enough and we are also not tackling end-of-life care well.

In Being Mortal, Atul Gawande says that fewer than one third of patients with an end-stage diagnosis discuss their goals and preferences with the clinicians when they come closer to the end of life. We are wasting too many resources on futile care. Gawande's Ariadne Lab came up with the serious illness conversation card. Such conversations almost never happen in Singapore. The focus is on allowing people to talk about what is most important when they are at the end-of-life and to avoid what is happening today. Seventy-seven per cent of Singaporeans want to die at home, yet only 27 per cent do so. Sixty-one per cent die in hospitals.

Ageism is also something omnipresent in the context of employment, the media, the roads, public transport, at home, in the community, advertisements, popular culture, shops that always cater for the younger set, and even casual conversations. Ageism is pervasive and it is self-fulfilling. If there is a universal belief that older people are a burden, they will quickly become a burden and that turns into a fact of life. Instead, we need to see the glass as half-full rather than half-empty. We focus so much on what we lose in old age when there is so much that we still have; in fact, what we still have is still growing. As a result, we are missing a lot of opportunities because we do not see older persons as being able to contribute to our society and being able to live with purpose.

Age is a self-fulfilling prophecy. Some researchers found that seniors with more positive self-perceptions of ageing, which is measured up to 23 years earlier, live seven and a half years more than those who have less positive self-perceptions of ageing. This advantage remained after accounting for differences in gender, socio-economic status, loneliness, functional status and so on. Many other studies show that as we become older, we become happier. Our ability to handle stress improves, we savour our relationships, we live life with more authenticity, we are better at emotional regulation, become more grateful and people develop the intrinsic urge to give back.

The concept of declining fluid cognitive ability as you grow older suggests that you cannot learn new things or problem-solve over time. Another more optimistic study shows that as you grow older, you become more distracted. Your cognitive control worsens and if you perform tasks that need focused attention, obviously your performance declines with lower cognitive control. However, if you focus on tasks that benefit from diffused attention, your performance heightens. In short, if you are more distracted, you are better at creative problem-solving and taking in new information.

We often use 65 years as a cut-off point for retirement, dependency and so on. Instead, we should shift the benchmark of 65 years because the 70-year-old in 2014 is behaving like a 65-year-old in 1999. In terms of the labour force participation rate, those above 70 accounted for 15.3 per cent of the labour force in 2014. That is even higher than the labour force participation rate in 1999 of those aged 65 years and above. Health-adjusted life expectancy at birth has increased about four years for both males and females. The old-age dependency ratio in 1999 — using the benchmark of 65 years — was 10.8 per cent. In contrast, the old-age dependency ratio in 2014 using the benchmark of 70 years was 9.9 per cent. This is an improvement. Seventy could be the "new" 65, but there will be oncoming issues.

Old age dependency ratio actually improved if 70 is the new 65!

	1999	2014
Life Expectancy at birth	77.6	82.6
Labour Force Participation Rate		
65 Years & Over	12.4%	25.2%
70 Years & Over	7.6%	15.3%
Health-Adjusted Life Expectancy at Birth		
Male	68	72
Female	71	75
Old Age Dependency Ratio		
65 Years & Over (per 100 aged 20-64)	10.8%	16.7%
70 Years & Over (per 100 aged 20-70)	6.5%	9.9%

Source: Department of Statistics, Ministry of Manpower, Estimates from Lancet data for 1990, 2006 and 2016

We should play, work and learn throughout our lives. But what jobs allow us to do this? I challenge employers. If the jobs for the middle-aged cannot allow them to live life in parallel today, then there is no chance for older people to work while enjoying life in the future.

Actress Jane Fonda is an amazing "age advocate" and she made a fantastic observation that one should not see "age as pathology" but "age as a potential". Basically, if we think about age while focusing on physical elements, then it is an arch because there is a decline. But if you think about age as moving towards authenticity, happiness and wisdom, then it is a staircase all the way to the end.

Here are some examples of how we can integrate the optimism, contributions and strengths of older people into society. One example is the "Ibasho" in Japan, started by Dr Emi Kiyota, an environmental gerontologist. It has been applied in Nepal and the Philippines. "Ibasho" means a place where you can feel like yourself. There are very few places in Singapore where older people can feel like themselves — where they do not lose respect from others in society, where they are with others and are contributing. In an "Ibasho," the older people serve drinks and snacks. The important thing is that they are valuable assets to the community. They have a voice and together with the facilitators, develop these projects. They become change agents and they care for other people instead of just being cared for.

I have, in my time, been focusing on developing assisted living facilities in Singapore. Assisted living is very different from nursing homes, and is usually for those who do not have severe care needs in terms of help with activities of daily living (ADLs). There is a sense of community and everyone contributes to the life of the place. Key considerations when designing an assisted living facility include respect for residents of nursing homes as those who can exercise choices and be empowered to do things for themselves and for other people.

The main problem with older people is not even finances or the physical self. It is loneliness. There is a need to build up the social capital of older people. First, among themselves. There is so much potential for mutual help and self-help. Second, with younger people. The fear that there will be a constant contestation over things like space is because younger people and older people do not come together to problem-solve. When they are able to do that, they offer solutions, not just to the problems inherent in ageing, but also to an array of other challenges that demand attention. So, when a senior mentors a youth, for example, it is a cure for loneliness for the older person and there is also guidance for the young. Age-friendly infrastructure can also be child-friendly infrastructure. We should not just focus on solutions for older people.

Older people are consumers too. We forget about that and we never advertise with them in mind or create enough products for them. "Genki Kaki" is an initiative of the Lien Foundation. We brought two older people to Japan to test out their eldercare facilities and to go to their malls, which cater to older people. So, we brought them to this mall where older people start their day by having exercises. The whole complex is geared towards them. It is so welcoming and of course, the two from Singapore said, "Would it not be nice if we had something like this at home?" The silver industry is a huge opportunity and if Singapore is an ageing population, we should be at the centre of this for the rest of the region.

We have also experimented with "Gym Tonic" — gyms for the older people using pneumatic exercise equipment. HUR is a supplier of incredible state-of-the-art exercise equipment from Finland. A radio frequency identification device (RFID) recognises the wearer and adjusts the weights according to what his or her physiotherapist has prescribed. With enough repetitions over time, the therapist can programme the equipment to automatically adjust the weights. We have been implementing this in many institutions. We have rolled this out for the community to fight frailty. This is very important because once you start being frail everything steadily goes downhill.

One of the things that we are building together with Khoo Chwee Neo Foundation and Peacehaven Nursing Home is the project "Jade Circle", which is part of Peacehaven. This is a nursing home concept, different from assisted living, but we are trying to transform it. On the inside there will be a cafe and a hairdresser. There will also be a mini-supermarket which is safe for even those who have dementia. All these will allow the residents go through the same routine that they have always done.

In short, we must change mindsets. This is critical. We must maintain optimism, act with urgency, and prototype quickly with seniors as part of the solution. We should not just do things for them. They must be part of the solution. Unlike race or religion which cannot be changed, we all will age. So, if we think long-term, we are doing things for ourselves and for the future. We will not do something that does not benefit the whole society overall. With this, we can create that "Golden Age of Ageing", the vision that I started with.

CHAPTER 20

Ageing with Vigour

TEO CHEE HEAN

We are now living much longer than before. In the 1950s, the expected lifespan was around 61 years. Today, those who are aged around 65 can expect to live another 21 years. These additional years of life are really a bonus, received from the investments that we have made in sanitation, healthcare, good housing and a good clean, safe and secure living environment. Children born today can expect to live up to around 83 years old. With improvements in biomedical sciences, we can only guess how many more bonus years today's children might have by the time they are in their 60s or 70s. Greater longevity is a bonus if we are well prepared for it. We can age with vigour if each one of us prepares himself or herself well, if we prepare ourselves well in our communities, and if all of us together, as a nation, are well prepared.

We are entering a phase where the number of seniors is increasing rapidly. The baby boomers are coming into their senior years. Today, we have about 500,000 seniors aged 65 and above. By 2030, this will double to around 900,000. The number of citizens aged 80 and above will also more than double from around 100,000 today to around 200,000 by 2030. In fact, our citizens aged 80 and above are one of the fastest-growing segments of our population. Baby boomers were born in fairly large cohorts of 50,000 to 60,000 whereas the cohorts today are almost half that, around 32,000 births a year, even though in the last three to four years we have had a higher number of marriage and births among citizens than we have had in the previous decade. The United Nations (UN) has described population ageing as one of the defining features of our times. Countries are seeing populations age at an unprecedented rate and the level of ageing will differ from country to country.

In Singapore, today, they are about 4.4 adults aged 20 to 64 (what we would conventionally call "working age") to every senior aged 65 and above. In Europe, it is about 3.0, and Japan, 2.0. Singapore will hit Europe's current levels of ageing by around 2020 and Japan's current levels by around 2040. We are also ageing much more rapidly than other countries. It took France over 100 years to transit from an ageing society, which by some demographers' definition is 7 per cent of the population, to an aged society with 14 per cent of the population aged 65 and over. It has taken us only 19 years and we crossed that mark last year. On the positive side, we are actually much better prepared than others.

The need to prepare for an ageing population could already be seen by the mid-1980s. Life expectancy was increasing and the baby boomers had already been born. However, in the mid-1980s, many people might not have been ready to think that far ahead and contemplate the range of measures that were needed to deal with this situation. Nevertheless, we were able to take several measures early, to set in place resilient institutions that are built on strong foundations and principles. These have now put us in a better position to look after ourselves and as a society as we age.

Now, one such pillar is the Central Provident Fund (CPF), which helps Singaporeans to save for their old age, cover medical expenses and purchase basic health insurance. This is a fully funded system and will be sustainable for generations to come. This is a fundamental difference and a fundamental strength. In many other countries, pension promises are not fully funded and pension payments have to be met from current government budgets, placing a great strain on the current working generation. The CPF system, as it was operating, was not good enough and it was improved significantly in 2009, with the introduction of CPF Life. CPF Life provides lifelong pay-outs for future cohorts of seniors by pooling together our longevity risk. In this way, our seniors are assured of monthly payments for as long as they live, compared to the previous CPF system, where seniors got a fixed amount but risked living beyond the time when their own CPF retirement accounts ran out. That is a very frightening position to be in and CPF Life deals with that problem. For those unable to save enough by themselves, we have targeted assistance through housing grants, Workfare and Silver Support.

As for healthcare, we have MediShield Life today, which provides lifelong universal health insurance coverage for all. Introduced in 2015, MediShield

Life made a significant improvement over the earlier MediShield, which only provided health insurance coverage up to the age of 92 on an opt-out basis. MediShield also did not cover pre-existing conditions. So MediShield Life deals with these three fundamental shortcomings of the old MediShield. MediShield Life now means that seniors need not worry about not qualifying for health insurance due to pre-existing conditions, or again living beyond the age when they can get health insurance. With MediShield Life and CPF Life, living longer is a blessing. The introduction of CPF Life and MediShield Life are therefore game changers. These national, social risk-pooling schemes mean that to a larger extent than before, we are all helping one another to cope better together with the uncertainties associated with ageing. So, with this national risk pooling, we are not facing ageing alone.

We are facing ageing together and we pool our risk of longevity together. Our healthcare expenditure to look after our seniors actually comes from three sources: sharing risk collectively through MediShield Life, our own Medisave accounts and cash payments, and also very significant subsidies from the government to hospitals and polyclinics for subsidised healthcare such as in our B2 and C wards. The doubling of our population of seniors by 2030 means that the subsidies that we provide from our government budget for healthcare will grow very substantially. Even if we assume that doctors and nurses have no more pay rises in the coming years and if our medical system uses exactly the same drugs and operates with exactly the same costs as today, just the doubling of the seniors means that the resources needed to support healthcare system from our budget will increase dramatically.

Today, the largest expenditure item in our government budget is defence, followed by education and health. Health today is around 2.4 per cent of gross domestic product (GDP). This is already a significant increase from 2007 when health was just around 0.8 per cent of GDP. That was when there were about 300,000 Singaporeans over the age of 65. Today, we have about 500,000 and by 2030 we will have 900,000 over the age of 65. So as a percentage of GDP, this is a three-fold increase in expenditure from the government budget and we could expect that health expenditure may overtake education in our government budget in the coming years. We will have to make sure that our budget remains on a sound footing so that we have the resources to take care of our seniors as they age and to make sure that we help our children take care of us. These measures, like CPF Life,

MediShield Life and a sound government budget sufficient to fund our current health care needs, have put us on a firmer footing than many other countries. We still need to be careful so that we maintain that sound foundation, those sound principles that have given us this firm footing as we develop policies for the future. Our past generations have given us these "bonus years", which I and those in my generation enjoy. It places all of us as a nation on a firmer footing to age with confidence and vigour. We must also continue to build on this for future generations. I think that it is our responsibility.

I have just outlined what all of us can do together at a national level but we also have to take ownership for what we can do collectively in our communities and what we can do as individuals to support our families and ourselves to age with vigour. It is not just something for the government to do or something for the government to take care of. We need to do it as a community, we need to do it ourselves and in our families. As a community, we can all play our part to enable our seniors to embrace the opportunities that come from longevity and live life to the fullest. For example, we have initiatives to enable those who want to work, to stay in work longer. We raised the re-employment age from 65 to 67 from July last year. Alongside this, we have introduced a special employment credit that helps companies to pay part of the wages of workers aged 55 and above, earning up to $4,000 a month. This today benefits about 340,000 workers and helps us to achieve a high rate of employment of workers between the ages 55 and 64. We are round about 67.3 per cent right now. This is comparable to the levels in Germany and Denmark, but I think we can still do better.

There are also grants to enable our companies to redesign workplaces and jobs — but these grants and credits are meaningful only when employers value and tap on the experience and skills that seniors can offer. Our seniors too have to do their part to keep up with the new skills that are required in the workplace. They need to make themselves relevant, useful and value adding. SkillsFuture and other programmes are targeted at this and we can also redesign jobs to have more flexible work arrangements so that there is part-time work, job sharing and working from home. Technology offers so much more opportunity. The gig economy, often talked of as something for millennials, is not just for the millennials. If we redesign jobs to be more flexible, seniors are one of the largest groups that can take part in this gig economy as well. So, only through a changed mind-set and a concerted effort, can we help make it possible for seniors to remain in the workforce for as long as they are able and willing to do so.

I visited Changi Airport and SATS recently. I met Dolly. Dolly is an automated, guided vehicle for food delivery. Workers no longer have to push heavy trolleys, weighing up to 200 kilogrammes. The Singapore Public Service is also doing its part. As at December 2016, we had close to 3,000 public officers now aged 65 and above. This is up from 500 in 2010. These officers continue to contribute well. In fact, our longest-serving public officer, Mr Puteh Bin Mahamood from the Elections Department, is 84 years old and first joined 70 years ago in 1947.

Within our communities, there is also much that we can do to build community spirit and look out for one another. The Japanese are very good at this. Japan is well known for having very strong community-based support. These younger seniors in the Nippon Active Life Club in Osaka helped to take care of senior-seniors enabling them to continue to live in their own homes, instead of moving to assisted care facilities. These younger seniors are "paying it forward". We can always stay young at heart, keep ourselves active and vigorous and encourage others to join in and do so too. One of my Pasir Ris residents, Uncle Chong, is 90 years old and continues to conduct weekly swimming lessons for other seniors, encouraging them to remain active and fit even in their advanced years. Another older lady in my constituency used to run the canteen when Changi Airport was being built and she cooked single-handedly. They remain active and support each other.

In 2016, we started the Community Networks for Seniors (CNS), to develop strong community-based support to complement family support. The community network reaches out to seniors to support them to age well in place. So CNS coordinates the efforts of government agencies, VWOs (Voluntary Welfare Organisations) and grassroots organisations to bring senior-centric programmes and services to their doorstep. Volunteers such as our pioneer generation ambassadors and grassroots leaders encourage our seniors to attend health screening and talks as well as exercises and social interest groups. We are also matching seniors living alone with befrienders and neighbours who can help them. Seniors living alone is another rapidly growing segment of our population. The goal is to build a close-knit community in our neighbourhoods where seniors can age happily, healthily and actively in place. To promote intergenerational bonding, we are also co-locating childcare and elder care facilities. The first such site is at Kampung Admiralty where a childcare centre and active ageing hub are located side-by-side. Over the next 10 years, we will extend this to some 10 new Housing and Development Board (HDB) housing precincts.

Finally, as individuals and as families, we also have to do our part to support our senior family members to age well and enjoy their silver years. The warm embrace of families plays an important role to provide meaning to life, support, mutual love and care. The government recognises this and, in fact, our policies are designed to encourage family members to help one another and to live close to another. We encourage children to live together or close together with their parents by giving priority for housing and grants. We have special incentives to encourage individuals to top-up the CPF accounts of loved ones.

Our tax policy encourages intergenerational support in terms of parent and grandparent caregiver reliefs. In addition, we need to rethink our own individual approach to life in ageing, so that we can all lead long, happy, healthy and purposeful lives. We can do this with lifelong learning, acquisition of new skills, keeping active through work and exercise, finding meaning through community and voluntary work and fulfilment with our families. Living longer does not mean being old for longer but means staying young for longer. So, we need to keep fit, keep learning and keep contributing. When I was 29, 30 years old, I thought that if I can keep running and jogging when I am in the 50s that would be fine. Today, I am in my 60s and I can still do it and I hope to continue doing it for as long as possible. It is the approach and attitude that we take towards ageing. So, instead of merely adding years to life, we should be adding life to years.

We do need a mind-set change in the way we think about ageing and stand the whole way we think about ageing on its head. We need a collective commitment at all levels. What can I in my family do? What can we do in our communities and workplaces? What can we all do together as a nation to prepare ourselves? Our pioneers laid a strong foundation for us. Each one of us and our families, businesses, employers, our community, need to shift toward a notion of ageing with vigour. To live a full life and life to the full and create a vibrant and vigorous Singapore for all ages.

CHAPTER 21

Misconceptions that Frame Singaporeans Living Longer as a Liability

KANWALJIT SOIN

In 2016, Singapore was ranked third in the world for the longest average life expectancy and second in the world for the longest average healthy life expectancy. Therefore, we are not only living longer, but we are living longer, healthier. Thus, we cannot equate biological age with chronological age. Seventy is the new 50. Fortunately, as we have grown older, we have also grown richer. Singapore's GDP per capita rose from just S$900 in 1970 to S$71,000 in 2016, one of the highest in the world. Despite the abundance of these good tidings, ageing in Singapore has generally been considered as a liability because of misconceptions about the ageing process and ageism. Policy planners, media, society in general and unfortunately some older people themselves are guilty of harbouring views which associate old age with physical decline, with financial dependence and with degraded mental functions. These misconceptions have clouded the promise of old age.

I will now cite a few misconceptions that some policymakers seem to have internalised and tend to perpetuate. The very important "Population White Paper", conceived by the National Population and Talent Division, to set the direction of our country's future, was presented in Parliament in 2013. Please note this very crucial but non-evidence-based paragraph in this vital document: "For society, a declining old-age support ratio would mean rising taxes and a heavier economic load on a smaller base of working-age

Singaporeans. Companies may not find enough workers". This population planning paper and many policy speeches have highlighted the adverse consequences of a declining old-age support ratio, or if expressed differently, an increasing old age dependency ratio. Both ratios are an incomplete, inaccurate and outmoded view of financial dependence in old age.

The old age support ratio indicates the number of working-age people — people aged 20–64 in the population — who are available to support one older person aged 65 or above. Here, we are assuming that those aged 20 to 64 are engaged productively and those who are over 65 would have to be suddenly supported from their 65th birthday onwards by their younger stalwarts. In reality, many Singaporeans over 65 are economically active and contribute either directly or indirectly to economic and social robustness. Also, if a retiree has saved enough money for his or her remaining life, should he or she be counted as dependent economically? We need alternative measures to reflect the true economic dependency of the elderly.

One such measure is a savings-adjusted old-age support ratio that requires an adjustment for savings available to the elderly. Or if you define those who must be supported as aged over 70 and not over 65, the old-age support ratio becomes much more favourable. With lower birth rates, total dependency ratio has gone down, but we hardly ever hear this fact being articulated. We only hear of old-age dependency ratio; however, it is but one part of the total dependency ratio. The same cut-off age of 65 is used to operationalise old-age dependency ratio even for 2030. There is no recognition of the cohort effects of better health and longer working lives of people in 2030. It is often assumed that the experience of the present can be extrapolated into the future. The 65-year olds of 2030 will be healthier, less dependent and more mentally agile than ever before, and so economic projections must take that into account.

Another alarmist view that is often articulated by policymakers is that, with an ageing population, business activity would slow and job and employment opportunities would shrink. In contrast to this pessimism about business affairs, global professional services firm Deloitte says "ageing populations will generate a growth cluster of new business opportunities for this region and Singapore in particular." The silver economy will see growth in private healthcare, travel, pharmaceuticals, biotechnology, insurance and retail industries. With relatively high levels of asset ownership among older

Singaporeans, there is an increased demand for the management of these assets, and this is generating opportunities in the financial services sector, insurance and legal industry. The Deloitte report further ranked Singapore third out of 15 Asia Pacific countries for silver market potential. With Singaporeans continuing to work and earning an income for a longer period, seniors are increasingly becoming consumers and paying at least Goods and Services Tax (GST).

Hence, older people are not just dependents, which is the only role in which they are cast. Policymakers often point to the intergenerational conflict arising from the financial dependency of ageing populations, but unlike other countries and thanks to the foresight of earlier policymakers, the reality here is quite different. The CPF system encourages self-reliance by making each individual responsible for his or her own retirement needs, rather than burdening future generations with ever increasing taxes and thus minimising potential intergenerational stresses as outlined by Professor Canning. We must also consider private intra-familial transfers, from older to younger generations — how many of us have helped our children to buy their first apartment or first car?

Ageism, in my opinion, is a mammoth misconception about the ageing process. Ageism is defined as a negative stereotyping of, and discrimination against, individuals or a group of individuals because of their age. Misperceptions regarding the ability, motivation and cognitive states of older persons abound among society and policymakers. Where cognition is concerned, research shows that psychological functions do not decline gradually in the healthy, elderly person. Instead, they plateau until a late age. This is due to improvement in crystallised intelligence as we grow older. This type of intelligence refers to the use of accumulated knowledge and experience in decision-making at older ages.

Now, I will point to some links between age discrimination and policies in Singapore and how they tend to convert Singaporeans from assets to liabilities. We are all aware that Singapore is not a welfare state. Social spending in Singapore only amounts to 5.5 per cent of GDP. In China, it is 8 per cent and it is an average of 21 per cent in other OECD countries. The social safety net in Singapore is built on the key principles of self-reliance and family as the two most important lines of support. Policymakers and the government have drilled this concept of self-reliance into our psyche and many older people want to continue to work. The presence of ageism and age discrimination, however, has trapped older Singaporeans between a rock and a hard place, where employment is concerned. The retirement age in Singapore is only 62. In the first place, why do we need a retirement age when there is no formal pension system? There is a heterogeneity where ageing is concerned. People do not age at the same rate and should not be retiring at the same age. Australia and the US have no mandatory retirement age as that has been abolished.

From 1 July 2017, employers must offer re-employment to eligible employees who turn 62 up to the age of 67. However, even if the employee is lucky enough to be re-employed and continues with the same job, the wages are often reduced and the contract is renewable annually. Also, termination of service can be done at any time without any reason by serving notice as stipulated in the contract. If the employer thinks that the employee cannot be offered re-employment, then the company can offer a one-off employment assistance of three and a half months of salary, and that is the end of the matter. The Ministry of Manpower has acknowledged that specific anti-discrimination laws may be needed to deal with age discrimination in employment here. However, companies argue that too much government protection is bad for business but the Ministry of Manpower has countered with the argument that the global competitiveness of places with anti-discrimination laws has remained relatively stable. Countries like the US, Britain, Germany, Hong Kong and Japan have been cited. Yet, the government is not willing to pass legislation to make re-employment compulsory till 67.

On the other side of the coin, older people are still expected to be self-reliant. In fact, because of age discrimination, many perfectly healthy, older workers feel that they have been forced by circumstances into leaving the labour force. Yet, we bemoan the lack of workers for our economy. In addition, being denied a job will impact on the CPF savings of these individuals and this may lead to financial dependency on the family and community. That age discrimination exists in employment has been acknowledged by our policymakers and by research published by the Institute of Policy Studies (IPS). In 2014 Mdm Halimah Yacob, then the Speaker of Parliament and now our President had this to say: "We are still very much an ageist society. Sometimes, people may not even know they are being ageist. I receive a lot of feedback from elderly job applicants and they say it is very difficult for them to get a job."

When Deputy Prime Minister Tharman Shanmugaratnam was speaking at the budget forum in 2015, he acknowledged that ageism in Singapore workplaces meant that experienced older workers were being shut out of jobs. He said: "I think we have to tackle ageism in Singapore. There is a sort of a quiet, unstated discrimination among the mid-careers and those who are in their 50s." IPS' latest survey in 2017 shows that there is an overwhelming agreement on age discrimination for workers aged 55 years and above, who are looking for work. Despite this big hurdle of age discrimination, older people still want to be self-reliant and the employment rate for local residents, aged 55 to 64, increased to 67 per cent in 2016, one of the highest compared to other OECD countries. For those between 65 and 69, it was 43 per cent; and for those over 70, it was 15 per cent.

The median age of our workforce is 43 years across all sectors and we can anticipate it to reach 47 years by 2020. Currently, one in three workers is already 50 years old and over. Soon, they will constitute most of our workforce. This is our reality — there is no place for age discrimination. How well we adapt our employment culture and how well we eliminate ageism from our employment practices will determine Singapore's future economic and social viability.

Media also plays an important role in the negative framing of the elderly. In television shows, for example, aunties and uncles are all too often portrayed as bumbling old fools. Our society of older people is frequently referred to in the media as a "silver tsunami" or a "demographic time bomb" as if it was a destructive force. The ways in which the elderly are represented in the media can have a lasting impact on social attitudes and this reinforces negative stereotypes held by both younger and older people. Sadly, this becomes a self-fulfilling prophecy for older people and can impact on older people's confidence and quality of life. The biggest problem for many older people is ageism rather than the process of ageing itself.

Let me now cite an example of when ignorance about ageism is not bliss. In 2016, the government unveiled its S$3 billion action plan for successful ageing. This is an impressive plan and provides a framework for preparing for our transition to becoming a super-aged society in 2030. Without a good hard look at the effects of ageism on the ability of individuals to age successfully, we may not manage the transition well. We need plans, policies and action, not just for active ageing, but also for understanding the causes of ageism and reducing all forms of age discrimination. The 2015 World Health Organization's *World Report on Ageing and Health* made this important observation and I quote: "Age-based stereotypes influence behaviours, policy development and even research. Addressing these by combating ageism must lie at the core of any public health response to population ageing." Alas, there is no mention of any action against ageism in Singapore's action plan for successful ageing.

While ageing is a dynamic process and is changing all the time, there is a structural lag of many years between the practice of public policy and the lived experiences of older people. Because of the stereotyping of older people as part of the past, we are often overlooked in society's future. In contrast, if older Singaporeans were considered as an asset, there will be a different orientation towards health and social expenditure for this group of citizens.